1 PETER

THE NIV APPLICATION COMMENTARY

From biblical text . . . to contemporary life

THE NIV
APPLICATION
COMMENTARY

From biblical text . . . to contemporary life

SCOT McKNIGHT

ZondervanPublishingHouse
Grand Rapids, Michigan

A Division of HarperCollinsPublishers

The NIV Application Commentary: 1 Peter
Copyright © 1996 by Scot McKnight

Requests for information should be addressed to:

Zondervan Publishing House
Grand Rapids, Michigan 49530

Library of Congress Cataloging-in-Publication Data

McKnight, Scot.
    1 Peter / Scot McKnight.
        p. cm.—(NIV application commentary)
    Includes bibliographical references and index.
    ISBN: 0–310–49290–4
    1. Bible. N.T. Peter, 1st—Commentaries. I. Bible. N.T. Peter, 1st. English. New International. 1996. II. Title. III. Series.
    BS2795.3.M38 1996
    227'.9207—dc20
                                       95–25254
                                              CIP

This edition printed on acid-free paper and meets the American National Standards Institute Z39.48 standard.

All Scripture quotations, unless otherwise indicated, are taken from the *Holy Bible: New International Version*®. NIV®. Copyright © 1973, 1978, 1984 by International Bible Society. Used by permission of Zondervan Publishing House. All rights reserved.

Edited by Verlyn D. Verbrugge

Printed in the United States of America

---

96 97 98 99 00 01 02 /❖ DC/ 10 9 8 7 6 5 4 3 2 1

Contents

For
Laura Elizabeth
and
Lukas Norman Matthew

NIV Application Commentary
Series Introduction

THE NIV APPLICATION COMMENTARY SERIES is unique. Most commentaries help us make the journey from the twentieth century back to the first century. They enable us to cross the barriers of time, culture, language, and geography that separate us from the biblical world. Yet they only offer a one-way ticket to the past and assume that we can somehow make the return journey on our own. Once they have explained the *original meaning* of a book or passage, these commentaries give us little or no help in exploring its *contemporary significance*. The information they offer is valuable, but the job is only half done.

Recently, a few commentaries have included some contemporary application as *one* of their goals. Yet that application is often sketchy or moralistic, and some volumes sound more like printed sermons than commentaries.

The primary goal of The NIV Application Commentary Series is to help you with the difficult but vital task of bringing an ancient message into a modern context. The series not only focuses on application as a finished product but also helps you think through the *process* of moving from the original meaning of a passage to its contemporary significance. These are commentaries, not popular expositions. They are works of reference, not devotional literature.

The format of the series is designed to achieve the goals of the series. Each passage is treated in three sections: *Original Meaning, Bridging Contexts,* and *Contemporary Significance.*

THIS SECTION HELPS you understand the meaning of the biblical text in its first-century context. All of the elements of traditional exegesis—in concise form—are discussed here. These include the historical, literary, and cultural context of the passage. The authors discuss matters related to grammar and syntax, and the meaning of biblical words. They also seek to explore the main ideas of the passage and how the biblical author develops those ideas.

After reading this section, you will understand the problems, questions, and concerns of the *original audience* and how the biblical author addressed those issues. This understanding is foundational to any legitimate application of the text today.

THIS SECTION BUILDS a bridge between the world of the Bible and the world of today, between the original context and the contemporary context, by focusing on both the timely and timeless aspects of the text.

God's Word is *timely*. The authors of Scripture spoke to specific situations, problems, and questions. Paul warned the Galatians about the consequences of circumcision and the dangers of trying to be justified by law (Gal. 5:2–5). The author of Hebrews tried to convince his readers that Christ is superior to Moses, the Aaronic priests, and the Old Testament sacrifices. John urged his readers to "test the spirits" of those who taught a form of incipient Gnosticism (1 John 4:1–6). In each of these cases, the timely nature of Scripture enables us to hear God's Word in situations that were *concrete* rather than abstract.

Yet the timely nature of Scripture also creates problems. Our situations, difficulties, and questions are not always directly related to those faced by the people in the Bible. Therefore, God's word to them does not always seem relevant to us. For example, when was the last time someone urged you to be circumcised, claiming that it was a necessary part of justification? How many people today care whether Christ is superior to the Aaronic priests? And how can a "test" designed to expose incipient Gnosticism be of any value in a modern culture?

Fortunately, Scripture is not only timely but *timeless*. Just as God spoke to the original audience, so he still speaks to us through the pages of Scripture. Because we share a common humanity with the people of the Bible, we discover a *universal dimension* in the problems they faced and the solutions God gave them. The timeless nature of Scripture enables it to speak with power in every time and in every culture.

Those who fail to recognize that Scripture is both timely and timeless run into a host of problems. For example, those who are intimidated by timely books such as Hebrews or Galatians might avoid reading them because they seem meaningless today. At the other extreme, those who are convinced of the timeless nature of Scripture, but who fail to discern its timely element, may "wax eloquent" about the Melchizedekian priesthood to a sleeping congregation.

The purpose of this section, therefore, is to help you discern what is timeless in the timely pages of the New Testament—and what is not. For example, if Paul's primary concern is not circumcision (as he tells us in Gal. 5:6), what *is* he concerned about? If discussions about the Aaronic priesthood or Melchizedek seem irrelevant today, what is of abiding value in these passages? If people try to "test the spirits" today with a test designed for a specific first-century heresy, what other biblical test might be more appropriate?

Yet this section does not merely uncover that which is timeless in a passage but also helps you to see *how* it is uncovered. The author of the commentary seeks to take what is implicit in the text and make it explicit, to take a process that normally is intuitive and explain it in a logical, orderly fashion. How do we know that circumcision is not Paul's primary concern? What clues in the text or its context help us realize that Paul's real concern is at a deeper level?

Of course, those passages in which the historical distance between us and the original readers is greatest require a longer treatment. Conversely, those passages in which the historical distance is smaller or seemingly nonexistent require less attention.

One final clarification. Because this section prepares the way for discussing the contemporary significance of the passage, there is not always a sharp distinction or a clear break between this section and the one that follows. Yet when both sections are read together, you should have a strong sense of moving from the world of the Bible to the world of today.

THIS SECTION ALLOWS the biblical message to speak with as much power today as it did when it was first written. How can you apply what you learned about Jerusalem, Ephesus, or Corinth to our present-day needs in Chicago, Los Angeles, or London? How can you take a message originally spoken in Greek and

Aramaic and communicate it clearly in our own language? How can you take the eternal truths originally spoken in a different time and culture and apply them to the similar-yet-different needs of our culture?

In order to achieve these goals, this section gives you help in several key areas.

First, it helps you identify contemporary situations, problems, or questions that are truly comparable to those faced by the original audience. Because contemporary situations are seldom identical to those faced in the first century, you must seek situations that are analogous if your applications are to be relevant.

Second, this section explores a variety of contexts in which the passage might be applied today. You will look at personal applications, but you will also be encouraged to think beyond private concerns to the society and culture at large.

Third, this section will alert you to any problems or difficulties you might encounter in seeking to apply the passage. And if there are several legitimate ways to apply a passage (areas in which Christians disagree), the author will bring these to your attention and help you think through the issues involved.

In seeking to achieve these goals, the contributors to this series attempt to avoid two extremes. They avoid making such specific applications that the commentary might quickly become dated. They also avoid discussing the significance of the passage in such a general way that it fails to engage contemporary life and culture.

Above all, contributors to this series have made a diligent effort not to sound moralistic or preachy. The NIV Application Commentary Series does not seek to provide ready-made sermon materials but rather tools, ideas, and insights that will help you communicate God's Word with power. If we help you to achieve that goal, then we have fulfilled the purpose for this series.

—The Editors

General Editor's Preface

TELEVISION AND NEWSPAPERS ARE FILLED these days with issues about religious freedom and the relationship between church and state. On the world scene the questions run the gamut from *Are Christians really free in China?* to *Can Christians avoid persecution in Islamic countries?* to *What is the role of Protestantism and Roman Catholicism in the Northern Ireland conflict?* In the United States, the questions center on issues like prayer in public schools, protection of religious minorities, and the Christian Right in politics. It is all but impossible to watch a television newscast or read the morning paper (or browse through increasing numbers of books in Barnes and Noble on contemporary issues) without running into such church/state issues.

As Scot McKnight so aptly points out in this commentary on 1 Peter, it is this concentration on the relationship between church and state in modern life that makes the first-century wisdom of this letter so relevant. Peter, in writing this text, had this relationship on the front burner of his mind. It is almost as if he were writing both to first-century Christians wondering about how to survive as aliens and strangers in the Roman empire and to twentieth-century Christians trying to live holy lives in a secularized, unholy culture. True, important circumstances have put these two communities, separated by 1900 years, on opposite ends of the social and economic spectra: first-century Christians were politically, socially, and economically disadvantaged, while twentieth-century American Christians have the numbers to be politically, socially, and economically powerful. Still, the two groups have much in common in trying to live lives of holy endurance in the face of suffering.

It is important to note a crucial difference between the perspectives given in our books and newspaper articles, however, and the timeless truth given by Peter. In the United States, for example, the public media, in commenting on both the world and national scene, always approach these issues from the point of view of human rights and legality. No matter how sympathetic to the religious dimensions of the controversies these writers are, they have no choice but to talk about United Nations policies on human rights and religious freedom, Thomas Jefferson's "wall of separation" between church and state, the stand that various politicians take on the key religio-political issues of the day, and the ideological makeup of the Supreme Court, the final legal arbiter of such issues.

As important as these perspectives are to Christians today, however, it is instructive to note that Peter does not approach these questions from the point of view of human rights and legality. Rather, he approaches them from the point of view of our relationship to God. He tells us that Christians survive in a hostile environment not by legal proceedings against persecutors but by endurance; not by imposing a lifestyle on others through law but by living holy lives that compel others to watch us; not by destroying unbelievers with sound bites and innuendo but by respecting them even as we witness to the eternal truths of the gospel.

For Peter, the burning questions of place, rights, and attitude have less to do with legal deeds to property than with being at home in a strange and temporary land; much less to do with "I'm okay, you're okay" relativism than with the gritty realities of family responsibilities and tough love; almost nothing to do with maximizing material advantages in the present and everything to do with seeing this world through the future-oriented lenses of Christian hope and promise. It is this spiritual/theological perspective that makes 1 Peter the primary resource for Christians trying to sort out their place in our modern world. And it is this perspective that Scot McKnight so capably opens up in the following pages for all to see and apply.

Terry C. Muck

Author's Preface

THIS REMARKABLE LETTER OF PETER has been with me at every major transition I have made in my academic life. The first class I ever taught, at Trinity Evangelical Divinity School in the academic year of 1980–81, when I was still a student, endured some lectures and meanderings on this letter, and the first class I taught after the same institution hired me was also a class that climaxed with a thorough look at 1 Peter. Even more important, as I was making the decision to become the Karl A. Olsson Professor of Religious Studies at North Park College, I was studying and writing up the results of my study on 1 Peter for this commentary. I will always remember 1 Peter for what I was doing; I hope this will do no disservice to its apostolic author.

One of the key transitions this commentary series serves is the one from the first century to the modern world. Its genius, of which I am thankful to be a part, is that it seriously considers the strategies that we as Christians use to make an ancient text relevant and powerful today. When the reader moves from the first section (Original Meaning) to the second and third sections (Bridging Contexts, Contemporary Significance), the worlds do change, as does the particularity of its meaning. I am not foolish enough to think that the second and third sections are the Word of God; that is reserved only for the first. These latter two sections, then, are human attempts to let the Word speak in modern words. This inevitably involves speaking to one's own context; if my context differs from yours, which it will often do, I ask only that you follow my meanderings and see if you can learn something from a brother who is seeking to be both faithful to the ancient Word while seeking to gain a hearing in the modern world.

The message of 1 Peter concerns how Christians are to live in a hostile environment, and live in such a way that they not only endure but also have a lasting impact for good on that environment. Our children, Laura Elizabeth and Lukas Norman Matthew, are at critical transitions in their own lives. Laura is now finishing high school and is about to enter college life at Wheaton College; Lukas is finishing his first year at high school. Each of them, in different ways, challenges Kris and me to relate the gospel of Jesus Christ to a massively changing suburban environment. I pray that both of them learn from this short letter of Peter how to live as Christians in their new worlds, as Kris and I have sought to do in our worlds. As a token of our prayers, I dedicate this book to them.

I want to thank Trinity once again for the academic and pastoral environment it has provided for me over the last eleven years. This book, I trust, will serve as a living memorial of what Trinity has done to me and for me. As I write this preface, on a sabbatical, I eagerly await the collegiality of the Humanities Division of North Park College and the fellowship of the Evangelical Covenant Church. Once again, I wish to express my thanks to Terry Muck, our general editor, but especially to Jack Kuhatschek, not only for envisioning this remarkable series of books, but also for his painstaking scrutiny of my manuscript. Time after time he made suggestions that improved my thinking about Peter and our world. Frank Thielman, the author of *Philippians* in this series, carefully read a draft of this manuscript and made many helpful and encouraging suggestions. Finally, I want to express my thanks to my lovely wife, Kris, who creates a home where a marriage is as joyful as it is meaningful. In our daily walks around Butler Lake near our home, I frequently bounce my latest ideas off her and, nearly always, I have something more to write about by the time we get back. In this way she has enriched my understanding of 1 Peter.

Scot McKnight
North Park College

Abbreviations

ABD	*Anchor Bible Dictionary*
AJS	*American Journal of Sociology*
BAGD	Bauer, Arndt, Gingrich, Danker, *A Greek-English Lexicon of the New Testament*
BDF	Blass, Debrunner, Funk, *A Greek Grammar of the New Testament*
CCCSG	Christian College Coalition Study Guides
CT	*Christianity Today*
DCA	*Dictionary of Christianity in America*
DPL	*Dictionary of Paul and his Letters*
EDNT	*Exegetical Dictionary of the New Testament*
FCGRW	First-Century Christianity in the Graeco-Roman World
GNTE	Guides to New Testament Exegesis
HAR	*Hebrew Annual Review*
JBL	*Journal of Biblical Literature*
JETS	*Journal of the Evangelical Theological Society*
JTS	*Journal of Theological Studies*
KJV	King James Version
LCC	Library of Christian Classics
LEC	Library of Early Christianity
NIDNTT	*New International Dictionary of New Testament Theology*
NIV	New International Version
NRSV	New Revised Standard Version
NTS	*New Testament Studies*
QD	Quaestiones disputatae
RSV	Revised Standard Version
SBG	Studies in Biblical Greek
SSNTMS	Society for the Study of the New Testament Monograph Series
TDNT	*Theological Dictionary of the New Testament*
TNTC	Tyndale New Testament Commentary
TynBul	*Tyndale Bulletin*
WTJ	*Westminster Theological Journal*

Introduction

EVEN AS I WRITE this introduction, Christians all over the world are posturing themselves over against their culture, their society, their local community with its leaders, "the world" as they perceive it. They are reading newspapers, listening to news broadcasts and watching television news report the latest events, sitting in business and power sessions, researching trends in think tanks, meeting together for discussions—all in an effort to discern what is going on in their society so they can live more responsibly, so they can reach out to their world, and so they can fight against disturbing and disquieting tendencies. Each one in his or her own way is trying to follow Jesus and live the Christian life.

Just how Christians are doing this varies considerably. Consider, for example, these widely different situations:

- the liberationist in Latin America, armed as he or she is with the gospel of liberation, contesting social injustices even to the point of violence.
- the quietist, pacifist "non-efforts" of the Old Order Mennonites or Amish, "armed" as they are with the gospel of peace and holy living, ready to suffer, even die, if society deems it necessary to force them to change their hallowed interpretations of godly living.
- the aggressive actions of the Christian Coalition (part of which was formerly the Moral Majority) or the New Right Wing Conservatives in North American politics, armed as they are with the historical arguments for the preservation of traditional American culture, Judeo-Christian ethics, and free enterprise, analyzing culture and assaulting the media with rapid-fire observations about creeping liberalism, secularism, and pluralism.
- the stance of Christians in countries recently set free from the restrictions of oppressive socialistic or communistic governments, such as Poland and Romania, who are now posturing themselves over against a culture that is changing so rapidly that

stances fluctuate weekly. They only know that they are Christians but are unsure of how they fit and how they will fit when the governmental structures begin to settle down.

- the normal activity of Christian citizens in Western democracies who, with no fanatical ideological tendency, simply exist within a society and try to live before God with a clean conscience, witnessing to the salvation of God in Christ, living honorably within their community, and striving to please God in whatever they do—even if they, too, are sometimes confused about how to live.

This is but a smattering of the alternatives Christians living in the world today have. We could go on to detail Christians in China, Indonesia, North Korea, or Japan. Each culture confronts believers in that culture with a different face, a face that nonetheless colors the presentation of the gospel and forces Christians to examine their strategies.[1]

A pressing concern for the entire sweep of church history has been to answer the question: "How should we then live?"[2] Is it to be the activist form taken by Martin Luther King Jr., who led the famous boycotts and marches for civil rights? Is it to be the Utopian communitarianism of the Hutterites? Is it to be the aggressive action of the Moral Majority of the 1980s?[3] Just how should Christians interact with society? To the shame of many modern Christians, this kind of question is simply not being asked, even while passionate activity

---

1. For a study of various Christians positions on how Christians interact with society, see M. Noll, *One Nation Under God? Christian Faith and Political Action in America* (San Francisco: Harper & Row, 1988); for more recent evangelical views, see A. Cerillo, Jr., and M. W. Dempster, *Salt and Light: Evangelical Political Thought in Modern America* (CCCSG 3; Grand Rapids: Baker, 1989); see also S. Bruce, *The Rise and Fall of the New Christian Right: Conservativ Protestant Politics in America 1978–1988* (Oxford: Clarendon, 1990). For the problem of the lack of serious thinking about politics among evangelicals, see M. Noll, *The Scandal of the Evangelical Mind* (Grand Rapids: Eerdmans, 1994), 149–75; see also 221–28. T. Sine, *Cease Fire* (Grand Rapids: Eerdmans, 1995) is an exceptionally insightful analysis of both the politically correct left and the political right. H. Richard Niebuhr, *Christ and Culture* (New York: Harper and Row, 1951), is a classic treatment of the church and society.

2. The words used here come from the title of Francis Schaeffer's book, *How Should We Then Live? The Rise and Decline of Western Thought and Culture* (Old Tappan, N.J.: Revell, 1976).

3. Behind some of conservative Christian activism is F. A. Schaeffer, *A Christian Manifesto* (Westchester, Ill.: Crossway, 1982).

assumes some theoretical basis—and passionate activity has not been lacking.

In contemporary evangelicalism, for instance, most are dyed-in-the-wool Republicans because, it is assumed, that is the Christian view.[4] Such shallow thinking masks an entire host of questions and issues that deserve careful thinking and extensive Christian debate.[5] Along the same line, most of these Christians believe that the issues are simple and that the answers can be found in the Bible with exceptional, and alarming, clarity. Such intuitive confidence, however, has not been part of the history of the church's discussions of the relationship of the church and society.

Church history has seen three dominant theological answers to this question of how Christians are to interact with society and culture. The first, *a counterculture of separatism*, has been consciously espoused since the Radical Reformation by various branches of the Anabaptists, including the Mennonites, the Amish, and the Hutterites.[6] The foundation for this view is its deep anchor into the teachings and lifestyle of Jesus, a foundation that is sadly missing in many reflections on the relationship of the church and society.[7] While only rarely cloistering themselves in separate communes, these Christians have contended that the church is a separate institution that should in no way allow interference from the state in governing its affairs. It was only a natural extension of this stance to find the Anabaptists not only prohibiting governmental interference, but also refusing to participate in many, if

---

4. See esp. M. Noll, *Scandal*, 149–75. New issues and platforms, of course, have entered in, but it is not hard to remember when many conservative Christians were heavily Democratic in voting orientation; see also Sine, *Cease Fire*.

5. See the essay of Os Guinness, "Mission in the Face of Modernity," in *The Gospel in the Modern World: A Tribute to John Stott*, ed. M. Eden, D. F. Wells (Downers Grove, Ill.: InterVarsity, 1991), 85–107; J. Wallis, *The Soul of Politics: A Practical and Prophetic Vision for Change* (Maryknoll, N.Y.: Orbis, 1994).

6. On this see C. J. Dyck, "Anabaptist Tradition and Vision," in *DCA*, 58–59; W. R. Estep, *The Anabaptist Story* (Grand Rapids: Eerdmans, 1975), esp. 179–202; the most definitive writer for Anabaptists today with respect to the church and state is John Howard Yoder. See esp. his *The Politics of Jesus: Vicit Agnus Noster* (2d ed.; Grand Rapids: Eerdmans, 1994); *The Christian Witness to the State* (Institute of Mennonite Studies Series Number 3; Newton, Kans.: Faith and Life, 1964).

7. See especially J. H. Yoder, *The Politics of Jesus*; see also R. J. Sider, *Christ and Violence* (Scottsdale, Pa.: Herald, 1979); J. Wallis, *The Call to Conversion: Recovering the Gospel for These Times* (San Francisco: Harper & Row, 1981).

---

not most, of society's ways and means. This naturally led at times to a severe separatism, though many of today's Mennonites, for instance, participate much more in political and social activities—even if often in their own particular ways. But what should be noted is that this view emerges from a people who have had both the practical experience of living an alternative vision for God's people and the theoretical benefit of sustained reflection on the issues from both political and theological angles.

While this separatist stance has been radical and rare, the majority of Christians in the history of the church, particularly since the development of the Industrial Revolution with its rapid secularization of society, have participated by seeking to *extend Christian society into secular society*, arguing that if it is God's will for the individual Christian, it surely is his will for all of society. This has been called the "Reformed view" of the relationship of the church and the state.[8] Here we find a stance of moving from individual Christian ethics to corporate political ethics in whatever manner is appropriate to a local society (from grassroots agitation to powerful acts of legislation). The history of American politics has been dotted with this sort of maneuvering: from Christian activism in the prohibition of alcohol to the attempt to block the teaching of atheistic evolutionism in public schools, from fighting against international warfare to blocking abortion clinics, and especially of late the attempt to lobby and influence major politicians through political rallies.[9]

A third view, rarely with strong political force, is the Lutheran view that there are *two realms*, the realm of the kingdom of God as found in the church and the realm of the state.[10] Lutheran politics contend that

---

8. An early formative statement is John Calvin, *Institutes of the Christian Religion;* ed. J. T. McNeill; trans. F. L. Battles (LCC 21; Philadelphia: Westminster, 1960), 4.20; see also N. Wolterstorff, *Until Justice and Peace Embrace* (Grand Rapids: Eerdmans, 1983); at a more popular level, Schaeffer, *A Christian Manifesto.*

9. Francis Schaeffer's book *How Should We Then Live?* is a classic example of this; however, I do not want the reader to think that this view is to be reserved for the New Right Wing Conservatives of contemporary American politics. This Reformed view is at the heart of both liberal and conservative politics: Extending one's personal ethics, whether Christian or not, into the political realm unites both ends of the spectrum here.

10. A profound statement of this view can be found in Mark Noll, *One Nation.* Noll's book details the weaknesses of the "Reformed view" (pp. 158–166) and proposes just how the Bible ought to be used in political argumentation (pp. 167–181). I recommend this book wholeheartedly as a good starting point for Christian discussion.

the relation between God and his *people* (the church) and the relation between God and the *world* are in fact two kinds of relationships. The strategy of God is different for society than for the church. As a part of evangelicalism for nearly thirty years now, I can say unequivocally that most evangelicals previously adopted a stance, however unwittingly Lutheran they may have been, in which they see the church and the state as governed by two different impulses—but today there has been more political activism than in the last forty years. This activism has led many to a more Reformed orientation. I wonder, however, if this switch in stances was made as a result of theoretical reflection or of some other motivation (economic?). Noll states: "If, in fact, there is a difference between God in relation to the individual and God in relation to the world, then a failure to observe the structural and systematic differences between personal moral vision and comprehensive public crusade becomes an important matter."[11]

Peter's Problem

IT IS NOT my intent either to propose an alternative or to resolve the differences among Christians in the academic and public discussions about how they are to be involved in society. Rather, it is to say that one of the earliest Christian documents reflecting on the problem of the relation of the Christian to the state is the First Letter of Peter. It is my contention that we can learn some enduring insights from studying this letter. In fact, the problem discussed in the previous section might be called "Peter's Problem": In light of the relationship of Christians to the Roman-led government of Asia Minor, how should Christians live in Peter's day? Any reading of 1 Peter brings this issue to the surface immediately. It begins in the first verse: "Peter, an apostle of Jesus Christ, to God's elect, *strangers in the world, scattered. . . .*" Peter's contentions are clear: Believers in Asia Minor are to live honorable and holy lives (1:14–16, 18, 22; 2:1, 5, 9, 11–12, 15, 20; 3:6, 15, 17; 4:1–6), they are to endure suffering (1:6–8; 2:18–25; 3:13–17; 4:1–6, 12–19; 5:8–9, 10), they are to live within social structures (2:13–17, 18–25; 3:1–6, 7, 8–12), and they are to be respectful of outsiders (2:11–12).

---

11. Noll, *One Nation*, 27.

We might be tempted, then, to think that the answer to Peter's problem was simple: Live holy, be good citizens, participate in society in your own way, endure suffering, and don't make waves. And then we might be tempted to follow this simple solution by suggesting that this is how we, as modern Western Christians, are to relate to society (live holy, endure suffering, and don't make waves). But this is surely far too simplistic, and I know of few Christians who adopt such a quietist stance over against society. No, this simplistic procedure will not do.

For one thing, Peter's social world differs considerably from ours. The three views I sketched above, for instance, are proposals in the history of the church that have been drawn up in social situations dramatically different from first-century Asia Minor. In fact, it might be said that *different social situations elicit different strategies for living within society.* For example, a beleaguered minority, suffering physically at the hands of a ruthless anti-Christian government, will not think of "extending its virtues" into political activity, any more than a dominant Christian majority will think of remaining separate from governmental and political activity when that same government is begging for its votes and input. Put more graphically, enfranchised Christians in Washington, D.C., Bonn, Edinburgh, and Geneva will think of society and Christian influence in society in completely different categories than those disenfranchised Christians in Bogota, Moscow, Saigon, and Cairo. But it is fundamental for each to plumb the depths of the scriptural witness to God's activities in the history of his people and how that people has related to the world around it.

Our goal is to study 1 Peter in such a way as to highlight Peter's proposals for "Christian life in a modern society." To accomplish this task requires three procedures: (1) We must study the ancient text itself and determine the original meaning of Peter's text; (2) we must reflect on how we, as modern Westerners, are to move that meaning into our world by bridging the contexts; and (3) I want to suggest some contemporary significance of that original meaning. We begin by looking more particularly at Peter's world and the world of his audience.

Peter's World

Social Situation

THOSE FOR WHOM Peter intended this letter were "scattered throughout Pontus, Galatia, Cappadocia, Asia and Bithynia," regions that comprised the Roman provinces of northwestern Asia Minor (modern
Turkey). It has been suggested that the order of the provinces reflects
the order in which the letter would have traveled and been read (beginning in the northern region, traveling southerly to Galatia and Cappadocia, and then returning back to Bithynia through the province of
Asia). We can be certain that the letter was taken to the major cities
in these provinces, cities that were thriving and growing according
the pulses of the Roman empire.

While it is possible that evidence like quotations from the Old Testament (e.g., 1:16, 24; 2:3, 6, 9–10, 12) and the use of designations for
Israel (1:1 ["elect"]; esp. 2:9–10) could indicate that the readers were
formerly members of non-Christian Judaism,[12] I am persuaded that
the readers were mostly Gentiles who had probably previously become
attached to Judaism through local synagogues and other forms of
Judaism.[13] Thus, their former life was a life of living in ignorance (1:14),
which was handed on to them by their fathers (1:18). That they were
formerly "not [my] people" (2:10) points in the same direction, as does
their earlier pagan lifestyle (4:2–4). Yet it is likely that the road to
Christianity for these Gentile pagans included a stop at the local synagogue, where they were instructed in the Torah and the ways of the
Jewish people. This permits an easy reference to the Old Testament

---

12. A fundamental misunderstanding in much of contemporary popular literature is the
assumption that to be Jewish is to be non-Christian. While we need to respect the differences between Judaism and Christianity, it remains a fact that earliest Christianity developed out of Judaism and the earliest Christians were both Jewish and Christian. Thus,
when in this book I use "Judaism" and "Jews," I mean by these terms "non-Christian Judaism"
and "Jews who do not believe in Jesus Messiah"—unless the context makes it clear that I
mean "Jewish Christians" and their "Messianic Judaism." See J. D. G. Dunn, *The Partings of
the Ways Between Christianity and Judaism and Their Significance for the Character of Christianity*
(Philadelphia: Trinity Press International, 1991); C. A. Evans and D. A. Hagner, eds., *Anti-
Semitism and Early Christianity: Issues of Polemic and Faith* (Minneapolis: Fortress, 1993).

13. On this, see M. Green, *Evangelism in the Early Church* (Grand Rapids: Eerdmans, 1970);
for the Jewish context, see S. McKnight, *A Light Among the Gentiles: Jewish Missionary Activity
in the Second Temple Period* (Minneapolis: Fortress, 1991).

for Peter. It is also likely that some of the Christian converts were formerly Jewish in race and heritage.

What is dramatically interesting about this audience is that though they came from a Gentile background, Peter addresses them as if they were Israel. That is, they have in some sense "replaced" national Israel as the people of God and are now the new and true Israel. From the beginning of the letter to the end Peter describes the church with terms that have been used in defining Israel. They are the "elect" and "scattered" ones (1:1) and a "holy priesthood" (2:5). Most prominent here is 2:9–10: "You are a chosen people, a royal priesthood, a holy nation, a people belonging to God. ... Once you were not a people, but now you are the people of God; once you had not received mercy, but now you have received mercy." This is the language of fulfillment and replacement.[14]

In general, then, we can safely conclude that the audience of Peter was comprised of Gentile converts to Christianity who had probably been proselytes to Judaism or at least God-fearers. Two other terms give us further insight into the nature of their social conditions: "*aliens and strangers* in the world" (2:11–12). While the letter reveals an audience that has some "free men" (2:16) and "slaves" (2:18–20), some wives without Christian husbands (3:1–6), and some Christian husbands and wives (3:7), the terms *aliens* and *strangers* may be the most revealing of all about the social location of the audience.

It is true that many commentators, sometimes with little thought about the options, interpret these two words as a metaphor for the Christian's earthly existence while he or she awaits the true heavenly home.[15] But the work of J. H. Elliott has demonstrated that these two terms refer as much (if not more) to their *social* situation as it does to their *spiritual* situation.[16] Thus, Elliott argues, the audience of Peter was

---

14. J. R. Michaels, *1 Peter*, devotes much attention to this topic in his commentary; see the summary on pp. xlix–lv (the reader of Michaels will notice that I see more displacement theology than Michaels).

15. An example is my (now former) colleague W. A. Grudem, *1 Peter* (TNTC; Grand Rapids: Eerdmans, 1988), 48–49, 114–15.

16. See his *A Home for the Homeless: A Social-Scientific Criticism of I Peter, Its Situation and Strategy*, 2d ed. (Minneapolis: Fortress, 1990), esp. 21–100; see also the summary in his "Peter, First Epistle of," in *ABD*, 5:273–74. Those who desire to interact with the fullest measure of evidence will need to read Elliott's book in its entirety. I know of no full-scale analysis of Elliott's examination of these terms and their social meaning.

a group of socially marginalized people who were "resident aliens" and "temporary residents" prior to, and independent of, their conversion to Christianity. In other words, in these two terms we have a window into the social condition of the readers of 1 Peter: They were disenfranchised workers laboring in the cracks of a network that largely excluded them, but they had found the meaning to their existence in the Christian family.

If Elliott's case is reasonable, as I think it is, that does not mean that the New Testament has no "pilgrimage theme," for surely this is the heartbeat of the Christian life in the letter to the Hebrews. But two questions surface: "Is such a theme taught in 1 Peter?" and "Do the above-mentioned terms reflect such a theme?" We need to answer these questions before we can go any further. We begin with the terms *aliens* and *strangers*. These terms[17] refer respectively to a social status, to "non-citizen residents in some place" (that is, a person residing in a place without rights) and to "temporary residents" in some place. Such a social displacement was normal in the history of Israel, even if it was the result of the hand of God himself (cf. Gen. 15:13). In the Roman empire these terms were used for the group of resident aliens who occupied a special wrung on the social ladder—below citizens and above the slaves and foreigners.[18]

> Legally, such aliens were restricted in regard to whom they could marry, the holding of land and succession of property, voting, and participation in certain associations and were subjected to higher taxes and severer forms of civil punishment. Set apart from their host society by their lack of local roots, their ethnic origin, language, culture, and political or religious loyalties, such strangers were commonly viewed as threats to established order and native well-being. Constant exposure to local fear and suspicion, ignorant slander, discrimination and manipulation was the regular lot of these social outsiders.[19]

The "homelessness" of these people, in other words, led them to a "new home": the church, the family of God, in which they found social

---

17. The Greek word for *alien* is *paroikos;* for *stranger, parepidemos.*
18. The Greek word for *foreigner* is *xenos.*
19. J. H. Elliott, "Peter, First Epistle of," 273.

acceptance and protection. In interpreting these two terms in social rather than spiritual or metaphorical categories, I do not pretend to think that the message of 1 Peter is entirely social and unspiritual. In fact, the reverse is the case. These social nobodies found that God, in his grace, had chosen them as members of his great family (a spiritual house). Furthermore, the analogy today is clearly to our "homelessness" in our society, whether that be spiritual isolation or social manipulation, and our "at-homeness" in God's family. Even more, it becomes important for the church of Jesus Christ to find the social cracks and those who have fallen through, and then to minister the gospel of God's acceptance to them, to show them that God's true family transcends and neglects the social boundaries that society constructs. The church needs to demonstrate itself to be the family where all can be accepted.

Indeed, Elliott himself allows that the terms we have been discussing may be both social (disenfranchised people) and metaphorical (earthly life while waiting for a heavenly home), but he contends that the social reality is nonetheless the core of the matter. I affirm his perception. That is, the metaphorical description of God's people derives from their social marginalization. I believe Elliott has proven his case beyond reasonable doubt, and a significant number of scholars today on 1 Peter agree with him.[20] In what follows, I will utilize his thesis that the converts to Christ in Asia Minor were socially deprived and that one of their great discoveries was that in the family of God they were reenfranchised.

Authorship and Date

IT IS CUSTOMARY for commentaries to include a section on authorship and original date of the book. Many readers tire of such a procedure— and for good reason, because frequently such sections cover old paths with little fresh light. In a commentary of this sort, a rationale needs to be provided for looking at these issues. The essential argument can be stated like this: Our commentary takes *history* as significant for interpretation; for that reason alone authorship and date may prove to be important. If we can determine these two issues, then we have a firm

---

20. See the survey of scholarship in his *Home for the Homeless*, xxvi–xxxii. See also below at 1:1–2.

grasp of the historical realities behind the text and informing the world of that text.

The foundation for this series of commentaries is that one must move from the ancient world to the modern world, using various ways and differing strategies to communicate the ancient message in a relevant way. This observation is grounded on the assumption that the ancient text was embedded in historical, cultural, social, and religious contexts that need to be appreciated if we are to understand the message of the book aright. Throughout the pages of this commentary the reader will be referred to ancient texts, to evidence from Peter's world, and to observations about cultural and social conditions that need to be understood properly before we can understand what Peter was saying. A famous saying, albeit in German, is regularly bandied about in discussions like this: "Willst den Dichter Du verstehen, musst in Dichters Lande gehen." This saying, attributed to Goethe, says, "If you want to understand an author, you have to go to his land." I agree wholeheartedly with this saying. Thus, at the end of this section on Peter's world, we must pause to survey the issues surrounding the authorship and date of 1 Peter.

Because the letter begins by saying that Peter wrote it, evidence must be presented by any who claim that Peter did not write it.[21] I do not consider this a heavy-handed presupposition. Instead, it is a simple methodological point: If the text says Peter wrote the letter, then to contend that he did not requires proof. If there is no solid counterproof, we can consider the ascription to be solid. Yet I do not want to argue, as a presupposition, that pseudonymity is not found in the Bible, for there can be differing motivations for writing something pseudonymously. On the other hand, if one argues that Peter did write the letter, then one should also provide evidence for that. A good place to begin (but only to begin) is with the letter's beginning and its supposed author.

---

21. That is, if a letter asserts that a certain author wrote the book (in this case, Peter), then there must be persuasive evidence against that assertion to discount the assertion. In this case, there must be evidence that pseudonymous letters were written in the early church (there were) and that this letter fits into that category. On all of this, see D. G. Meade, *Pseudonymity and Canon* (Grand Rapids: Eerdmans, 1987); K. Aland, "The Problem of Anonymity and Pseudonymity in Christian Literature of the First Two Centuries," *JTS* 12 (1961): 39–49; B. M. Metzger, "Literary Forgeries and Canonical Pseudepigrapha," *JBL* 91 (1972): 3–24. A conservative classic is D. Guthrie, "Epistolary Pseudepigraphy," Appendix C in his *New Testament Introduction*, 4th ed. (Downers Grove, Ill.: InterVarsity, 1990), 1011–28.

Besides the name at the outset of the book, there are elements that confirm Peter as the author of the book. (1) The author has seen the sufferings of Jesus (2:21–24; 5:1). (2) Similarities between the teachings of Jesus and 1 Peter support an author who spent time with Jesus (cf. Luke 12:35 and 1 Peter 1:13; Luke 11:2 and 1 Peter 1:17; Matt. 5:16 and 1 Peter 2:12; Luke 6:28 and 1 Peter 3:9; Matt. 5:10 and 1 Peter 3:14). (3) There are also similarities between Peter's speeches in Acts and 1 Peter (cf. Acts 5:30, 10:39 and 1 Peter 2:24; Acts 2:23 and 1 Peter 1:20).[22] (4) One might also mention the rather vague, but sometimes suggested, idea that the theology and church organization of 1 Peter are early and consistent with what Peter would have taught.

Some, however, have argued that the Greek style of 1 Peter is simply too accomplished for Peter.[23] As Acts 4:13 states, "When they saw the courage of Peter and John and realized that they were *unschooled*, ordinary men, they were astonished and they took note that these men had been with Jesus." Could an "unschooled" man like Peter have written this book in such good Greek? The argument is solid but not unimpeachable. In fact, evidence from Acts suggests that Peter was in fact eloquent for someone who had not been educated (in the rabbinic manner?); this eloquence satisfies the evidence of 1 Peter. Furthermore, some contend that 1 Peter 5:12 describes Silas as contributing to the letter—perhaps polishing Peter's ideas (see comments). In short, while the major obstacle to Petrine authorship style[24] is serious enough that it must be given fair attention, the preponderance of evidence commends the traditional authorship. I will assume that Peter[25] did in fact write this letter.[26]

---

22. For other parallels, see John Drane, *Introducing the New Testament* (San Francisco: Harper & Row, 1986), 437.

23. Other arguments include (1) affinities to *1 Clement* (ca. A.D. 96), (2) the seeming spread of the gospel throughout Asia Minor and the need for sufficient time for such a spread, (3) a shift in attitudes toward the government from Romans 13 to 1 Peter, and (4 late use of the term "Babylon" (5:13), since parallels to this metaphorical description of Rome are found only after A.D. 70 (after Peter's presumed death).

24. I have been teaching 1 Peter in Greek to students at Trinity off and on since 1981, and I can affirm that our students are stumped over and over by the difficulty of Peter's style.

25. J. Jeremias: "those who today would defend the inauthenticity of 1 Peter are faced with no easy task" (*New Testament Theology: The Proclamation of Jesus* [New York: Charles Scribner's Sons, 1971], 307 n. 4).

26. For more complete studies, see D. Guthrie, *New Testament Introduction*, 762–81 (who responds to criticisms of the traditional viewpoint); Michaels, *1 Peter*, lv–lxvii. For an artic-

If Peter can be argued reasonably to be the author, then our letter was written prior to A.D. 64 or 65, when Peter was martyred at the hands of Nero. In light of the number of references to suffering and persecution in 1 Peter, we maintain that Peter wrote this letter near the outset of Nero's persecution of the church—perhaps between 62 and 65. Indeed, Peter's conciliatory attitude toward the state (2:13–17) and his optimism about Christian life in the context of an unbelieving society (2:11–3:12) suggest that Peter wrote this letter near the beginning of Nero's persecutions and that it is an early strategy for coping with serious problems from the state. We even dare to suggest that if Peter had waited five more years to write this letter, it would have been rearranged considerably. (And Peter could not have written it!)

Writing sometime in the early 60s, then, Peter, through his letter-carrier (or fellow author) Silas, encourages a series of small churches throughout northwestern Asia Minor by asserting their particular Christian identity (the family of God), by exhorting them to love one another, and by explaining to them the apparent inevitable tension that being a Christian will generate in a society that does not look tolerably on religious innovations.

Peter's Message

THE ESSENTIAL MESSAGE of Peter can be categorized into three separate features: (1) salvation, (2) church, and (3) the Christian life.[27] Peter's letter is an exhortation (5:12) to socially disenfranchised Christians to live steadfastly before God with faithfulness, holiness, and love. This steadfastness may lead to suffering, but a genuine understanding of persecution permits them to face it head-on and go forward faithfully. But the foundation of their faithfulness is an understanding of their salvation that Peter paints graphically at the beginning of his letter.

---

ulate and balanced defense of a later date and by an author other than Peter, cf. Elliott, "Peter, First Epistle of," 276–78.

27. See G. E. Ladd, *A Theology of the New Testament*, rev. D. A. Hagner (Grand Rapids: Eerdmans, 1993), 640–48.

Salvation

PETER USES A host of words to describe what has happened to those who enter the family of God. In particular, he draws deeply from the cultic imagery of the temple with its rituals and worship to express this matter. They have been sprinkled with blood (1:2), they have been ransomed (1:18–19), they have been purified (1:22), they have tasted God (2:3), they have been healed (2:24), and they have been presented before God (3:18). He draws on family imagery when he speaks of their new birth (1:3, 23; 2:2, 24; 3:7, 18), their inheritance (1:4–5), and their blessing (3:9). The two terms used most frequently are "salvation" (1:5, 9, 10; 2:2; 3:20–21; 4:18) and "grace" (1:10, 13; 3:7; 5:5, 10, 12).

That this understanding of salvation is the foundation of his ethical exhortation to faithfulness in the face of persecution can be seen in how these two themes are interwoven in the introductory section of the letter (1:3–12). There Peter praises God for their salvation and future hope, a future that is secured by God, and he rejoices in their current suffering because he knows what it will do for them as they await their final salvation, a salvation that was predicted long ago. The interweaving of these two themes—to the point of extreme grammatical complexity!—highlights how tied together these themes are for the apostle.

A similar twisting together of suffering and salvation can be seen in 2:18–25: Peter exhorts slaves not to rebel against even scurrilous masters because, after all, Jesus suffered in the same manner and he trusted God. But Peter's description of Jesus, the Great Example, tails off into a description of his saving work (2:24–25). Similarly in 3:18–22, the example of Jesus is described with reference to his saving ministry. Fittingly, in a deft combination of ethical exhortation rooted in the salvation of God, Peter's final prayer wish is that the "God of all grace, who called you to his eternal glory in Christ, after you have suffered a little while, will himself restore you and make you strong, firm and steadfast" (5:10).

Church[28]

AS MENTIONED ABOVE, the church (a term Peter does not use) displaces/replaces Israel in the favor of God as the new, true people of God (see comments at 2:8). Peter has raided the Old Testament for vocabulary about the new people of God. After describing them as the "elect" (1:1), the apostle lays himself down in a bed of images in chapter 2: "living stones" (2:5), "spiritual house" (2:5), "holy priesthood" (2:5); further, they are a "chosen people, a royal priesthood, a holy nation, a people belonging to God ... people of God ... [those who] have received mercy" (2:9–10).

In addition to these, some scholars today argue that the dominant image of the church in 1 Peter is *the family of God*.[29] The church is a "spiritual house" (2:5) or the "family of God" (4:17). As with other New Testament letters, the directions for specific groups of people are arranged around a family structure (2:11–3:12), revealing that Peter sees the church as a family of God. God is the Father (1:2, 3, 17), who gives birth (1:3) to the new children of God (1:14; 2:2), who in turn form a brotherhood (2:17; 5:9) that practices brotherly love (1:22; 3:8). This new home would have been spiritually and psychologically important to the homeless Christians of Asia Minor, for it was here that they found social acceptance and spiritual nurture. In short, they found a place they could call "home."

Peter leaves behind only residual traces of any church *organization*. The churches are led by the apostles who give directions to "elders" (5:1–4), who, Peter enjoins, are to lead the churches circumspectly and lovingly. While it is probable that these churches met to commemorate the Lord's Supper, only the rite of baptism is mentioned (3:21).[30]

---

28. See the full historical analysis of P. D. Hanson, *The People Called: The Growth of Community in the Bible* (San Francisco: Harper & Row, 1986), which regrettably has no section on 1 Peter; P. S. Minear, *Images of the Church in the New Testament* (Philadelphia: Westminster, 1975); D. Watson, *I Believe in the Church* (Grand Rapids: Eerdmans, 1978), 51–175; H. C. Kee, *Who Are the People of God? Early Christian Models of Community* (New Haven: Yale Univ. Press, 1995), esp. 124–29.

29. See J. H. Elliott, *Home for the Homeless*, 165–266; "Peter, First Epistle of," 275–76.

30. It has been argued that the bulk of 1 Peter is a "baptismal liturgy," but this theory has fallen out of favor recently. For discussions, see F. L. Cross, *1 Peter: A Paschal Liturgy* (London: Mowbray, 1954); F. W. Beare, *1 Peter*, 25–28, 220–26 (in favor of seeing 1:3–4:11 as a baptismal discourse); J. N. D. Kelly, *Epistles of Peter and Jude*, 15–20 (who argues against such a theory). For possible allusions to baptism, see W. A. Grudem, *1 Peter*, 40–41.

Christian Life[31]

GROUNDED IN THE salvation that the believers find in Christ through their new birth (1:3), the Christian life is an inevitable manifestation of that salvation. The exhortations in 1 Peter are rooted in this experience. Thus, after detailing salvation and its privileges (1:3–12), Peter exhorts his readers to practice hope (1:13), holiness (1:14–16), fear before God (1:17–21), love (1:22–24), and growth (2:1–8). The key word at 1:13 is "therefore": because of salvation, *therefore* pursue these Christian virtues. For Peter, ethics apart from a grounding in salvation is of no concern because a moral life forms the reverse side of salvation. In the words of Wolfgang Schrage, "Without new birth, there is no new obedience. Without hope, there is no basis for Christian life."[32]

The *social context* of the Christian life is crucial in 1 Peter: The audience is socially disenfranchised and has found a home in the family of God. They are experiencing persecution, both because of their social location and their spiritual orientation, and Peter's exhortations concentrate on their need to endure unjust suffering, just as Jesus did (1:6; 2:18–25; 3:13–17; 4:1–6, 12–19; 5:8–10).[33] Without doubt, this social context influences his entire letter to such a degree that his message must be rearranged dramatically in order to speak to a situation where Christians experience little social suffering.

Peter's perspective on the Christian life is that Christians are *to live for the salvation that is to come*, another indication of the social context of this family of God. God, who judges justly (1:7, 9, 17; 2:12, 23; 3:12; 4:5, 17–19), will reward those who faithfully endure suffering for his sake (1:7, 13; 4:13, 14). After all, they are only temporary residents in their social location (1:1); this provides a key for them to understand that they are to live for the future. As they pursue faith (1:5, 8–9, 21; 2:6–7; 5:9), hope (1:3, 13, 21; 3:5, 15), and joy (1:6, 8; 4:13), they are to be secure in God's protection of them (1:5). Their *primary social group* has become the church, the family of God, where they are to love

---

31. See R. Schnackenburg, *The Moral Teaching of the New Testament*, trans. J. Holland-Smith and W. J. O'Hara (New York: Seabury, 1965), 365–71; W. Schrage, *The Ethics of the New Testament*, trans. D. E. Green (Philadelphia: Fortress, 1988), 268–78.

32. Schrage, *Ethics*, 271.

33. See L. Goppelt, *Theology of the New Testament. Volume 2: The Variety and Unity of the Apostolic Witness to Christ*, trans. J. E. Alsup, ed. J. Roloff (Grand Rapids: Eerdmans, 1982), 174–75.

one another (1:22; 2:17; 3:8–12; 4:8–9; 5:14), be humble (3:4, 15; 5:6), submit to one another (3:1–7; 5:1–4, 5), and serve one another (4:10–11). Above all, they are to be sensitive in their communication with one another (2:1; 4:7–11).

A clear ethical orientation for Peter is that God's family is to be *holy and pure*. They are to obey God (1:2, 13, 22), be holy because God is holy (1:14–16, 18, 22; 2:1–2, 5, 9, 11–12, 15, 20; 3:6, 15, 17; 4:1–6), and live righteous lives (2:24; 3:13; 4:18). Such holiness will serve as a convincing demonstration to outsiders of God's salvation (2:11–12, 13–17, 18–25; 3:1–6); their lives, then, are a means of evangelism (2:12, 15; 3:1–6, 16), though such lives are to be accompanied by their verbal witness (1:12, 25; 2:9; 3:15; 4:6).

In essence, then, Peter's letter is an exhortation to holy endurance of suffering because these Christians have experienced the salvation of God and because that salvation is promised to them in all fullness when the final day arrives. Having received salvation and having been empowered by God with a new life, they must orient their lives toward the future revelation of Christ, love their fellow Christians, and maintain a holy life.

Outline of 1 Peter

MOST OUTLINES OF New Testament books are more precise and organized than careful study seems to justify or demand.[34] Furthermore, outlines involve subjective judgments that cannot demonstrate an appropriate sensitivity to other (just as careful) judgments. The following outline will serve as our guide throughout the book; I heartily urge that students of 1 Peter struggle with its structure themselves.

---

34. Thus, N. Brox writes: "When one reads 1 Peter without interruption (as it is intended to be), it leaves behind a genuinely vague impression concerning both its form and its contents" (*Der erste Petrusbrief*, 15; translation mine); so also A. Schlatter, as quoted by L. Goppelt: "A predetermined plan [from the author] cannot be found because one never existed" (*1 Peter*, 15). See the discussion of C. H. Talbert, "Once Again: The Plan of 1 Peter," in *Perspectives on First Peter*, ed. C. H. Talbert (National Association of Baptist Professors of Religion Special Studies Series 9; Macon, Ga.: Mercer Univ. Press, 1986), 141–51.

Peter's Relevance

APPLYING 1 PETER TO our world is not as simple as it might seem. If we assume that the letter was (1) sent to those who were socially marginalized (for whatever reasons), (2) encouraging them to endure persecution and to live holy, loving lives because (3) they were in God's family and (4) their salvation was being protected by God until the revelation of Christ, we can probably assert up front that the first and second aspects of this message are virtually irrelevant to the bulk of West-ern readers. Furthermore, the assurance that our salvation is being pro-tected by God is anchored to the context of suffering, making it difficult to apply today.

Nonetheless, to speak of disenfranchised people (whether as the result of social status or spiritual orientation does not matter here) is immediately to limit the message of Peter for the Western world, espe-cially for the majority of Christians living in our country. For more than a decade I have met once a week with a dozen or so students, who have never once raised a concern about persecution or outright suffering for their faith. At the same time, in one of the earliest classes I taught at Trinity when I raised this issue of the "irrelevancy" of some of the main elements of Peter's message, two of my students—one from Yugoslavia (who was pastoring at that time over a dozen separate churches) and the other from Indonesia—explained to me that 1 Peter was the most popular New Testament book among Christians in their countries.

I must admit I have never met any Christians in the United States who have told me that 1 Peter was their favorite book or even high on the priority list. Most Christians enjoy Psalms and Proverbs, many Christians enjoy Philippians or 1 John, active countercultural types like the teachings of Jesus (especially the Sermon on the Mount), academic-theological types like Romans, charismatic types like Acts, practical types like James—but few people raise their hands in Sunday school classes and ask the teacher to expound 1 Peter. Why? The answer is simple: Too much of it is centered on aspects of Christian existence that are far from most Western Christian experiences: social marginalization and suffering.

Does this mean we should actively pursue suffering? Just how we might do this is another matter (should we be more obnoxious in our presentation of the gospel, or should we be less pleasant?), but the pursuit of suffering is clearly not what we ought to be doing. For the letter to make sense to us does not mean we have to suffer. I suppose it would be healthy for us to learn about suffering so that, if a life of suffering ever became more typical for Western Christians, we would be better prepared. But this seems almost silly. No, we must simply admit that the suffering context of the letter makes it more distant for us than for those of our Christian brothers and sisters who are suffer-ing. Making the suffering passages relevant to our world, however, is not something we ought to neglect. In the commentary I will attempt to do this.

What about disenfranchisement? Should we pursue this situation so that 1 Peter can meet our needs? I would say, to begin with, that though this letter is to the socially disenfranchised, it is not an encouragement to live in such a social status. The author does not praise the lower classes, the dispossessed, and (in a Tolstoyan manner) the glory of the proletariat peasant class.[35] He does not offer a sentimental honoring of the beauty of poverty and oppression. Nor does this letter encourage the Christians of Asia Minor to go out and bring in social dropouts. In other words, it is not Peter's intent to encourage people to become social castaways or to critique the upper classes, the powerful, and the wealthy. His is not a religion of the disinherited, though his message is clearly articulated *for* the disinherited. Rather, this *was their condition*, and Peter *explains how Christians ought to live in that condition in light of God's future salvation.*

And surely, one of the fundamental aspects of his teaching is to inculcate in his audience *a true Christian identity.*[36] He wants his readers to understand, appreciate, and appropriate their special relationship to God (as a result of their salvation) and their new relationship to others in the universal family of God. Put differently, he does not want them to focus on their social marginalization or on persecution because of their faith; rather, he wants them to see that no matter what happens, God loves them, protects them, and has promised that when the End comes, they will be vindicated and glorified. Consequently, they can rejoice now with an inexpressible delight in God's goodness (1:8–9). Thus, Peter intends his readers to understand who they are before God so that they can be who they are in society.

The other elements of Peter's message, of course, are not hard to find relevant: to live loving, holy lives; to find in the church the fam-

---

35. In about the middle of his life, Leo Tolstoy, the famous Russian novelist and idealist, converted to Christian idealism. From that point on he renounced his possessions (though he lived on a large estate) and the royalties from his bestsellers (though his wife and family received them), and he adopted peasant dress. Beside the oddity of his personality and his genius, this sentimental attachment to peasants caused no end of grief in his marriage. See the insightful study of W. L. Shirer, *Love and Hatred: The Troubled Marriage of Leo and Sonya Tolstoy* (New York: Simon & Schuster, 1994).

36. A good book in this regard is D. Keyes, *Beyond Identity: Finding Your Self in the Image and Character of God* (Ann Arbor, Mich.: Servant, 1984).

ily of God; and to appreciate God's protection. These we will find as contemporary now as they were then, even if they emerge from a different social context than ours. First Peter, then, addresses a special situation that is different from ours but which, nonetheless, has much to offer our social context.

The issue facing the Christians in Asia Minor was disturbingly simple: How should we live in this context of social exclusion and persecution? Should we escape into a more sheltered world? Should we withdraw from society? Should we turn a cold shoulder to our world? Should we denounce society in poetic and prophetic tones? How then should we live? Peter's letter is a window into a situation that even throws light on our world; his letter is one of the first struggles in the church with society. It formed some of the conversation that continues to this day, and in our examination of it, we will reap great reward.

Annotated Bibliography

IN THIS COMMENTARY, I have tried to limit myself to studies that most of my (imagined) readers would have access to. Hence, I have tried to omit citation of scholarly and foreign language studies. On the other hand, I have compensated for this omission by continually citing the major commentaries so that my readers do not have to look up other viewpoints on a regular basis. Of the works on 1 Peter, my favorites are: Beare (whom I read first, while a seminarian), Selwyn (whose work influenced my first lectures on 1 Peter), Goppelt (who was the first German commentator I read), and Michaels (the most recent comprehensive study). I also found Marshall's exposition very helpful. Outside the commentary genre, I find Elliott's book to be profound and nearly irrefutable at the level of his main theses. First Peter has been anointed with an abundance of wonderful commentaries and studies. I am grateful for the many I have been privileged to read.

Beare, F. W. *The First Epistle of Peter: The Greek Text with Introduction and Notes*. 3d ed. Oxford: Basil Blackwell, 1970. An insightful, provocative, and suggestive exegesis of 1 Peter. Beare's commentary is written for those who can read Greek, but, with effort, those without Greek can generally understand his points. Beare accepts the theory that the letter is rooted in a baptismal context. He compares the ideas of Peter with Paul throughout.

Best, E. *1 Peter*. NCB. Grand Rapids: Eerdmans, 1971. Helpful and charming work on 1 Peter. Best always has one hand on the text and the other on church life. It is only slightly dated.

Bigg, C. *A Critical and Exegetical Commentary on Epistles of St. Peter and St. Jude*. ICC. Edinburgh: T. and T. Clark, 1902. For six decades, this was the definitive commentary on 1 Peter. Consequently, Bigg shaped the conversation that continues to this day. One departs from old friends only reluctantly. Bigg has always been at my side. This one is only for those with expertise in Greek.

Brox, N. *Der erste Petrusbrief*. EKKNT 21. Koln: Benziger/Neukirchener, 1979. Exhaustive, comprehensive, critical commentary. It takes into consideration all the latest theories about 1 Peter and the development of early Christian beliefs and practices. Useful for those who can read German, it deserves to be translated into English. Brox is Germany's leading scholar on pseudepigraphy.

Clowney, E. *The Message of 1 Peter*. The Bible Speaks Today, ed. J. W. R. Stott. Downers Grove, Ill.: InterVarsity, 1988. A readable exposition of the message of 1 Peter. Clowney attempts to synthesize the message of Peter with major themes in the Bible. Unfortunately, he does not give Elliott a careful reading.

Cranfield, C. E. B. *The First Epistle of Peter*. London: SCM, 1950. This lucid exposition by a brilliant New Testament scholar is unfortunately difficult to obtain. Full of both exegetical and homiletical insights. It is now slightly dated.

Davids, P. H. *The First Epistle of Peter*. NICNT, ed. G. D. Fee. Grand Rapids: Eerdmans, 1990. Solid exegesis of 1 Peter, with helpful introductory essays. Davids' essays on theology are especially useful for the expositor.

Elliott, J. H. *A Home for the Homeless: A Social-Scientific Criticism of 1 Peter, Its Situation and Strategy*. Minneapolis: Fortress, 1990. Scholarly examination of the meaning of 1 Peter in its social context in Asia Minor. This commentary is especially useful for its study of "aliens and strangers."

Goppelt, L. *A Commentary on 1 Peter*. Ed. F. Hahn. Trans. J. E. Alsup. Grand Rapids: Eerdmans, 1993. Profound commentary by a brilliant German theologian of the previous generation (orig. published in 1978). Though heavily influenced by debates about 1 Peter in Europe, Goppelt's commentary is still exceedingly useful for the patient reader. Occasionally it relates items in 1 Peter to discoveries of the Dead Sea Scrolls.

Grudem, W. *1 Peter*. TNTC. Grand Rapids: Eerdmans, 1988. A useful exposition of 1 Peter, with special attention to word studies and synthesizing theological themes in their larger context. Grudem offers an extensive additional note that treats the notoriously difficult text on Christ's preaching to the spirits (1 Peter 3:18–22).

Kelly, J. N. D. *The Epistles of Peter and Jude*. Black's NTC. London: Adam & Charles Black, 1969. A brilliant commentary by a patristics specialist, the best one available of those based on English translations. Time and time again, Kelly offers insightful observations on the message and significance of Peter's theology. He is influenced to some degree by the baptismal theory of 1 Peter's origins and often finds tantalizing parallels in early Christian writings.

Luther, M. *Commentary on Peter and Jude*. Grand Rapids: Kregel, 1990 [reprint ed.]. The great Reformer's insights on 1 Peter, though not as profound as his exegesis of Romans and Galatians, are still helpful. This commentary is hard to use because Luther did not make a distinction between an explanation of the text and theologizing for his churches. But that is what made Luther who he was.

Marshall, I. H. *1 Peter*. InterVarsity Press NT Comentary, ed. G. R. Osborne. Downers Grove, Ill.: InterVarsity, 1991. A lucid, readable commentary that both expounds 1 Peter and applies its message to our world. Marshall is currently the "veteran" of evangelical scholars in Great Britain.

Michaels, J. Ramsey. *1 Peter*. WBC 49. Waco, Tex.: Word, 1988. The best scholarly commentary available on 1 Peter today. It is exegetical, comprehensive, and rich in bibliography. Michaels is cautious about the relationship of Peter's Christians to the Jewish people.

Selwyn, E. G. *The First Epistle of St. Peter. The Greek Text, with Introduction, Notes, and Essays*. London: Macmillan, 1961. A magisterial commentary, only for those with an ability to use Greek. For years, this was the only serious commentary in English, though it has now been largely replaced by Michaels and Goppelt. It is still of use for the patient observer; his essays are permanently useful.

1 Peter 1:1–2

※

ETER, AN APOSTLE of Jesus Christ,
To God's elect, strangers in the world, scattered
throughout Pontus, Galatia, Cappadocia, Asia
and Bithynia, ²who have been chosen according to the
foreknowledge of God the Father, through the sanctifying work of the Spirit, for obedience to Jesus Christ and
sprinkling by his blood:
Grace and peace be yours in abundance.

PETER'S SALUTATION[1] is one of the richest
greetings to open a letter in the New Testament. It contains pastoral warmth and theological sweep. Whereas some salutations
orient themselves around Christology (Rom. 1:1–7), salvation (Gal.
1:1–5), or the church (1 Cor. 1:1–3), and others are "bare bones"
greetings (e.g., Eph. 1:1–2; Col. 1:1–2; 1 Thess. 1:1–2; 1 Tim. 1:1–
2), Peter's salutation contains both a penetrating description of the
audience and a theological explanation of how they became Christians.
While Paul's greetings are frequently tinged with a necessity to defend
himself, Peter's apostolic status is not under question, leaving his title
a simple, humble claim to authority (cf. 1 Peter 1:1; 5:1). As with other
New Testament letters,[2] the themes of the salutation become central
to the letter itself: the status of the people of God and the salvation
God provides for them. Peter's letter has been categorized with other
ancient hortatory (paraenetic) letters.[3]

---

1. One of the main words for greeting in Latin is *salutatio* ("salute").

2. On letters, see S. K. Stowers, *Letter Writing in Greco-Roman Antiquity* (LEC 5; Philadel-
phia: Westminster, 1986); W. G. Doty, *Letters in Primitive Christianity* (Philadelphia: Fortress,
1973); S. McKnight, "More Than Mere Mail," *Moody Monthly* 88/89 (May 1988): 36–38.
See also the summary of D. E. Aune, *The New Testament in Its Literary Environment* (LEC 8;
Philadelphia: Westminster, 1987), 158–225; S. K. Stowers, "Letters (Hebrew; Aramaic;
Greek and Latin)," *ABD*, 4:282–93.

3. See Stowers, *Letter Writing*, 91–152. Stowers finds several kinds of "Letters of Exhortation and Advice": paraenetic (exhortation and dissuasion), advice, protreptic (exhortation
to a way of life), admonition, rebuke, reproach, and consolation. We run amok, however,

Letters of the ancient world began with the author's name and any descriptions needed (here: "Peter, an apostle of Jesus Christ"), the addressee and any necessary descriptions (here: "To God's elect . . ."), and the greeting proper (here: "Grace and peace be yours in abundance"). Thus, there are three parts. Peter expands the *addressee* to include a threefold breakdown: the believers in Asia Minor are who they are (1) *"according to* the foreknowledge of God the Father," (2) *"through* the sanctifying work of the Spirit," (3) *"for* obedience to Jesus Christ and sprinkling by his blood." The italicized prepositions highlight the triadic description of these believers, and each is connected to a different member of the Trinity.

The Sender. Peter has been categorized in popular writings and sermons as impetuous and impulsive, but we know far too little about him to know whether such psychological descriptions are fair. We do know that he was a fisherman on the northern shore of Galilee, he was called by Jesus to follow him (cf. Luke 5:1–11; John 1:35–42), he become the leader of the apostolic band (Matt. 10:2), he was the first to perceive Jesus as the Messiah (Matt. 16:17–19; Mark 8:27–33), he tried to walk on water (Matt. 14:28–31), he denied Jesus (Luke 22:21–23, 31–34, 54–71), he was restored (John 21:15–19), he was a primary leader of the new church formed at Pentecost (Acts 2–5), he received a magnificent vision about the unity of God's people (Acts 10–11), he was miraculously released from prison (Acts 12:1–17), and he continued to have a ministry as far as Rome (cf. Acts 12:18–19; 15; Gal. 2:7–8; 1 Cor. 1:12; 9:5; 1 Peter; 2 Peter). We know that Peter's ministry in Rome was so extensive that Roman Catholics see the foundation of their church in his ministry there; we also know that Peter's ministry has become far too divisive of an issue between Roman Catholics and Protestants.[4]

---

if we think reductionistically, contending that 1 Peter has to have only one trait. Rather, while Peter's first letter is clearly paraenetic, it contains other methods of exhortation and advice.

4. See O. Cullmann, *Peter: Disciple-Apostle-Martyr: A Historical and Theological Study*, trans. F. V. Filson (Philadelphia: Westminster, 1953); O. Karrer, *Peter and the Church: An Examination of Cullmann's Thesis* (QD 8; New York: Herder and Herder, 1963); R. E. Brown, K. P. Donfried, and J. Reumann, *Peter in the New Testament: A Collaborative Assessment by Protestant and Roman Catholic Scholars* (Minneapolis: Augsburg / New York: Paulist, 1973); C. P. Thiede, *Simon Peter: From Galilee to Rome* (Exeter: Paternoster, 1986).

Perhaps more important for the interpretation of our letter, we can discern in Peter an "about-face" over the question of Jesus' death: from outright rejection (Matt. 16:22) and denial (Luke 22:54–71), to restoration (John 21), to preaching the death and vindication of Jesus (Acts 2), to finding in the death of Jesus the ultimate paradigm of Christian existence (1 Peter 2:18–25). This trail of Peter's conversion is what lies beneath our letter: a Peter who found in Jesus' death and resurrection the secret of life. Another feature of his life that is fundamental for understanding his letter is that his original name was "Simon" and only through a special calling by Jesus was it changed to "Cephas" (or "Peter").[5] His name change included Jesus' prediction of his role in the development of the early church: Simon would be a "foundation," a "rock" (*petros*), upon whom the church would be built. In light of this, Peter developed the metaphor of Christians as "living stones" (2:4–8).

Peter was an "apostle of Jesus Christ." An apostle[6] is one who was personally called by Jesus to a special ministry of founding the church; the corollary of that calling is that an apostle represents, as an ambassador does a president, the one who sent him. Peter, like the other apostles, was a personal representative of Jesus, and how people responded to Peter reflected how they responded to Jesus (cf. Matt. 10:40–42). Yet we should note that Peter does not brandish his authority like a saber; rather, he states his title here and then uses the more humble power of rhetoric and persuasion. Not until 5:12 do we again see his authority, unless it be noted (as it probably can be) in his use of commands and prohibitions. In fact, Peter identifies himself with the leaders of the various churches (5:1).[7] Nonetheless, the "letter is to be seen, not as the pious opinions of a well-wishing friend, but as the authoritative word of one who speaks for the Lord of the church himself."[8]

The Addressees. The geographical location of Peter's churches is not as important as the terms he uses to describe their social and spiritual

---

5. "Cephas" is an Aramaic word that is translated into Greek by "Peter."

6. See K. H. Rengstorf, "ἀπόστολος," *TDNT*, 1:407–47; J.-A. Bühner, "ἀπόστολος," *EDNT*, 1:142–46; H. D. Betz, "Apostle," *ABD*, 1:309–11; P. W. Barnett, "Apostle," *DPL*, 45–51.

7. C. E. B. Cranfield, *First Peter*, 12: "So here in our letter the word 'apostle' is essentially an exceedingly humble word; for it directs attention away from the Apostle's person to Him, whose Apostle he is, from the one sent to the One that has sent him."

8. P. Davids, *1 Peter*, 46.

status: "To God's[9] elect, strangers[10] in the world, scattered[11] throughout Pontus, Galatia, Cappadocia, Asia and Bithynia, who have been
chosen according to the foreknowledge of God the Father, through the
sanctifying work of the Spirit, for obedience to Jesus Christ and sprinkling by his blood." Another translation, one that I will refer to occasionally in the discussion that follows, is "To the sojourning elect[12]
who are scattered throughout . . ." (pers. trans.).

To be "elect" means to receive God's grace; this benefit is the result
of God's initiative, not ours.[13] In other words, God has called us to his
love and grace, he has prompted our faith through the regenerating
work of the Holy Spirit, and he claims our allegiance (cf. John 15:16;
Rom. 8:28; 1 Cor. 1:9; Eph. 4:1; 2 Thess. 2:14; 2 Tim. 1:9; 1 Peter
1:15; 2:4, 6, 9, 21; 3:9; 5:10). To be one of God's elect is a source of
joy and comfort (for we know God's will cannot be thwarted) and of
exhortation and demand (for we know God is working in us to enable
us to do his will).

---

9. Actually, "God's" is not in the original Greek text; the word is, however, implied.
Adding words like this tends to focus the expression in ways that are not always accurate.
In this instance, a social-ecclesiological focus is lost when "God's" is added.

10. In the Greek the words for "elect" and "strangers" are in the same case (dative) and
their relationship is such that one is not sure which is the noun and which is the adjective.
Thus, is it "sojourning elect ones" or "elect sojourners"? The NIV has decided that "strangers"
is an adjective and "elect" is the noun. Furthermore, it has added "in the world" to "strangers"
as an interpretation of the term "strangers" in such a manner that the *only possible* meaning
one can infer from this expression is a spiritual status. As mentioned in the introduction, this
term probably refers to a social status. Thus, while I would agree that the NIV's rendering
is a tolerable interpretation, I believe the translators have gone beyond their limits here by
forcing the expression into only one possible meaning. When terms are ambiguous, it is usually best to leave them ambiguous rather than trying to be more specific than the author.

11. The Greek word *diaspora* is translated by "scattered" (from which we get Diaspora).

12. I prefer the term "sojourners" over "strangers" because, in American English, the latter speaks of weirdness and oddity; the former, at least, conveys the notion of "temporary
residency away from home." Another good term would be "exiles." The term "elect" is the
noun and the adjective "sojourning" is placed after it for a smoother transition to "scattered
throughout. . . ." See Michaels, *1 Peter*, 7; "chosen sojourners" is preferred in Grudem, *1 Peter*,
47—48.

13. This issue has, of course, been a divisive issue among theologians; Calvinistic views
may be found in A. A. Hoekema, *Saved by Grace* (Grand Rapids: Eerdmans, 1989), 68—92;
L. Berkhof, *Systematic Theology* (4th ed.; Grand Rapids: Eerdmans, 1972), 109—25, 415—22,
454—79; an Arminian view can be seen in J. R. Williams, *Renewal Theology: Salvation, the Holy
Spirit, and Christian Living* (Grand Rapids: Zondervan, 1990), 13—33. Williams helps at the pastoral level in correcting potential errors and misunderstandings of this important doctrine.

The Meaning of "Aliens and Strangers": A Brief Study. Not only did Peter's churches enjoy a special status with God; Peter uses another term that goes a long way in helping us to understand the social location of his readers. In the introduction I observed that this term "strangers" (or "sojourners") can refer either metaphorically to their temporary residence on earth as they await final salvation (NIV)—the so-called pilgrimage theme—or literally to the social location in their communities. It is important to pause for a brief study of this term and another one like it, "aliens" (2:11), and of the idea of a pilgrimage theme in this letter. By looking at more than one term at a time, we will have a wider grasp of what Peter is saying and will avoid the hazard of being concerned with only one term apart from its larger contexts.

First, I must observe that the inertia of convention propels us in the direction of a metaphorical sense to these terms. Most popular and scholarly works interpret 1 Peter 1:1 and 2:11 as describing the Christian pilgrimage on earth. Many commentators assume this view without further reflection[14] and give little space to arguing against the unconventional view.[15] Progress in interpretation can never be gained if we simply repeat habitual interpretations; instead, we must look again at the evidence to see what it says. If we arrive at an unconventional conclusion, we may be breaking free from unnecessary restrictions, though we may also be simply wrong. But such are the implications of exploring interpretations.

Second, there is no doubt that the literal meaning of these terms refers to people in specifically low social conditions. The Greek word for "foreigners" or "aliens" (*paroikos*) refers to people who reside in a given place without the legal protection and rights provided for citizens (i.e., noncitizen residents); the Greek word for "strangers" (*parepidemos*) refers to people who reside in a place but who stay there

---

14. A clear example of this is P. Davids, *1 Peter*, 46–47. In spite of writing his commentary during the time when Elliott's ideas about "foreigners and strangers" were being hotly debated and the trend was moving toward Elliott, Davids never once raises the issue in his commentary. Instead, he assumes that the terms are metaphorical. So also the (otherwise) fine study of B. W. Winter, *Seek the Welfare of the City: Christians as Benefactors and Citizens* (FCGRW; Grand Rapids: Eerdmans, 1994), 12.

15. Thus, Elliott, *Home for the Homeless*, xxviii–xxx (review of the recent discussion).

only for a brief time (temporary residents).[16] This is the literal senses of these two terms; when used metaphorically (in the rare instances when they are found this way), they emphasize, in some nonliteral sense, sojourning in a place temporarily or being found as an alien in some location.

Third, the issue here, then, is *whether there is evidence that the terms in question are being used metaphorically.* Good metaphors are drawn from reality, from the hustle and bustle of normal life. Here we have two terms drawn from perceptions of the social rank and how society works. However, a standard principle of interpretation insists that words be taken literally unless there is something in the context that tips the reader off to a metaphorical use of a term. For example, it strains our reading to think that "slaves" in 1 Peter 2:18 does not refer to actual social status but instead to our "slave-minds" and that we are being exhorted to submit to reason, for nothing in the text makes us think that anything other than a social class is in view.[17] The questions we must face, then, are simple: Is there evidence for a metaphorical use here either in the type of literature we are examining[18] or in the immediate context? And how do we discern the difference between a literal meaning and a metaphorical one?

The late G. B. Caird, in his masterful book on language and interpretation,[19] proposes four tests to discern when a given word or phrase is being used metaphorically. (1) At times the biblical author makes an explicit statement that a given expression is metaphorical, as when he uses the word "like," states that such-and-such is an allegory (Gal. 4:24), or adds a qualifier that shows something other than the literal

---

16. Thus, the use of the expression "aliens and strangers" in the NIV (2:11) has little chance of informing the reader of the nuances involved in the original expressions. Although not perfect, I prefer the expression "aliens and sojourners." A nearly exhaustive listing of translation possibilities can be found in J. H. Elliott, *Home for the Homeless,* 39–41.

17. Philo of Alexandria, a first-century Jewish philosopher in Alexandria, did just this sort of thing with Old Testament narratives. For an introduction, see especially E. Schürer, *The History of the Jewish People in the Age of Jesus Christ (175 B.C.–A.D. 135),* rev. ed. G. Vermes, F. Millar, and M. Goodman (Edinburgh: T. & T. Clark, 1987), 3.2:809–89.

18. That is, it is normal to find metaphors in apocalyptic literature (like Revelation) or in poetry (like Psalms and the Song of Solomon); narrative and letters, on the other hand, are not as full of metaphors. Reading a letter makes us think naturally of the literal sense to referential terms of a personal nature. However, this does not exclude the use of metaphors.

19. G. B. Caird, *The Language and Imagery of the Bible* (Philadelphia: Westminster, 1980), 183–97.

sense is intended (Matt, 5:3—"poor in spirit"; Eph. 2:14—"wall of hostility"; 1 Peter 1:13—"the loins of your mind"[20]). (2) Sometimes an expression is impossible to understand literally. For example, the believers in Asia Minor are not literally "a royal priesthood" (2:9), their leaders are not really "shepherding flocks of real sheep" but are leading the believers the way a shepherd leads his flocks (5:2), and it is not their literal "brothers" who are suffering throughout the world but their spiritual brothers (5:9). (3) There must be a certain amount of correspondence between an expression and the reality itself for something to be literal; when the correspondence is low, then we have a clue to the use of a metaphor. Thus, just as it is unlikely that Peter was in "Babylon" (5:13), so it is unlikely that Jesus will appear the second time in a Shepherd's garb (5:4). (4) Sometimes the expression is developed so highly and intensively that it is easy to detect metaphorical imagery. Clearly, Peter is raiding architectural metaphors when he speaks of the church in 2:4—8, to the point that one gets lost in the mixing of metaphors (see also 2:9—10).

In light of this brief analysis, we can ask whether the terms "aliens and strangers" betray any of these clues. First, there is no explicit statement in 1 Peter that the references in 1:1, 17 and 2:11 are to be understood metaphorically. In 1:1, the addressees are "strangers ... scattered throughout" the Diaspora; there is no qualifier here that suggests anything but a literal meaning. Inasmuch as "scattered throughout" leads into a literal description of geography, so we are led to think that "strangers" has the same literal sense.[21] The other two references, however, contain some ambiguity. First Peter 1:17 says, "Live your lives as strangers here in reverent fear."[22] If the readers truly are socially isolated (for whatever reasons), this expression can be literal and makes sense that way; if, however, they are upper-class elites, there is evidence for a pilgrimage theme. But we have no evidence to suggest that a metaphor is being used. Slight ambiguity, however, could be felt in a contrast between life "now" (not "here") and life "in the future"

---

20. The NIV eliminates this ancient metaphor by translating "your minds"; the original Greek has literally, "gird up the loins of your mind."

21. This is why the NIV's addition of "in the world" is unfair, for it has no evidence in the context; the evidence that we do have points in the opposite direction.

22. Literally, "live the duration of your sojourn in fear." "Here" has been added in the NIV according to the translators' perception of a pilgrimage theme.

(1:20–21). This *could* be evidence for a modifier being present. Finally, the use of "as" with "aliens and strangers" in 2:11 is perhaps significant evidence for a conscious use of a metaphor. There is, however, a problem. Does "as" mean (1) "I urge you, as if you were foreigners and strangers," or (2) "I urge you, because you are literally foreigners and strangers"?[23] The text does not give us a clue as to which of these we should choose. I conclude, therefore, that there is no unambiguous evidence in 1 Peter for a pilgrimage use of these two terms (though there is some evidence).

The second, third, and fourth tests turn up nothing for our concerns. There is nothing impossible at the literal level for any of the references cited above; each could be literal with no problem. The evidence in 1 Peter does not admit of a low correspondence between the condition of the readers and the actual terms used, nor does Peter run wild in developing this imagery (he simply states it each time). Thus, the tests for determining a metaphor do not yield any clear evidence that the expression "aliens and strangers" must be understood as a metaphor. I am not saying it is impossible or wrong to interpret these expressions metaphorically, but I maintain that such a view is highly conventional in modern reading and has little (if anything) to offer on its own behalf. Because of a lack of evidence for such a view,[24] we ought to see here a literal expression. The evidence, then, leads us to think that the expressions in 1 Peter are literal, describing the readers' social location.

Finally, was the addressees' literal status as "aliens and strangers" caused by their becoming Christians or by their already being "aliens and strangers" prior to believing? That is, did they suffer social exclusion because of their faith, or were they already targets of persecution, who simply became easier targets when they embraced the faith? Without engaging in a lengthy discussion, it seems best to say that

---

23. An analysis of "as" expressions in 1 Peter is not entirely clear. When the noun of the "as" expression is literal, the order "verb/noun" then "as" is found 13/14 times (cf. 2:12, 13, 15, 16 [2x]; 3:6, 7; 4:10, 11, 12, 15 [2x], 16; 5:3). However, a clear metaphorical usage of "as" can be found in either order (cf. 1:14, 19, 24 [2x]; 2:2, 5, 16, 25; 3:7; 5:8). The order would only slightly favor a literal sense in 2:11.

24. There is no evidence outside of these terms in 1 Peter that the author is working with a pilgrimage theme either; this counts against seeing a pilgrimage theme in the first line of the letter, where central themes are often present. That the readers were (literally) socially excluded, however, is found throughout 1 Peter.

there is no evidence (from 1 Peter) that becoming a Christian in Asia Minor involved a drop in social class (though I am certain such a thing happened frequently);[25] nor is there a shred of evidence from 1 Peter that these believers had at one time been people of power or status. When Peter lists their stations in life (e.g., "slaves" and either "wives" or "husbands"), there is a noticeable absence of other vocations or stations in life. One suspects that these descriptions probably obtain because they did not have any more powerful vocation.

This group of churches, in other words, was composed almost entirely of persons drawn from the slave classes and the disenfranchised.[26] We should, however, contend that the reason the believers were literally "aliens and strangers" was twofold: (1) They were socially marginalized people, and (2) their faith led to an association that had no social acceptance and therefore, at the very least, exacerbated their social conditions.

As well, their homelessness would have naturally been a picture of their spiritual status. They were not only castaways because of their social status; they were also castaways because of their commitment to Jesus, to a life of holiness, and to a group of similarly disenfranchised people—the church. We are, then, to see in this description a picture of hard-working, poor people who had no rights and no protection but who, through the grace of God, had found life in Christ and fellowship in the family of God. Thus in 1:1–2, Peter gives both their spiritual status ("elect") and their social location ("sojourners" in the Diaspora[27]). The gospel of salvation in Christ took root in Asia

---

25. It is possible, but by no means clear, that 1 Peter 4:4 might indicate some kind of social ostracism; it does not clearly indicate, however, that the Christians experienced a drop in social status.

26. Although this is speculative, we might suggest that the temptation to "lord it over others" (5:3) would be especially acute for those who have never had power. However, if the study of Winter is accurate here, 2:14–15 may indicate the presence of people wealthy enough to be benefactors to the society; see his *Seek the Welfare of the City*, 25–40. But there is no evidence either that they were meeting in the homes of the wealthy nor that their meetings were so large that they had to be at a villa owned by someone of considerable substance. Rather, the only impressions we gain are small cell groups meeting in homes.

27. What we have here is a Jewish perspective on geography: anyone who lives outside of Judea is "in the Diaspora." There is no indication in Peter that the word *diaspora* (NIV "scattered") is a metaphor for the world and that his addressees' real home was heaven. The word is used clearly for a geographical location in John 7:35 (cf. also Acts 8:1, 4; 11:19; throughout the Old Testament), though it is used metaphorically in James 1:1 (even there,

Minor particularly among the disenfranchised and gave Peter and the early church an important angle on ministry and theology.

....

The Experience of These Believers. The socially marginalized believers of the Diaspora are who they are (1) *"according to* the foreknowledge of God the Father," (2) *"through* the sanctifying work of the Spirit," (3) *"for* obedience to Jesus Christ and sprinkling by his blood." We need to look at each of these expressions. At the outset, observe that each one describes, in a different way and from the angle of a different member of the Trinity,[28] the complex nature of conversion.

According to the NIV, these Diaspora Christians have been chosen[29] "according to the foreknowledge of God the Father." Theological debates have issued forth from this expression and others like it. Is God's election (and predestination) *based* on his knowledge that certain people will believe (which gives the human decision paramount importance),[30] or is God's foreknowledge the determinative factor in choosing certain individuals to be part of his people? If these two options were the only options, then surely the second is to be preferred: God's foreknowledge is more than prescience (knowing ahead of time), for it is effective, active, and determinative.[31]

However, it is not altogether clear that "according to" is to be restricted only to "elect." In fact, with the number of words and the additional description of the addressees as "sojourning" between "elect" and "according to," some have suggested that "according to" modifies

---

the meaning is hotly disputed). So far as I can tell, the term did not become a common Christian description for a Christian's location in the world in the early church.

28. That the order is Father, Spirit, and then Son may reflect the order of their experience.

29. The NIV of 1:2 renders *kata*, "according to," with "who have been chosen according to." The "who have been chosen" phrase is a legitimate inference from the word "elect" in 1:1 and is useful because of the number of words between "elect" and "according to."

30. I would also add that if election is based on the knowledge that God has of those who will believe, then election as a category has almost no meaning. (Such a view is sometimes called "conditional election.") Why would we say that God has elected someone who has already chosen him? What kind of election would this be? Another alternative is experiential: humans, finding in Jesus Christ that their life now has grounded meaning, infer that their experience was preceded by God's working. In this case, election describes their experience of God's working in their lives.

31. So also J. R. Michaels, *1 Peter*, 10—11.

all that goes before: thus, Peter is an apostle of Jesus Christ *and* the Diaspora Christians are elect *and* the Diaspora Christians are sojourning throughout Asia Minor *according to the foreknowledge of God the Father.*[32] Moreover, the highly formulaic nature of verse 2 (with its three prepositions and references to Father, Spirit, and Son) may well suggest the adoption of a set liturgical formula, so that the author is not trying to define "elect" in specific categories but rather is simply writing in a formal, liturgical manner that may well run ahead of precise thinking.[33] While it is not easy to decide here, as long as we understand "foreknowledge" as determinative (rather than confirmative of human choice) and as long as we see that "elect" is described by the "sojourning in the Diaspora" phrase, it is probably best to see all three prepositional phrases in verse 2 as modifying "elect."

Second, the believers in Asia Minor are what they are "by the sanctifying work of the Spirit." Both theological reasoning and spiritual experience confirm that God prompts us to believe through the convicting and regenerating work of his Spirit. The process of sanctification, a word drawn from Old Testament tabernacle and temple worship,[34] involves God's setting his people apart and the lifelong work of his Spirit to effect God's will on earth. Unfortunately, popular theology teaches that sanctification is something that happens *after* conversion and justification; first one is justified and then, throughout life and into glory, he or she is sanctified. This is not a biblical understanding of *sanctification.* The term refers to three features of Christian existence: the initial separation from sin (clearly in 1:2; cf. Acts 20:32; 26:18; 1 Cor. 1:2, 30; 6:11; 2 Thess. 2:13), the hard work of growing in holiness throughout life (Rom. 8:13; 2 Cor. 3:18; 7:1; 1 Thess. 5:23; Heb. 12:10, 14), and the final act of God when he makes his holy people completely holy for eternity (Eph. 5:25–27).[35] Peter is referring here, then, almost exclusively to the first dimension

---

32. So also W. A. Grudem, *1 Peter,* 50.

33. Interesting allusions to liturgical formulas at Qumran are suggested by L. Goppelt; see his *1 Peter,* 70–72.

34. See H. Seebass and C. Brown, "Holy, etc.," *NIDNTT,* 2:223–32, esp. 224–28.

35. On all of this see, esp. P. Toon, *Justification and Sanctification* (Westchester, Ill.: Crossways, 1983); *Born Again: A Biblical and Theological Study of Regeneration* (Grand Rapids: Baker, 1987); A. A. Hoekema, *Saved by Grace,* 192–233. The radical distinction between conversion and subsequent sanctification is probably why Leon Morris has never examined this term in his numerous studies on the atonement (but cf. Heb. 10:29!).

of our sanctification: God's gracious act of turning sinners into his people. Later, he emphasizes the lifelong process of sanctification (cf. 1:14–16, 22; 2:1–2, 9–10, 11–12; 4:3–4).

Third, the addressees are who they are for a purpose: "for obedience to Jesus Christ and sprinkling by his blood" (or "for obedience and sprinkling with the blood of Jesus Christ").[36] These believers have been chosen by God *so that they may be obedient,* that is, so that they may respond to the demand of the gospel and become children of obedience (1:14) and pure children of God (1:22).[37] The use of the word "obedience" for the initial response to the demand of the gospel is found elsewhere in the New Testament (cf. Rom. 1:5; 6:16; 15:18; 16:26; 2 Cor. 7:15; 10:6; 2 Thess. 1:8; 1 Peter 1:22 with 2:8; 4:17). And these people were chosen so that they could be sprinkled with the new blood of the covenant established by the death of Jesus (cf. Ex. 24:3–8; Heb. 9:18–21; 10:22; 12:24).[38]

In sum, then, Peter sees the electing work of God as leading to the *conversion* of the disenfranchised sojourners of Asia Minor. Each of the three prepositional phrases in verse 2 is predominantly a reference to conversion, to the act of God's saving these people. They were effectively called and spiritually made holy, and this election led to their obedience to God's call and to forgiveness under the new covenant.

---

36. The Greek expression is literally: "for obedience and sprinkling of blood of Jesus Christ." It has been suggested that whereas "of blood" goes with "sprinkling," the "of Jesus Christ" goes with "obedience"; thus, the expression is in the form of a chiasm (repeating something in reverse order; i.e., A B B A). Others suggest that two goals are mentioned here: converting obedience and sprinkling of the blood of Jesus (consecration). Once again, the NIV is too loose with the force of the expressions. "Obedience" is used here for the initial response to the gospel as demand on our lives (as in Acts 6:7; Rom. 1:5; 16:26; see also 1 Peter 1:14, 22, 23–25), and it is more than post-conversion obedience to Jesus Christ; the sprinkling is clearly with the blood of Jesus Christ. Grammatically, it is best to assign "Jesus Christ" exclusively with sprinkling in this context.

37. See the excellent discussion of J. R. Michaels, *1 Peter,* 11–12. Observe that "obedience" precedes "sprinkling" here; this confirms that converting obedience is in view. See also J. N. D. Kelly, *Peter and Jude,* 43–44; E. Best, *1 Peter,* 71; L. Goppelt, *1 Peter,* 74; N. Brox, *Der erste Petrusbrief,* 58; P. Davids, *1 Peter,* 48–49.

38. See here J. R. Michaels, *1 Peter,* 12–13. Others have seen other themes present: the sprinkling of baptism (F. W. Beare, *First Peter,* 77), the covenant's blessing of forgiveness (E. G. Selwyn, *First Peter,* 120–21; L. Goppelt, *1 Peter,* 74–75, with a baptismal context), or a post-conversion purification (W. A. Grudem, *1 Peter,* 52–54). Grudem argues against covenant entrance because the term "sprinkling" follows obedience, but this argument falls if "obedience" is seen as a conversion term.

While the first two emphasize God's work, the last expression empha-sizes the believer's response.[39]

The Greeting Itself. As with other letters in the New Testament, the addressees are greeted in both a customary Greco-Roman way ("grace") and in a Jewish way ("peace"). Especially under the influence of early Christian and Jewish theology, these two terms exemplify not only friendliness to others but the rootedness of that friendliness in the gra-cious and peacemaking ways of God.

IT WOULD NOT be normal for modern West-erners to take a letter from the ancient world, say one from Pliny to Calpurnia Hispulla (about his recent marriage), and apply it to our day (assume Pliny's insights about marriage are true for us). Why do we do this for the Bible? How can we take a letter from Peter, a first-century apostle of Jesus Christ, to Christians in Asia Minor who were socially excluded and assume that it is also written to us? While I do not pretend that such a maneuver is simple or that it ought to be done without further ado, I do believe that what Peter wrote is as advanta-geous for us as the Old Testament was for Paul and his readers (cf. 1 Cor. 10:6, 11).

My assumption of the usefulness of Scripture is based on three foundations. (1) *Scriptural.* Paul teaches that God gave us the record of his dealings with his people in order that it may be useful to his peo-ple in the ages to come (see 2 Tim. 3:16–17). (2) *Anthropological.* Since we are all created in the image of God, what was good for God's peo-ple long ago is good for us now because we, as they, are humans. It is only Western arrogance that makes us think we have such a higher level of development that we can look down at the ancients. To con-firm our point about the likeness of humans, one need only read Proverbs or one of the Greek tragedies or comedies to see that what vexed and delighted them is the same as what vexes and delights us. (3) *Ecclesiological.* Members of the church of Christ, both ancient and modern, are one. While we admit to differences between our world and theirs, the first-century church comprises our ancestors in the faith.

---

39. This theme of salvation continues from 1:3–12.

And while we will apply the Bible in different ways because of changes that have taken place and because of differences in our culture, they remain our spiritual ancestors, who have bequeathed to us the faith once and for all delivered to the saints of God.

These foundations, however, do not mean that "things are the same"; for surely this working assumption would be foolish. Adjustments have to be made, in the same way as we change our data for a new word-processing program. Most, if not all, of us do not live in Asia Minor (it has changed immensely anyway), and we are probably not socially excluded (at least to the same degree that they were). But nonetheless, what was written was written for Christians of all ages.

We need here to look more directly at the Petrine notion of *social exclusion*. The Christians of Asia Minor were socially excluded either (1) because they were already nothing more than social sojourners and foreigners, or (2) because they became Christians and so "joined" a disenfranchised religion. Applying this first sense of social exclusion could work in different directions. We could seek to be socially excluded by gaining a station in life that is less than desirable. It is true that the history of the church has found such people; but noble as their desire to follow Jesus is, this is hardly what God expects from us, for the biblical principle seems to be that God wants us to follow him in whatever vocation we have (1 Cor. 7:17–24).[40] This form of application is wooden, overly literal, and forced. As the Christians of Asia Minor did not *seek* lowly wrungs on the ladder of society, so we should not.

Another way of applying such a position of social exclusion is to minister to those who are on the fringes of society. This, I believe, is a valid *extension* of what Peter is saying, *but it is still not what Peter is saying*. Not once in 1 or 2 Peter does the apostle urge his fellow Christians to look for, find, and convert the socially excluded. However noble such a ministry would have been, this is not his point in calling his readers "aliens and strangers."

Most Christians, I am sure, believe that ministry to the socially

---

40. See J. A. Bernbaum, S. M. Steer, *Why Work? Careers and Employment in Biblical Perspective* (CCCSG 2; Grand Rapids: Baker, 1986); see also G. Agrell, *Work, Toil and Sustenance: An Examination of the View of Work in the New Testament, Taking into Consideration Views Found in Old Testament, Intertestamental, and Early Rabbinic Writings* (Lund: Håkan Ohlssons, 1976).

excluded (AIDS victims, the poor, the homeless, many African-Americans, Cuban refugees, etc.) is demanded by the nature of the gospel (it is for all) and the image of God in everyone. Inasmuch as the original readers of 1 Peter were social outcasts, that letter does crystallize a model for the church to minister to those who are socially deprived as an extension of Peter's concerns. If we simply, in our imagination, wrote in the words "Cuban refugees who are Christians," this point becomes clearer. The letter, then, is not primarily an exhortation to minister to Cuban refugees, but a letter to Cuban refugees in the hope that they will be able to learn from Peter how to live *as Cuban refugees* in their environment. On the other hand, while the letter is not an exhortation to work with such a group of people, it is certainly natural to extend the letter's message in that direction.

In my judgment, if the first sense of social exclusion is accurate, then the primary application is in another direction, namely, the importance of establishing our identity on the basis of who we are in God's family rather than who we are in social perceptions. What we find here is Peter's attempt to make sense of his readers' present social location in the Roman empire in the light of their new-found social location in the family of God. Because they are members of God's household, their social location as outcasts has no bearing on who they are in the fullness of reality, on who they are in God's estimation, or on who they are in the context of God's ultimate designs for history. While they are socially strange and foreign in Asia Minor, while they are excluded, powerless, and homeless in the Roman empire, in God's family they are citizens, they are included, they are royalty (2:9–10), and they are at home as God's people. True applications, analogies, and appropriations of Peter's category of "aliens and strangers" move in the direction of one's identity, new group consciousness, and cohesion.

If the second sense of the socially excluded is correct (excluded because of an association with Christianity), then other avenues need exploration. Then it is Peter's message that no matter what social location believers find themselves in, they are still in God's family, and their fundamental means of coping with the stresses and persecutions of society is to see themselves as God's people who are being prepared for God's final kingdom (cf. 1:3–12). Problems immediately arise for many Western Christians, of course, because they find that when they embrace the gospel and follow Jesus Christ in obedience, they are not persecuted; instead, they remain accepted and acceptable in our still somewhat Christian society. What does this letter say to Christians who are obedient but not persecuted?

The first observation is the most important but rarely said in evangelical circles: The social exclusion dimension of 1 Peter simply does not apply because so many Christians walk obediently with the Lord and do not, at least very often, experience social exclusion. This inevitably means that some things in 1 Peter are not as important for such a group as it might be for those who are being persecuted. A second observation, however, is that it is rare for Christians to live obediently even in the Western world without experiencing some kind of social exclusion at some point in their lives or at some level of existence—even if it does not go as far as outright persecution. What we are doing here is trading on the notion of "social exclusion for being a Christian." Even if we cannot identify one kind of social exclusion (persecution; cf. 1:6; 4:1–6, 12–18) with another (e.g., prevention of career advancement), they remain generically the same: Christians often find that their faith jeopardizes elements and dimensions of their lives (physical, material, social, etc.).

In this discussion about applying this letter to our world, we need to pause for some minor considerations. Our use of Peter's letter should not be one of slavish imitation. This can be seen in several ways. Peter's letter does not mean we need to write letters to Christian groups, and it certainly does not mean we have to start our letters in the same way Peter did. After all, no two letters in the New Testament are written in identical ways. It does not mean that we have to find the socially excluded and minister to them. It does not mean that we have to go to Asia Minor or that we need to divide our ministries into five areas (as Peter wrote to churches in five provinces). Peter did not write to give us a stereotype of Christian ministry, though it is altogether clear that we can learn from this great Christian leader. One of the dangers of canonizing letters of the early church, as has been done for 1 Peter, is that its sanctity becomes perversely stereotypical and exemplary. While it is wise to follow the best at something, it is perverse to follow it in a literal, unimaginative manner.

Applying the Bible to our day can be difficult because one of the problems in using the New Testament for our own day and throughout the history of the church is what sociologists call "reification."[41] This term means turning human relationships and observations into rigid, dehumanized, and immutable laws. While it is a fact that sufficiently heated water turns into steam and eventually all the water is turned into the property of gas (this is a natural law), it is not a fact (to the same degree) that treating others lovingly will inevitably lead others to treat us in a loving manner. We reify love and a relationship when we suggest that love always begets love (even if, in God's design, it is supposed to). We reify parenting principles when we lay it down as law, as a preacher I recently heard did, that if we teach our kids to love God, we are guaranteed that every one of our kids will love God, on the basis of Proverbs 22:6: "Train a child in the way he should go, and when he is old he will not turn from it."

We reify different nationalities and races when we ascribe to them a static quality that is "always true": Irish are hot-tempered, Scottish are stubborn, Americans are brash, and Italians are emotional. We reify pastors when we expect each to be identical; we reify political leaders when we expect each to perform the same functions. We reify the role of the father when, because he is father, he cannot apologize to his children; we reify the role of children when parents never take their feelings and ideas into consideration (because they are, after all, only children); we reify the role of mother when we think mothers cannot work outside the home. As for the issue about women's ministries, it is not hard to see that the church (even in the twentieth century) has reified the role that women had in the first century (a modern projection of what women were like both in Judea and the Diaspora) and made that role normative and determinative for roles today. The Amish have reified the dress of eighteenth-century central Europe and made that the stopping point of change. The examples could go on.

Reification also takes place in theology and interpretation, not to mention application. Two examples from our passage may be taken to illustrate my point. First, frequently interpreters of our passage find in verse 2 three points about conversion: God's effectual call through his determinative knowledge, the Spirit's regenerative work, and the Son's

---

41. A brief discussion can be found in P. Berger, T. Luckmann, *The Social Construction of Reality: A Treatise in the Sociology of Knowledge* (New York: Doubleday/Anchor Books, 1967), 89–92; A. Giddens, *The Constitution of Society: Outline of the Theory of Structuration* (Berkeley: Univ. of California Press, 1984), 25–26, esp. 179–80.

covenant-binding death that secures our salvation. We "reify" this text when we treat this as the "order of salvation" that is always and immutably followed in God's working with humans. So reified does this become at times that we think that someone who has suddenly begun to obey Jesus Christ but who has not apprehended the regenerative work of the Spirit has not truly been converted and must (amazingly!) back up in the "law of order" to the regenerative stage in order to be truly converted.[42] A quick glance at 1:3 shows that Peter can connect regeneration with the Father and the Son! Clearly, Peter was not reifying his terms and categories. Pastors and teachers ought to consider their own notes to see how often they have "reified" a text in such a way that it has become an absolutely hardened system. Any reconsideration must take place in the context of the whole of the Bible because other texts might put "hardened systems" to the chase.

A second example from our verses can be seen in the kinds of extrapolations that have been occasionally made from the expression "to God's elect" (1:1). The theme of election is important in the Bible and to theologizing in the history of the church; furthermore, for many Christians God's election is fundamental to their contentment. What I wish to point out here is that there are also many Christians who have been severely shaken in their faith (even to the point of a resigned abandonment of the faith) because of a reification of this category of Christian thought. When taken out of context and planted in a garden of sterile ideas and insensitive theology, a reified doctrine of election can be damaging to the gospel and to Christian existence. When election is understood apart from a biblical perspective on human responsibility, it is misunderstood and the gospel message itself is perverted. God never "forces" unbelievers to believe against their will. However true election is, it is not some insensitive and nondialectical

---

42. A. A. Hoekema, *Saved by Grace*, takes a step forward for Reformed theology when he recognizes that the process of salvation is complexive and not consecutive; see his discussion on pp. 11–27. On p. 16 he gets it right: "the various phases of the way of salvation are not to be thought of as a series of successive steps, each of which replaces the preceding, but rather as various simultaneous aspects of the process of salvation which, after they have begun, continue side by side." Hoekema's discussion of the "spiritual" versus "carnal" Christian provides another example of reifying observations of Paul. The people with whom Hoekema disagrees provide for us examples of those who may, at times, reify certain biblical statements into systems that are not fully biblical.

act of God; the biblical message always understands humans as participating and responding to God in freedom and choice. When election becomes "violent" and "abusive" of human will, it is no longer biblically accurate; rather, it is an example of reification.

True and accurate interpretation of the Bible always takes care to interpret words and ideas in their immediate and fuller context and with all the necessary qualifications that prevent misunderstanding.[43] To avoid reification in interpretation two things are necessary: (1) a contextual sensitivity that permits an interpretation that is logically and theologically accurate in the context of the whole Bible and larger truth, and (2) a flexibility in application that accounts for changing social circumstances and development in our understanding.

Reification is an important category for those who interpret the Bible. We reify biblical texts most often when we are engaged in heated debates about what we think are important points. The Calvinist and the Arminian are surely guilty of overemphasizing and overusing certain points, just as covenant and dispensational theologians do the same when they debate one another. Often it is the balanced interpreter who gets it right biblically but who also seems not to fit quite right into some systematic category. Reification, then, ought to be seen at times as a category useful to some ideology. Biblical theology is always willing to suspend judgment so that the biblical witness receives its full share of influence.

ONE FRUITFUL LINE of bringing the message of 1 Peter into our world is to examine what was meant by "social exclusion" and how that might apply in our world. In my judgment, the social exclusion for the Christians in Asia Minor was intensified by their conversion to Jesus Christ—certainly they were not put to death simply because of the social class (though it was possible that people of such status were not privileged to normal rights). In this case, the expression "social exclusion" refers mostly to a social status (the homeless). However, in what follows I will examine the implications for

---

43. It has been said many times over that Calvin's followers were more Calvinistic than the master. What we have is an example of people reifying Calvin's thoughts into hardened, inflexible "laws of theology."

today of an interpretation of "aliens and strangers" that makes this realistic social exclusion the result of having become followers of Jesus.

In the Western world I can think of no group to whom "social exclusion" might apply any better than to God-fearing Christians on university campuses. However many qualifiers are needed, it remains a piece of history that nearly all major Western universities were originally designed primarily to prepare clergy for the tasks of ministry. This is clearly the case with American universities. Surely, various denominational skirmishes were involved, the precise role for the university in the burgeoning American culture was disputed, and the relationship of "secular" and "sacred" disciplines was hotly debated. These debates notwithstanding, the formation of our university system was determined by religious needs.

Furthermore, most of my readers are probably aware that American history involved a massive split in its Protestant community, the so-called Modernist-Fundamentalist Controversy, with the disastrous result of two communities who for several decades in this century had little or no interactive relationship. Traditional theology was having a hard time surviving at American universities. While the fundamentalists retreated on the whole into separate Bible institutes and colleges, the modernists assumed the leading role in the universities. The result of this history is a university system that has had almost no creative thinking from American conservative Christians and an evangelicalism that developed a mentality that the intellectual life was unhelpful to the churches and unworthy of serious Christian devotion.[44]

Now a word to our universities and evangelicals on those campuses. Whether there is some justification or not, contemporary traditional Christian faith is frequently out of place at American universities. I am not talking about campus impact through campus ministries, like InterVarsity, nor about the religious impact that cam-

---

44. Two brilliant books covering aspects of these paragraphs are M. Noll, *The Scandal of the Evangelical Mind* (Grand Rapids: Eerdmans, 1994); G. M. Marsden, *The Soul of the American University* (New York: Oxford Univ. Press, 1994). Christianity in England did not go through the same kind of polarization and, as a result, many American students have gone and still go to Great Britain for doctoral work (including the present writer). On this see M. Noll, *Between Faith and Criticism: Evangelicals, Scholarship, and the Bible in America*, 2d ed. (Grand Rapids: Baker, 1991), 62–90, 91–121; A. McGrath, *Evangelicalism and the Future of Christianity* (Downers Grove, Ill.: InterVarsity, 1995), who speaks optimistically, yet realistically, to the issue of the viability of evangelicalism.

pus churches have on campuses, like Oxford Bible Fellowship in Miami University (Oxford, Ohio). Rather, I am talking about the intolerance, almost fascist at times, of religiously conservative ideas that deserve to be debated by leading intellectuals and that deserve a place of hearing in the marketplace of ideas. This is what a university is supposed to be—a place where *all* ideas compete against one another.[45] An alarming statistic indicating this massive (and tragic) polarization is the almost total absence of conservative theologians in American university posts and their almost total congregating in Protestant evangelical colleges and seminaries.

The watchword for American universities is no longer simply truth; rather, the watchword today seems to be pluralism or toleration. In fact, it is a sad story about many American universities that traditional ideas (no matter how well-founded and adaptable they may be for today's culture) are out, while novel ideas (no matter how radical and illogical) are in. Education becomes indoctrination into the ideas of recent special interest groups. These ideas need to be heard, but not at the expense of all other ideas or of not pursuing truth.[46] Let me reiterate (and not to please special interest groups): It is educationally important to be exposed to all sides and to alter our programs and curricula as we learn and grow; but it is educationally disastrous to think that the newest books are better than the classics unless they are truly better—scholars and time will guide us here.

As I said above, Christians who take a stand for truth and who believe that God's Word provides a unitary perspective for all disciplines will find the university road rocky and uphill—the whole way. They will more often than not find themselves socially, morally, and intellectually excluded. They may be branded as obscurantist dinosaurs and may even find it difficult to present their ideas in the open market. Furthermore, it comes as no surprise that Christian students who take a stand against casual sexual relations, undisciplined use of time, and partaking of drugs and alcohol will find even less acceptance, just

---

45. See J. Pelikan, *The Idea of a University: A Reexamination* (New Haven, Conn.: Yale Univ. Press, 1992).

46. A penetrating book on this theme is D. D'Souza, *Illiberal Education: The Politics of Race and Sex on Campus* (New York: The Free Press [Macmillan], 1991). See also the insightful study by Tom Oden, based on his own experience, in *Requiem* (Nahsville, Tenn.: Abingdon, 1995); see also W. H. Willimon and T. H. Naylor, *The Abandoned Generation: Rethinking Higher Education* (Grand Rapids: Eerdmans, 1995).

---

as Peter's churches did (4:4). Such students will find less social acceptance and so will become marginalized by the majority, who find these activities the essence of weekend recreation. I speak here from ten years of counseling and discussing life with students who have had such experiences throughout North America.

I find this situation of our students (and faculty members and those seeking faculty positions) similar to the situation facing the Christians in Asia Minor. They were socially excluded, at the least, because they were Christians.[47] What is Peter's word to our students who are finding themselves excluded? It is twofold: (1) Maintain the course of a loving, holy lifestyle, and (2) find your identity in being part of God's family, not in being part of a society that does not accept you. It ought to be noticed that Peter does not tell them to be coarse, rude, and arrogant, nor does he tell them to segregate themselves into separated communes. Rather, he tells them to live their godly lives right in the midst of the society that rejects them, always ready to answer people with a reason for their hope (3:15). He informs them that their very lives are a witness to God's glory (2:11–12).

Furthermore, Peter tells them that their family, their social group, is the church, not society. There they are to find their social acceptance. They should see that they are part of a worldwide movement, God's household, the church, which is being persecuted throughout the world. What this means for Christian university students is that they are to seek out fellowship with other Christians who can sustain their spiritual and social needs while they remain faithfully integrated in their campuses as witnesses to God's love in Christ.

While this first attempt at updating the message of 1 Peter with respect to social exclusion has focused on the university experience of Christians who seek to be faithful to Jesus while growing up in such a massively different environment from home, we will have more than ample opportunity to explore the same theme from different angles (the business world, morality, etc.) in other places. To go into each of these fields here would make it more than difficult to explore direct analogies for our world in those texts that deal with suffering and social exclusion.

---

47. I do not have space here to explore applications of a strictly social nature. I will pursue those lines at 2:11–12 below.

What then does this salutation say about *the relationship of the Christian to society?* Fundamentally, it gives us the general perspective of Peter for Christians who find themselves excluded and oppressed socially. That perspective is that *their primary group is God's family* ("God's elect") *and their secondary group is society.* Peter does not address them as "the socially excluded" but as "God's elect"; their social standing was completely absorbed by their spiritual calling. His directions throughout the letter are concerned with their Christian identity and their Christian family (the church) *and how they were to live as Christians within their social setting.*

With the rising influence of Christian attempts at political activism in the Western world, particularly in the United States, Peter offers two pieces of advice: (1) Act as Christians and in a Christian manner, and (2) understand that your identity is your church, not your social group. Each of these could easily be developed at length; here we offer only brief remarks.

(1) As for Christian behavior, I find Christian activism to be both good and bad. It is good that Christians are attempting to influence society with the values of the kingdom. Democratic politics, where the one with the most votes wins, are extremely valuable for expressing the rights of the majority and for hearing the voices of the minorities. I am thrilled that Christians are agitating, and I am not speaking here just of the New Right or the Radical Left Evangelicals (like Jim Wallis). I am glad that both are attempting to reach into the community with the message of biblical Christianity, even if at times there are excesses and misunderstandings. I do perceive something exceedingly grotesque, however, when I hear of people murdering "abortion doctors" in the name of Christ and when I see on television divisive animosities being expressed in hateful slogans bantered about on boycott signs. What I like about Western politics is that, if a given position agitates enough and garners the majority, that position gets its chance in the public forum. What I do not like is people, in the name of Christ, claiming to be following Jesus and appearing to most observers to be acting in a manner unworthy of the gospel.[48]

Furthermore, it is not the case that Christians have definitive, biblical "Christian answers" for everything that arises. The arrogance

---

48. See especially T. Sine, *Cease Fire* (Grand Rapids: Eerdmans, 1995).

and self-assuredness that are too frequently found in "Christian politicians," while making that politician's personal hopes obvious, do little to further the work of Christ. Just as we do not have definitive answers on taxation, so we do not have absolute answers for the issues involving international strife. While we clearly have definitive answers about racism and civil rights, we do not have (in my judgment) absolute answers about capitalism and social welfare. The problem here is that too many people contend their view is *the only Christian view* on this matter, whether it is the radical left or the capitalist right.[49]

(2) No matter who wins and which position gains the upper hand, the Christian cannot be depressed because, regardless of the intensity of the problem, he or she remains in God's hands as God's elect and finds the primary social group in the church of God. This is an area Peter develops, perhaps because he found no other consolation. The socially excluded had no recourse to political democracy or representation in Asia Minor. Nonetheless, his insight here is enduring and penetrating. Do we find our primary identity in being Americans or Canadians or being Christians? Do we find our consolation in that we are Irish, Scottish, English, German, Italian, Russian, or South African, or do we find our principal root in our connection to God in Christ and in the new people of God, the church? Peter exhorts his churches to find their identity in that they are God's elect and that they have a socially satisfying group. Do we find this same identity?

---

49. A brief introduction to such debates can be found in R. G. Clouse, *Wealth and Poverty: Four Christian Views of Economics* (Downers Grove, Ill.: InterVarsity, 1984); J. A. Bernbaum, *Economic Justice and the State: A Debate Between Ronald H. Nash and Eric H. Beversluis* (CCCSG 1; Grand Rapids: Baker / Washington, D.C.: Christian College Coalition, 1986); C. M. Gay, *With Liberty and Justice for Whom? The Recent Debate Over Capitalism* (Grand Rapids: Eerdmans, 1991); F. Schaeffer, *Is Capitalism Christian? Toward a Christian Perspective on Economics* (Westchester, Ill.: Crossway, 1985). One of Tom Sine's best insights is his insistence that too many evangelicals have assumed and argued that the gospel is identical with free market capitalism; see his *Cease Fire.*

1 Peter 1:3–12

PRAISE BE TO the God and Father of our Lord Jesus Christ! In his great mercy he has given us new birth into a living hope through the resurrection of Jesus Christ from the dead, ⁴and into an inheritance that can never perish, spoil or fade—kept in heaven for you, ⁵who through faith are shielded by God's power until the coming of the salvation that is ready to be revealed in the last time. ⁶In this you greatly rejoice, though now for a little while you may have had to suffer grief in all kinds of trials. ⁷These have come so that your faith—of greater worth than gold, which perishes even though refined by fire—may be proved genuine and may result in praise, glory and honor when Jesus Christ is revealed. ⁸Though you have not seen him, you love him; and even though you do not see him now, you believe in him and are filled with an inexpressible and glorious joy, ⁹for you are receiving the goal of your faith, the salvation of your souls.

¹⁰Concerning this salvation, the prophets, who spoke of the grace that was to come to you, searched intently and with the greatest care, ¹¹trying to find out the time and circumstances to which the Spirit of Christ in them was pointing when he predicted the sufferings of Christ and the glories that would follow. ¹²It was revealed to them that they were not serving themselves but you, when they spoke of the things that have now been told you by those who have preached the gospel to you by the Holy Spirit sent from heaven. Even angels long to look into these things.

PETER HAD LEARNED in the synagogue and from other pious Jews how to pray. The typical Jewish prayer, called the *Shemoneh Esreh* ("The Eighteen Benedictions"), was a series of "blessings of God." Thus, when Peter begins to pray, he does so in this customary Jewish manner.[1]

Grammatically, our passage is one massive run-on sentence. While such lengthy sentences (ten verses!) tweak the nose of modern English teachers, Peter's grammar is wonderfully elegant as well as profoundly expressive of the grandeur of his subject: salvation. We may unravel the grammar as follows: Peter blesses the Father for the *new birth* he grants his people (v. 3a), *which* leads to their majestic hope of *final salvation* (vv. 3b–5); this *expectation of final salvation* leads them to rejoice, in spite of suffering, about that final day of *Jesus Christ* (vv. 6–7); this very *Jesus Christ* they both love and trust, while they rejoice as they await that final day of *salvation* (vv. 8–9); that very *salvation* was the subject of inquiry and longing for the ancient prophets of Israel, though they did not live to see its fulfillment (vv. 10–12). The words in italics demonstrate how one idea leads to a fuller digression on that idea, leading to more and more digressions—all in one breath and in one glorious doxology.

Put more graphically, the following outline suggests both the scope and the digressory nature of these verses:

1. Praise Expressed (vv. 3–5)
2. Digression on Joy Despite Their Suffering (vv. 6–7)
3. Digression on Love and Joy in Anticipation of End (vv. 8–9)
4. Digression on the Prophetic Search for Salvation (vv. 10–12)

Thus, our passage is essentially a eulogy to the Father that overflows into a fuller eulogy touching on the joyful expectation of salvation, on how that expectation can sustain Christians in suffering, and on how

---

1. On Jewish prayer, see J. H. Charlesworth, M. Harding, and M. Kiley, *The Lord's Prayer and Other Prayer Texts from the Graeco-Roman Era* (Valley Forge, Pa.: Trinity Press International, 1994), with extensive bibliography. See also E. Schürer, *The History of the Jewish People in the Age of Jesus Christ*, ed. G. Vermes (Edinburgh: T. & T. Clark, 1973–1987), 2.423–463. The *Shemoneh Esreh* can be found on pp. 454–63. See also E. P. Sanders, *Judaism: Practice and Belief. 63 BCE–66 CE* (Philadelphia: Trinity Press International, 1992), 195–208.

privileged they ought to feel about being the ones who get to enjoy that salvation after millennia of expectation. Run-ons express it best!

Peter begins with the theme of salvation because he has already made conversion/salvation the foundation of his salutation (1:1–2). There, it will be remembered, he focused on three dimensions of the great process of salvation: the determining knowledge of God, the sanctifying work of the Holy Spirit, and the obedience-generating covenant of Jesus Christ, the Son of God. With this salvation in mind, Peter now sets their social condition (i.e., social exclusion) into the grand scheme of God's salvation. He will proceed to talk about ethics and lifestyle, but before he doing so, he must make clear the foundation. That foundation is the salvation of God, and it is only on this foundation that Peter constructs the life of the church.

While it has been popular since the Enlightenment in the Western world to reduce Christianity to morality and ethics (especially in the United States through the rise of Jeffersonian morality and liberal Protestantism's ethic of tolerant love), Peter will not let ethics come to the fore until he speaks of salvation, the foundation of morality. He blesses God for salvation; in light of that salvation, he goes on to say, "*Therefore*, live a good life" (see 1:13–2:10).

Praise Expressed (1:3–5). It is perhaps easiest to see the grammar and logic of these verses if we diagram the verses graphically (the translation is mine to facilitate this diagram).

Blessed be the God
and   Father of[2] our Lord Jesus Christ
                who gave us new birth
                      (1) according to his great mercy
                      (2) unto a living hope
                          through the resurrection of Jesus Christ from
                            the dead
                      (3) unto an imperishable, unspoiling and
                          unfading inheritance
                      which [inheritance] is kept in heaven for you
                        by God's power
                      through faith in the salvation prepared to be
                      revealed at the end.

---

2. The expression "Father of " gave rise to the heresy known as Arianism, in which it was argued that God the Father actually generated the Son and, therefore, the Son is not eternal. But this expression describes the subordination of the Son to the Father by choice, not in essence.

As can be seen, the sentence is simple in that it is a statement of praise to God, and the blessing is directed to the God *and* Father. This God and Father is blessed because he has given us a new birth. This new birth is the result of his mercy, which grows into a living hope; that hope is defined[3] as an inheritance. Put differently, Peter blesses the God and Father because of salvation and its manifold benefits.

The new birth God has given to Peter and his readers, changing their status before God (2:24; 3:18, 21; Titus 3:5) and their lifestyle before others (1 Peter 1:22–23), theologians call *regeneration*. It is part of the large drama of cosmic regeneration (Matt. 19:28) that finds its climax in the glorious final existence (Rev. 19–22). Thus, through the new creation work of Jesus as a result of his resurrection, the new life the church receives through him is part of that grand act of a new creation. Furthermore, it is fundamental for New Testament teaching to see this work of creation as a work of the Holy Spirit (John 16:7–11), though that dimension is not mentioned here by Peter (but cf. 1 Peter 1:2, 12; 3:18; 4:6).[4]

Peter tells the readers that they have benefited from this new birth because of God's "mercy."[5] *Mercy* is that pity God shows toward humans in spite of their sin and because of their total helplessness to right their wrongs; God permits them to be part of the special people of his favor (2:10). This great new birth sets off a chain reaction in his plan of redemption: His mercy stimulates their new birth, and their new birth stimulates a "living[6] hope." This orientation toward the future that God will bring through Christ constantly appears in this letter (e.g., 1:3, 13, 21; 3:5, 15). It is not so much that believers are now liv-

---

3. Some have seen the prepositional phrases as coordinates: "unto a living hope," "unto an inheritance," and "unto salvation." However, it is best to see them consecutively: "unto a living hope," which is defined by "unto an inheritance," which is conditioned upon a faith "in that final salvation."

4. See esp. P. Toon, *Born Again: A Biblical and Theological Study of Regeneration* (Grand Rapids: Baker, 1987).

5. The grammar here is eloquent. Literally, it is "Praise to the God and Father . . . who, according to his great mercy, gave us new birth." The intrusion of "according to . . ." between "who" and "gave us" is a classical touch that brings out even more forcefully the important connection between God's mercy and his granting of the new birth. "According to" shows the ground of the new birth.

6. "Living" refers either to their "living" hope over against the "dead" hopes of paganism or, more likely, to their "living" hope now that they have been given a "new life" in Christ (see J. R. Michaels, *1 Peter*, 19).

ing "full of hope," but that they have a fixed "hope," a clear vision of what God will do for them in the future.[7]

The chain reaction continues: Not only does the new birth stimulate a "living hope," but that living hope is defined by "an inheritance that can never perish, spoil or fade" (1:4). The children of God, who have received new birth, can look forward to a special inheritance[8] because they are God's children. That inheritance is their completed salvation (1:3, 4, 5, 6–9) and eternal life in the kingdom of God, where they will enjoy worship, praise, and blessing directed toward the Father, Son, and Spirit. This inheritance is kept for God's people in heaven, guarded by God's power (1:5). The only condition God sets for his people is that they must have faith (1:5); no biblical author guarantees final salvation apart from faith. This faith is a faith in "the salvation[9] that is ready to be revealed in the last time." In sum, the new birth gives rise to a living hope that is defined as an inheritance that is guarded by faith in that final salvation.

Digression on Joy Despite Their Suffering (1:6–7). Abruptly, Peter begins to comment on the joy that suffering believers have as they contemplate that final day: "In this[10] you greatly rejoice" (1:6). That is, contemplating salvation and its forthcoming climax generates great joy[11] in the hearts of the believers, a joy so great they can endure suffering. The *problem* facing these Christians in Asia Minor is that they are suffering "grief in all kinds of trials" (1:6)—even if it is "now for a little while." But Peter wants them to see the *purpose* of their suffering, "so that

---

7. Thus, their "hope" is their "salvation" (1:5) and their "inheritance" (1:4). Using the word "hope" here does not suggest any element of doubt, as it might in English when we say, "I hope I will be found acceptable to God."

8. Peter defines the "inheritance" as something "that can never perish, spoil or fade." F. W. Beare put it beautifully when, following the "alpha privatives" of the Greek construction, he wrote: "the inheritance is untouched by death, unstained by evil, unimpaired by time" (*1 Peter*, 83–84).

9. Grammatically, "in salvation" (lit., "unto salvation") can modify either "given us a new birth" (1:3), "shielded," or "faith." The proximity to the latter makes this the best option. The NIV prefers "shielded."

10. A question arises over the grammar here: "this" could go with "salvation," but such a connection would be grammatically difficult ("salvation" is feminine while "this" is masculine or neuter); with "God" in 1:3, but a reference back three verses without warning would be highly unusual; with the entirety of 1:3–5 or with "last time" at the very end of 1:5. Grammatically, this last solution is preferable.

11. On this verb, see J. N. D. Kelly, *Peter and Jude*, 53; P. Davids, *1 Peter*, 55.

your faith—of greater worth than gold, which perishes even though refined by fire—may be proved genuine and may result in praise, glory and honor when Jesus Christ is revealed" (1:7). Whereas gold perishes when it is refined by fire, their faith will endure the fire of persecution, and will be proved genuine at the last day. Like James in James 1:3, Peter sees in suffering a situation from which the believers can learn and grow.

These verses depict the heart of Peter: He began theologically with praising God for his great benefits of salvation, but then he pauses pastorally to show that the Christians in Asia Minor can be exceedingly glad about the final day of salvation even though they are presently enduring various kinds of trials. They can be glad because they will survive this trial and find themselves in the glorious situation of salvation. This pause is a pastoral digression and, like many pastors I have heard, it leads to yet another digression.

Digression on Love and Joy in Anticipation of the End (1:8–9). Since his readers will be found acceptable to God[12] on the day when Jesus Christ is revealed, Peter turns to the present relationship of these Christians to Jesus. Their *current response* is that they love Christ in spite of not having seen him; furthermore, though they believe in him and still do not see him, they are "filled with an inexpressible and glorious joy" (1:8).[13] Peter sees this response to the Lord as so potent that he describes it as the inauguration[14] of their final salvation: "for you are receiving the goal of your faith, the salvation of your souls" (1:9).

Digression on the Prophetic Search for Salvation (1:10–12). Now comes yet another digression, this one stimulated by Peter's mentioning of "the salvation of your souls." Peter contends that this salvation, which the

---

12. A paraphrase of "may result in [Gk. *eis*] praise, glory and honor when Jesus Christ is revealed."

13. The vivid contrast between "faith" and "sight" occasionally forms the foundation of New Testament exhortations (see John 20:29; Rom. 8:24–25; 2 Cor. 5:7; Heb. 11:1, 7, 8–10, 13–16, 39–40).

14. Some have thrown all the tenses of 1:8–9 into a future sense: "you will rejoice . . . when you receive." Not only did Peter avoid future tenses here and chose present tenses, he probably did so because he wanted to emphasize the inaugural nature of the Christian experience. In the present, believers can experience a foretaste of the future. On "receiving" as correspondence between earthly obedience and heavenly decision, see 1 Peter 5:4; cf. also 2 Cor. 5:10; Eph. 6:8; Col. 3:25. Here, obviously, the final state of people is determined by their faithful love and endurance of suffering.

Asian Christians have enjoyed and for which they earnestly hope, is the very salvation that the ancient prophets (cf. Matt. 13:17) were seeking in all its details but never found. Peter's ultimate point is to demonstrate the privilege of enjoying salvation in his era, the privilege of living in the "A.D." rather than the "B.C." era.

Thus, Peter begins with the *prophetic inquiry* (1:10). To emphasize the diligence and intensity of the ancient prophets,[15] Peter uses two terms, "searched intently and with the greatest care"[16] (he includes a cognate of the second word in v. 11). Their passion, whether they knew the exact longing of their hearts or not, was the grace that the Asian Christians found in Christ.

Verse 11 gives the *topic* of the prophets' inquiry.[17] They spoke about God's final salvation and the judgments that preceded that final day. Precisely when and under what circumstances such events were to occur they did not know, but they did inquire into such matters.[18] Peter writes that it was "the Spirit of Christ in them" that prompted their inquiry, and ultimately, they were investigating "the sufferings of Christ and the glories that would follow." It only makes sense for us to think, since we have so many Jewish prophecies that do not state these facts in outright fashion, that Peter is here clarifying for his readers the ultimate visions of the Jewish prophets, not explaining the precise details of their prophecies.

No matter how intense their search or profound their vision, Peter insists that these prophets, like John the Baptist after them, only served a preliminary role in the plan of God (1:12). They were preparing the world and God's people for a later time—and that later time is now (cf. 2:10, 21, 24, 25; 3:6, 9) for Peter. This is the great privilege of the church age: the enjoyment of the inauguration of God's salvation in Christ. It is so great that even the angels are looking down to gain a

---

15. Peter does not seem to have any particular prophets in mind; his expression refers to the entirety of the Jewish prophetic tradition.

16. The two Greek words are *ekzeteo* and *exeraunao*, the first signifying "seeking out and searching," the second "inquiring carefully" (as when, for instance, invading military personnel inquire from house to house; see Josephus, *Jewish War*, 4.654). See Psalm 119:2 (where the Septuagint uses these two terms for those who seek the Lord in obedience); John 5:39; 7:52.

17. See on this W. A. Grudem, *1 Peter*, 69–70.

18. See the fuller discussion of J. R. Michaels, *1 Peter*, 41–43; for a slightly different view, see Grudem, *1 Peter*, 74–75.

view,[19] like wedding attendees attempting to steal a glance at the bride before her appearance. The angels are brought in here, not to invite us to speculate about their activities, but to press on our minds the privileges of salvation; neither the prophets nor the angels experience what the church assumes and enjoys.

Bridging Contexts

THIS TEXT RAISES at least four issues that we could explore: the praise and worship of God, Christian hope, suffering, and the privilege of salvation. In this section, I will look at suffering, while in the "Contemporary Significance" section below, I will look more at salvation. However, in separating the two topics, we cannot separate them totally. For Peter, the reason the Christians were suffering was because they had the results of salvation in their lives, and their Christian living was now grating against a sinful society. Thus, our angle here is how suffering flows from salvation. Suffering, when properly understood and applied, is the wake following behind salvation's boat.

An obvious point of departure for application concerns the suffering of the believers in Asia Minor, along with Peter's instructions on how to perceive and endure such sufferings, and then contrast this point with the lack of suffering that takes place in the postmodern West. I begin by contending that our *lack* of suffering is, in part, due to a *lack of nerve* on the part of the church to challenge our contemporary world with the message of the cross and to live according to the teachings of Jesus with uncompromising rigor. While the Bible never states that every Christian of every age will always suffer, Paul does state that "everyone who wants to live a godly life in Christ Jesus will be persecuted" (2 Tim. 3:12). I take this to be not an absolute prediction by Paul for all ages, but a general principle that is rooted in the nature of a fallen world, the kind of statement made so often in Proverbs. As a guiding principle, then, those who live faithful lives in an unbelieving world will find opposition to both their ideas and their practices.

There are, of course, exceptions. One simply has to imagine a fairly Christianized society (e.g., early nineteenth century United States in

---

19. On this verb see F. J. A. Hort, *1 Peter*, 62–64; J. R. Michaels, *1 Peter*, 49.

the specific communities), where most of one's family and contacts were upright, godly men and women. In such a community one could live a godly life and not be persecuted. But this is not the case today for most readers of this book.

In other words, I am arguing that suffering, while it may not be as much a part of the everyday fabric of our lives as it was when Peter was writing, should probably be more a part of our lives than it is. True, ours is an age of toleration and pluralism. These two characteristic virtues clearly retard a society's inclination to persecute. Nor is our society as intense about its religious beliefs as other parts of the world, which inculcate both a quicker and more physical response to strange ideas and practices. But even if we bracket out our Western civility, the contrast between the Christian community's belief in the gospel as well as its commitment to holy living and our culture's unbelief in the gospel and its permissiveness *ought to generate more sparks* than it does. I contend that one of the reasons there are so few sparks is because the fires of commitment and unswerving confession of the truth of the gospel are too frequently set on low flame, as if the church grows best if it only simmers rather than boils.

Accordingly, one of the reasons it is hard to apply this feature of 1 Peter to our world is our own problem. We should not then accuse the text of being hopelessly irrelevant; we can only accuse ourselves of being dormant and sleepy. I would also suggest, however, that we *must recognize the change of cultures and the distance of time*. First-century Asia Minor was made up of totally different kinds of people and religious groups from what we encounter today. With the moving ahead in time and the total change of society—that is, with our concentration of people into cities with a capitalistic culture (modernization), with our disintegration of a theological center for ascertaining meaning and morality (secularization), and with our multiplication of options and denial of the superiority of any one option (pluralization)—there is good reason for stepping back and saying that our culture and Peter's culture are simply different and, therefore, his message about suffering will have to make some adaptations.[20]

---

20. I might add, however, that a comparison of the role the church played in society in Peter's day and the role our churches play may not manifest as great a difference as one might find between Peter's day and either the Catholic villages of the post-Industrial Revolution in Italy or post-Reformation Scotland. Those communities had large churches at the center

If indeed ours is a more tolerant time and if in certain places the church of Christ has much more significance in its culture, then it must be granted that the times have changed. Peter's churches enjoyed neither toleration nor significance. Therefore, we cannot expect the same amount or the same degree of suffering as is found in our letter. In the Western world Christians cannot be put to death (legally) simply for believing that Jesus is Lord or for living according to his teachings. We can proclaim the gospel with boldness and live godly lives without fear of suffering as a result. But Christians were put to death in Peter's day for such beliefs and for living a holy life.[21]

What we must not do, however, in this context is *to demythologize the conditions of suffering*. Because we want to be accurate in our interpretation, we can never degrade the writings of the early church, a suffering community, by suggesting that "suffering is not the issue" and that what is at issue is "faithful living." Furthermore, we assault the sensitivities of suffering believers the world over (and throughout the history of the church) when we trivialize the meaning of suffering. How do we do this? At the popular level, I have heard suffering texts trivialized into stresses in life, like the psychological pressure on the student who is preparing for an exam or the emotional drain that an interview with the boss might bring. I have heard it trivialized into "bad breaks in life," like having a flat tire on a vacation trip or being too far away when a loved one dies. I have heard it trivialized even further when some moderns find suffering to be losing some sports event or not gaining an advancement at work.

While no sensitive or thinking person would want to minimize the reality of stress or the tragedy of losing members of one's family, such events are not true counterparts to suffering in the early church. While we recognize differences between our world and Peter's, we are not entitled to trivialize the suffering of that church by finding cheap analogies and then pretend that such things are suffering for faithful-

---

of their cities and villages, right in the heart of the community, whereas neither Peter's world nor ours permits churches to enjoy the same status and centrality.

21. For the context of 1 Peter one needs to read about the Roman empire under Nero. See F. Hooper, *Roman Realities* (Detroit: Wayne State Univ. Press, 1979), 380–91; a more extensive analysis can be found in M. Grant, *Nero: Emperor in Revolt* (New York: American Heritage, 1970). See also W. H. C. Frend, *Martrydom and Persecution in the Early Church* (Oxford: Blackwell, 1965).

ness to the Lord. Peter was addressing the impact salvation had on one's life and how that changed life (and status) ran counter to the culture in which these Christians lived.

Accordingly, what we need to find in our world, if we want to apply this message to our situation with biblical fidelity, are *analogies of experience that correspond significantly to first-century suffering*. What would these look like? No matter what happens, it qualifies for "being suffering" only if the opposition occurs *exclusively because someone is a Christian*. This is why we have to link suffering and salvation together. Flat tires happen because of sharp objects and thin tires, not because someone is a Christian. Bad events in life happen to good, God-fearing people, but bad events in life are not necessarily events of persecution. We need to find events that occur against people as a result of human opposition, that occur solely because of that person's stand for the gospel of salvation and a decision to proclaim the gospel in word and deed. As an extension of this, sometimes Christians may be opposed at a more indirect level (say politically) because of a stand for the gospel of Jesus. Thus, a Christian stand at the personal level may bring opposition at another level.[22]

I recently spent some time with a young athlete who had some rough experiences at his local high school with his "former" friends. As a senior he had a track record of drinking and drugs but was converted to Christ. His conversion made a sudden and immediate impact on his life, so much that he found himself on an island. After games, he was no longer invited to the parties; during games, he was no longer given the same opportunities to shoot the basketball; and in the hallways at school, he was no longer a "hit" with either the girls or his friends. He came to me for consolation. I explained that at least part of this was suffering and that he needed to guard against retaliatory speech and bitter attitudes. He began to see, in a painful way, that commitment to Christ can involve suffering. Here is an example of "bad events" occurring *because this young man was a Christian*. If he had become arrogant and obnoxious and these things occurred, one could not rightly call it suffering (2:20). But when such things happen as a result of one's

---

22. I have seen conservatives oppose more liberal Christians at a political level when the liberal group was doing something for "all the right reasons" and their actions were noble and good; the opposition, one suspects, was generated at another level. And I have seen liberal groups oppose conservative political statements for the same kind of reasons.

faithful devotion to Jesus, then we can find fruitful analogies to Peter's advice to suffering believers (even if we respect the differences).

ONE OF PETER'S major themes is salvation, and this salvation is what led the believers of Asia Minor to experience suffering. Not only did we see this theme in 1:1–2, but it emerges at several places in 1:3–12. I want to look at two dimensions of this theme: *the necessity of salvation* and *the denial many express today for the need of salvation.*

Our world is so pluralistic that it has become anticultural to speak of *the necessity of salvation.* Furthermore, we have been easily led astray into following socially significant ministries rather than following the path of salvation as the road Christians should travel. The centrality of salvation, a cardinal doctrine of the Christian faith, is offensive to our culture. As a result, suffering often accompanies the preaching of salvation. Thus, the need to refocus our energies on the message of salvation stems in part from our fear of some form of cultural persecution.

Pluralism is the result of the modernizing and secularizing forces in our world. These forces drove from the center of our lives the values and theology that held the various branches of knowledge and behavior in some kind of unity for the masses of the Western world. Once those central forces were driven out, what remained were options but not truth. Furthermore, religious convictions were driven from the public into the private sphere of life, where one can believe what one wants without interference, debate, or prejudice. But such views and affections are not for the public because toleration dominates public discourse. A typical adage of religious pluralism is that "all religions lead to the same God and to heaven." While it would be foolish to think that religious pluralism exhausts the pluralisms of our day, it is this kind of pluralism that confronts the readers of the Bible the most today.[23]

The second problem staring Peter's message in the face today is the pervasive *lack/denial of a sense of any need for salvation* in contemporary

---

23. Two other major features of modern pluralism include materialism and naturalism. For a judicious critique, see J. R. W. Stott, *The Contemporary Christian*, 296–320.

society. To speak of such a need is to be old-fashioned in some sense. At the root of this denial is a view that sees people as essentially good, though possibly hurting through some sickness or victimization, but not one as sinners in the sight of God who need divine grace and re-creation. Accordingly, to speak to our society of the need for salvation in order to be acceptable to God is to speak, too often I fear, a language that our culture simply does not hear. While centuries have been crossed since Peter wrote this letter, this strangeness of the message of salvation remains similar. And as this strangeness led to suffering for the early Christians, so also it leads to suffering in our world.

How does Peter's message of salvation fit into all of this? To begin with, we need to see how Peter describes salvation. It is a "new birth" (1:3) that has already been experienced and is being integrated into lives at an inaugural level (1:9) by people who have received the Holy Spirit through the proclamation of the gospel (1:12); yet it is also their "living hope" (1:3)—an "inheritance" (1:4) and a "salvation" that is still future (1:5). Peter tells us that the ancient prophets researched this salvation and that its components were the death of Jesus and his sub-sequent glories (1:10–12). In other words, for Peter, salvation meant the benefits believers have found, do find, and will find because of their faith in the work of Jesus Christ and the blessed Holy Spirit. And this salvation is an experience *only* for those who put their faith and focus their obedience on Jesus Christ (1:2, 14, 21). Thus, his message is an exclusivist message: It finds salvation in Christ alone and only for those who trust and obey him.

The church is an exclusive and a privileged[24] community because it is a saved community. It is not a social organization, structured to provide its participants with opportunities for social interaction. It is not organized in this sense at all; rather, it is a group of people who have been called by God to trust in him, obey him, and associate with others that have the same calling, trust, and obedience. Any church today

---

24. First-century Christians, such as Peter, experienced the privilege of the salvation Christ brought in a way unlike any Christians who followed them. They, as it were, knew what it was like to live prior to the era of the Holy Spirit and in the era of the Holy Spirit. Consequently, they knew the "privilege" in a way unlike the way we know it. However, through imagination and the reading of the Bible in a historical manner, we can glimpse (like the angels) their sense of privilege and begin to appreciate even more our historical privilege.

that does not immediately "advertise" itself in this way does not understand what it means to be "in the church." From beginning to end, the church desires salvation through Christ and through the attending work of the Holy Spirit. It preaches that salvation begins with a "new birth," continues through the ministry of the gospel, and climaxes at the final day when that praise, honor, and glory are expressed. Whether it stems from the fear of sounding dogmatic or from a desire for respect, any church that denies its calling to announce salvation in Christ alone is denying its primary God-given mission.

We might begin by saying that it takes nerve and backbone to announce this message in our day, just as it did in Peter's day. But this is our task in making our text significant to our contemporaries. Peter's text is about salvation, and we need to think about how to proclaim salvation in our world. Our first problem is that we fear what others might say, worry over whether or not our message is palatable, and fret over our acceptance. "And so we settle for the kind of friendliness within which all absolutes perish either for lack of interest or because of the demands of the social etiquette."[25]

But such a courting of our culture is not the way to lead others to the marriage supper of the Lamb or to woo our world (it leads, in fact to disrespect). A compassionate announcement is profoundly effective while a timid and fearful suggestion about the gospel falls into one more slot in the pluralistic organization. We need to ask God for the courage to proclaim his truth with boldness and love and to announce his truth to a society that is crippled with options. Like someone sitting down in a restaurant who becomes overwhelmed by the number of options on the menu, knows that no chef makes all things well, and finally (in frustration) blurts out to the waiter, "What does your chef make best?"—so we need to announce the goodness of God in his revelation of Christ to those who are befuddled by the menu of pluralistic options available today.

This fear of others and our lack of being stubbornly committed to the truth of Scripture have led some churches today to have virtually no such thing as a "theological confession" or set of "church beliefs" to which its members must subscribe in order to become members. Yet the church is the place where salvation is proclaimed. Indeed, the his-

---

25. D. F. Wells, *No Place for Truth*, 75.

tory of doctrinal debates records some ugly arguments over minor issues that fractured churches and denominations. But in our haste to run away from being stained with having a reputation for doctrinal divisiveness, it is possible to avoid the central doctrines that define the church. We need to advocate "what Christians believe"[26] and then hold to it. Salvation is at the heart of what Christians believe.

A second problem is that Christians, the church, and Christian organizations are easily led off the track of leading people to salvation by following lines that contribute to the well-being of society. It is not that social services are unimportant, for they are critical for the health of our society. It is not that teaching other nations the principles of farming or computing is not useful, for these things do help. It is not that offering psychological counseling is not fundamental for people who are emotionally hurting, for psychology aids our ministries. It is rather that social services are never a substitute for the process of salvation but are instead preparatory to the consequences of salvation. Focusing on the consequences to the neglect of the cause (salvation) distorts the message and ruins the church. Furthermore, the history of the church proves dramatically that when Christians get out of balance here, it is always the message of salvation that gets lost.

Take, for instance, the history of the YMCA/YWCA. These were at one time thoroughly godly organizations, designed to lead men and women into the faith, to educate them theologically, and to provide them with fellowship. But they have succumbed to the spirit of social services—so much so that most of us could be forgiven if we ask why the letter "C" remains on the signs.[27] I speak here of getting off the track that Peter built long ago, the track of salvation in Christ, which can be specifically related to our desire not to bear the brunt of standing up for the gospel. The connection between salvation and suffering, seen so vividly in Peter's churches, remains a vital link to

---

26. This, in fact, is the title of a textbook on theology by A. F. Johnson and R. E. Webber, *What Christians Believe: A Biblical and Historical Summary* (Grand Rapids: Zondervan, 1989), which they claim brings together "a theology that affirms the unity we have in the essentials, yet allows for the diversity we hold in matters of secondary importance" (ix). I can't think of a better way of educating young theologians than in a theology that is affirmed by the church at large.

27. See C. H. Hopkins, *History of the Y.M.C.A in North America* (New York: Association Press, 1951); I obtained this reference from G. M. Marsden, *The Soul of the American University* (New York: Oxford, 1994), esp. 343.

this day even when we do not see the same kinds of opposition to the gospel.

To be sure, the history of the church in the United States has witnessed an incredible inability to hold in balance the preaching of salvation and social work. Evangelicals have largely focused on the former while liberal Protestantism has worked on the latter; perhaps only the Roman Catholics have remained balanced in this regard. Because of our history, the point I am making could be misunderstood as one more criticism of the so-called social gospel. This would be a gross misunderstanding, for I believe the message of salvation inevitably entails with it a desire for social transformation. But the tasks are not identical and the priority of the Bible is clearly in favor of the message of salvation. Peter's letter reminds us once more of the centrality of the ministry of salvation through Christ for the church.

The word "centrality" here is important. In ministering the message of salvation to our world, it would be helpful for us to think not in terms of an assembly line (as we capitalists are prone to do), but in terms of a wheel in which the hub is salvation, the spokes the various ministries, and the outer rim our society. Salvation is central and remains central, regardless of the order of our activity. But the minute the spoke becomes dislodged from the hub, the life of salvation can no longer flow to our society.

Our world, with its pluralistic contours, deserves to hear the clarity of Peter's message. Our world both deserves it and needs it, because it is God's world and because God has brought his Son into the world so that this very world might know truth, the truth that can set us free and give us a center for finding meaning in our culture. It may be the case that we, along with Peter's churches, will suffer for standing up bold for the message of salvation, but we are called to proclaim God's salvation.

1 Peter 1:13–25

THEREFORE, PREPARE YOUR minds for action; be self-controlled; set your hope fully on the grace to be given you when Jesus Christ is revealed. ¹⁴As obedient children, do not conform to the evil desires you had when you lived in ignorance. ¹⁵But just as he who called you is holy, so be holy in all you do; ¹⁶for it is written: "Be holy, because I am holy."

¹⁷Since you call on a Father who judges each man's work impartially, live your lives as strangers here in reverent fear. ¹⁸For you know that it was not with perishable things such as silver or gold that you were redeemed from the empty way of life handed down to you from your forefathers, ¹⁹but with the precious blood of Christ, a lamb without blemish or defect. ²⁰He was chosen before the creation of the world, but was revealed in these last times for your sake. ²¹Through him you believe in God, who raised him from the dead and glorified him, and so your faith and hope are in God.

²²Now that you have purified yourselves by obeying the truth so that you have sincere love for your brothers, love one another deeply, from the heart. ²³For you have been born again, not of perishable seed, but of imperishable, through the living and enduring word of God. ²⁴For,

"All men are like grass,
    and all their glory is like the flowers of the field;
the grass withers and the flowers fall,
²⁵   but the word of the Lord stands forever."

And this is the word that was preached to you.

Original Meaning

PETER BEGAN THIS letter by singing the praises of the God who had given such a great salvation to the Christians of Asia Minor. Reflection on this salvation now leads him to the heart of his letter: an exhortation on how to live in society as Christians who are oppressed and excluded. His order follows a pattern throughout the whole Bible: Theology prompts ethics. That is, beliefs about God and experiences with God undergird beliefs about what is right and wrong. At 1:13 Peter says, "Therefore"—that is, since you have received the great benefits of salvation, among which are a new birth, a living hope, and an assured inheritance—you ought to be different in how you live. The theme of this passage, indeed 1:13–2:10 (with further implications until the end of the letter), is *the difference salvation brings to the life of the Christian.*

This particular unit (1:13–25) is not a tightly woven unit of logic (as can be found frequently in Paul's letters), but is rather a series of ethical reflections on the difference salvation should make in believer's life. Peter exhorts his readers in four areas, each of which is grounded in a reflection about salvation. (1) He exhorts them to *hope* (1:13), grounding this exhortation in the salvation of 1:3–12 (cf. "therefore"). (2) He exhorts them to *holiness* (1:14–16), grounding this exhortation in the assumption that they are "obedient children," an expression denoting their conversion (see below), and in the character of God (1:15–16). (3) He exhorts them to *fear God* (1:17–21), grounding this exhortation in their new relationship to God—they can address the very Judge of the Universe as their Father (v. 17), and they have been redeemed by the precious blood of the Lamb of God (vv. 18–21). (4) He exhorts them to *love one another* (1:22–25), grounding this exhortation in their purification (1:22) and in their regeneration (1:23–25).

Our section, then, contains a series of reflections about Christian ethics for believers living within an unbelieving society, but it also presents a profound, if not elegant, deliberation on the foundation of Christian ethics. This reflective stance of Peter is not some self-conscious piece of theological gamesmanship or of doctrinal speculation; rather, in the heat of the battle for human lives, Peter knows (from his biblical heritage and the teachings of Jesus) how to ground his exhortations in the character and actions of God, and he does so. Put differently, this is not groundless advice that Peter hopes his readers will like; this is *theological* ethics. Each of these ethical directives (hope, holiness, fear of God, love) deserves more treatment than space permits in this format. Accordingly, I have tried to provide the reader with sources where the discussion can be pursued further.

First Exhortation: Hope (1:13)

PETER'S EXHORTATION TO hope has three parts: two metaphorical images, preparing the reader for the main verb, "set your hope."[1] His first image is captivating: "Prepare your minds for action" translates an ancient image that literally reads, "gird up the loins of your mind."[2] This image is drawn from the ancient (and still modern for some in the Middle East) form of dress in which a man's long outer "shirt" draped down to his ankles, obviously preventing agile and quick motions and strenuous work. As a result, when such actions were needed, a man tucked his shirt into his belt and thus "girded himself for action" (cf. 1 Kings 18:46; Jer. 1:17; Luke 17:8; John 21:18; Acts 12:8). Peter applies the metaphor to mental behavior with the added word "of your minds" (see Luke 12:35).[3] Thus, the NIV rendering captures the image with "prepare your minds for action." C. E. B. Cranfield suggested that we translate it as "rolling up the shirt-sleeves of your mind," or "taking off the coat of your mind."[4] Given our fitness craze, we might translate it today, "Take off your mental warm-up so your mind can move freely." In light of Peter's emphasis on hope in 1:3–12 and the subordinate nature of this image to the verb "set your hope," this mental activity involves perceiving this world as transitory and orienting itself around the future hope that God will bring about at the day of Jesus

---

1. The sentence can be translated literally from the Greek as follows: "Therefore, girding up the loins of your mind, being completely sober, set your hope. . . ." Since the only finite verb is "set your hope," it is grammatically better to understand the first two metaphorical (participial) clauses as subordinate to the main verb, containing images for the same idea as is found in the main verb. In other words, "prepare your minds for action" and "be self-controlled" are metaphors for "set your hope." See the discussion of L. Goppelt, *1 Peter*, 107–9. Many today, however, take the participles as imperatival participles; on this, see the discussions of D. Daube, "Participle and Imperative in 1 Peter," in E. G. Selwyn, *1 Peter*, 467–88; J. N. D. Kelly, *Peter and Jude*, 67–68.

2. So roughly the RSV and KJV.

3. See also at Job 38:3; Eph. 6:14.

4. C. E. B. Cranfield, *First Peter*, 32.

Christ (see 1:13b).[5] Peter wants his churches to maintain a loose grip on this world and a tight grip on the world to come.

The second image is "be totally self-controlled."[6] This image is drawn from the all-too-realistic world of drunkenness; drunks have no control over themselves or their body. Peter's expression is metaphorical[7] in that believers are to be totally in tune with God's plan in history, so much so that they set their hope on the future and live in light of that day. People who look into the future and want to live completely in light of God's will do not want their eyes blurred by sin or other distractions (cf. 4:7; 5:8; 1 Thess. 5:6, 8; 2 Tim. 4:5).

Christians must be ready to do mental work and be totally focused on God's plan; that is, they must "set [their] hope [fully][8] on the grace to be given you when Jesus Christ is revealed." Living for the future is fundamental for Peter, and a brief sketch of his theology here provides the most important context. Even if believers have begun to share in the salvation of God (1:9), that salvation is presented as only complete in the future (1:5). There will be a penetrating evaluation by God (1:7, 9, 17; 2:12, 23; 3:12; 4:5–6, 17–19) when Jesus is fully revealed (1:7, 13; 4:13). After the judgment, the faithful followers of Jesus will share his glory (5:1, 4) and receive the full compensation of grace (1:17; 4:13, 14). Peter urges his readers to see history the way God has planned it. Though now they may suffer unjustly at the hands of evil people, someday Christ will return and justice will be fully established. As a result, Christians are to live in light of that day

---

5. This limiting of the kind of mental activity that concerns Peter stands against some interpretations that find here every (and almost any) kind of mental activity, like the importance of theology, exegesis, Bible study, or serious grappling with social issues in which we find ourselves. A *general* exhortation to mental preparation does not seem to be in order in this context. See the discussion in J. R. Michaels, *1 Peter*, 54–55; so also L. Goppelt, *1 Peter*, 108–9; N. Brox, *Der erste Petrusbrief*, 74–75.

6. In Greek, this participle is immediately followed by "fully." Debate has arisen over whether or not "fully" is to be understood as a modifier of what precedes (thus, "be *totally* self-controlled") or of what follows ("set your hope *fully*"). In light of Peter's preference for adverbs ending with *-os* to follow the verb they modify rather than to precede it (see 1:22; 2:19, 23; 5:2 [4x]), it seems best to translate "be totally self-controlled." So also F. J. A. Hort, *1 Peter*, 65; F. W. Beare, *1 Peter*, 96; J. R. Michaels, *1 Peter*, 55; I. H. Marshall, *1 Peter*, 51.

7. It is unlikely that Peter is speaking literally here in the sense of urging that his readers be "teetotalers."

8. See note 6.

of manifested grace. If they think fellowship in the family of God and tasting of Jesus are good now (2:3), they need to think even more about the future when better things await them. What they can only praise God for now they will then know personally in all its glory (cf. 1:3–12).

Second Exhortation: Holiness (1:14–16)

VERSES 14–16 BEGIN with an assumption of salvation (v. 14a), give the command to holiness (vv. 14b–15), and then return once again to the assumption of salvation (v. 16). The expression "as obedient children" returns to the foundation of ethics in salvation. The obedience mentioned at 1:2 as the response believers make to the gospel (cf. also 1:22) is clearly an expression for conversion. It is only because in modern discussion the term *obedience* describes how converts behave after conversion that we miss the meaning of this term here.[9]

The exhortation to holiness begins with a negative statement ("do not conform to the evil desires you had when you lived in ignorance") that is subordinate[10] to a positive one that follows ("just as he who called you is holy, so be holy in all you do"). As Paul urged the Romans not to be conformed to this world (Rom. 12:2), so Peter urges his readers not to be conformed to their former passions, which dominated their lives prior to their entrance into God's family. Since they are now children of obedience (1:14a), they are to be holy, just as God is holy. We can assume that Peter has in mind here the similarity children are to have to their parents.

God, who is different and unlike anything the Israelites had ever seen or would see, is altogether holy (Ex. 3:5; 15:11; Lev. 20:26; Ps. 99; Hos. 11:9; cf. Luke 4:34; John 6:69; Rev. 1:16–17). Because he had drawn Israel into a special relationship with himself, he expected his people to reflect his nature, including his holiness (Ex. 19:6; Col. 1:2). Those who lived according to God's commandments and will were considered holy because they were morally excellent (cf. Lev. 20:7–

---

9. J. N. D. Kelly, *Peter and Jude*, 67; J. R. Michaels, *1 Peter*, 56–57; P. Davids, *1 Peter*, 67.

10. Once again, the negative here is a participle; in my judgment, it is not an imperatival participle (so also D. Daube, "Participle and Imperative in 1 Peter," 482); thus, the negative functions as a subordinate idea to the positive command to be holy.

8; Hab. 1:12–13).[11] The fundamental connection made here is twofold: Christians should be holy both because they have been converted (1:14a) and because they are children of a God who is himself altogether holy (1:15–16). In fact, Peter prefaces and concludes the exhortation to holiness with a description of God as holy (1:15a, 16). I can think of no section in the Bible that involves more interweaving of ethical exhortation and theological foundations for ethics than these three verses.

Third Exhortation: Fear of God (1:17–21)

THE FLOW OF thought here again emphasizes the foundation of ethics. Peter begins with the foundation for living in the fear of God (1:17a), then exhorts his readers to live that way (1:17b), and finally reflects again on the foundation for living in that fear, this time as it relates to their redemption (1:18–21).

Put simply, Peter says that if believers call as Father the one who judges indiscriminately, penetratingly, and absolutely honestly, then they had better live in fear of this God, for he is altogether holy and will judge justly. The notion of God as Judge underlies many exhortations to obedience in the Bible. Furthermore, if there is a God, if the God of Israel and Jesus are the true one God, and if this God is altogether holy, it follows that this God must judge if he is to allow anyone in his presence. He cannot tolerate any sin, for sin is repulsive to his holiness. The God of the Bible is the Judge of all (cf. Gen. 18:25; Ps. 75:7; Acts 5:1–10; Heb. 12:23; Revelation), and, as Peter says, he is "ready to judge the living and the dead" (1 Peter 4:5) with a judgment that begins "with the family of God" (4:17). This judgment is according to their works, because these works are the logical result of one's relationship to God (Matt. 16:27; 25:31–46; Rom. 2:6–11; 14:9–12; 1 Cor. 3:10–15; 2 Cor. 5:10).[12] As Stephen Travis has said, "The final judgment means God's underlining and ratification of the rela-

---

11. For a brief survey of the holiness of God, cf. J. R. Williams, *Renewal Theology. Volume 1: God, the World and Redemption* (Grand Rapids: Zondervan, 1988), 59–63; N. Snaith, *The Distinctive Ideas of the Old Testament* (New York: Schocken, 1964), 21–50.

12. See J. I. Packer, *Knowing God*, 2d ed. (Downers Grove, Ill.: InterVarsity, 1993), esp. 138–47; W. A. Grudem, *Systematic Theology: An Introduction to Biblical Doctrine* (Grand Rapids: Zondervan, 1994), 1140–57.

tionship or non-relationship with him which men have chosen in this life."[13]

Knowing that God is judge and that he judges with absolute fairness[14] drives us to live in a healthy fear and awe of him (cf. 2:17, 18; 3:2, 15; see Prov. 1:7; Matt. 10:28; 2 Cor. 5:11; 7:1; Eph. 5:21; Phil. 2:12; 1 Tim. 5:20; Heb. 4:1; 10:31).[15] This can only refer to the constant knowledge the child of God (1 Peter 1:14) has that whatever he or she is about to think or do is subject to the scrutiny of God's penetrating holiness and love. And when his beautiful holy love checks our thoughts and our actions, we live in the light of his character and in the fear of him, regardless of social conditions.[16] This fear is neither dread nor anxiety; rather, it is the healthy response of a human being before an altogether different kind of being, God, and is a sign of spiritual health and gratitude. This holy Judge we now call "Father," a term indicating intimacy and love but also respect and submission. That is, though we now call God "Father" (cf. 1:14), as Jesus taught (Matt. 6:9), we must not let that familiarity with God degrade his holiness, for God is just and his judgment will be just.

To this fear of the Judge Peter adds a second motive for a life of obedience: the nature of redemption (1:18–21). The *former life* of his addressees was an "empty way of life handed down to you from your forefathers." What had been considered venerable tradition was now considered "empty" (cf. Jer. 10:15; Acts 14:15; Rom. 1:21; 8:20; 1 Cor. 3:20; Eph. 4:17); thus, a new tradition, one rooted in Jesus and the apostolic testimony, was needed.[17]

---

13. Stephen H. Travis, *Christian Hope and the Future* (Downers Grove, Ill.: InterVarsity, 1980), 121. The last chapter is a good survey of the New Testament teaching on judgment.

14. The Greek word here is *aprosopolmptos*, which describes receiving a person without regard to showing any favoritism because of the benefits he or she may provide (Deut. 10:17; 2 Chron. 19:7; Rom. 2:11; Eph. 6:9; Col. 3:25). Cf. James 2:1 for the opposite characteristic in humans.

15. On fear, see esp. M. Luther, *Peter and Jude*, 70; J. N. D. Kelly, *Peter and Jude*, 71; L. Goppelt, *1 Peter*, 111–13; P. Davids, *1 Peter*, 70–71. See also J. Murray, *Principles of Conduct* (Grand Rapids: Eerdmans, 1957), 229–42.

16. The expression "as strangers here" reflects the terms of 1:1 and 2:11. As discussed in the introduction and at 1:1, this term may describe his readers' social conditions literally (a view we have adopted throughout) or a metaphorical description of "life on earth."

17. On this see esp. W. C. van Unnik, "The Critique of Paganism in I Peter 1:19," in *Neotestamentica et Semitica: Studies in Honour of Matthew Black*, ed. E. E. Ellis and M. Wilcox (Edinburgh: T. & T. Clark, 1969), 129–42; J. R. Michaels, *1 Peter*, 64–65.

From this former life believers have been *redeemed*, that is, purchased with a price—the blood of Jesus Christ.[18] The plight of humans is moral offense (Rom. 1:18–3:20; Eph. 1:7; Col. 1:14), sinfulness, and bondage to that vicious condition (Rom. 7:1–6; Gal. 3:13; 4:5; Titus 2:14; 1 Peter 1:18); the price paid is the atoning death of God's Son (Mark 10:45; Rom. 3:21–26; 5:1–11; Gal. 3:13; 4:4–5; 2 Cor. 5:21; Titus 2:14). As a result, we are now back in God's ownership as his servants, free from sin and death (Rom. 6; 8; 1 Cor. 6:19–20; 7:22–23; Gal. 5:1). Since we know we have been redeemed by the precious blood of Christ, we should be grateful to God for our new family and live in fear and holiness before him.

Reflection on the redemption accomplished by Christ leads Peter to reflect further on Christ: "He was chosen before the creation of the world, but was revealed in these last times for your sake" (1:20). Furthermore, this same Christ is the agent in our developing faith and hope in God (1:21).

Fourth Exhortation: Love One Another (1:22–25)

PETER'S FINAL EXHORTATION is again rooted in the "before and after" of conversion: Since you have been purified, love one another, because you have been born again. The *foundation* for love that Peter builds on is that "you have purified yourselves by obeying the truth so that you have sincere love for your brothers" (1:22). Their purification was by means of the sprinkling (cf. 1:2; also Ex. 19:10; Acts 21:24, 26; 1 John 3:3), and they responded to God by obeying the truth of the gospel (1 Peter 1:2, 14).[19] The result of obeying the truth was that they were ushered into the realm of brotherly love.[20]

Almost redundantly, Peter exhorts his addressees to "love one another deeply, from the heart" (1:22). The word "deeply" (found also

---

18. On *redemption*, a metaphor drawn from the commercial world, see L. L. Morris, *The Atonement: Its Meaning and Significance* (Downers Grove, Ill.: InterVarsity, 1983), 106–31; J. R. W. Stott, *The Cross of Christ* (Downers Grove, Ill.: InterVarsity, 1986), 175–82. On blood, the definitive study is A. M. Stibbs, *The Meaning of "Blood" in Scripture* (London: Tyndale, 1948); but see also L. L. Morris, *The Apostolic Preaching of the Cross* (Grand Rapids: Eerdmans, 1965), 112–28.

19. See J. R. Michaels, *1 Peter*, 74–75; L. Goppelt, *1 Peter*, 125–26; P. Davids, *1 Peter*, 76.

20. The Greek grammar in *eis philadelphian anupocriton* indicates that brotherly love flows from their purification.

at 4:8) speaks of the effort required for that love, the depth of it for one another, and the duration of it (until the end). The word is frequently associated with characteristics of prayer: fervency, constancy, and effort (cf. Luke 22:44; Acts 12:5).[21] Peter expects his churches to be filled with people who love one another in that way, who try to understand one another, who give the other person the benefit of the doubt, and who reach out to others in the same love. But, as Howard Snyder says,

> The church today is suffering a *fellowship* crisis. . . . In a world of big, impersonal institutions, the church often looks like just another big, impersonal institution. . . . One seldom finds within the institutionalized church today that winsome intimacy among people where masks are dropped, honesty prevails, and that sense of communication and community beyond the human abounds—where there is literally the fellowship *of* and *in* the Holy Spirit.[22]

Peter wants churches filled with people who love one another and where intimacy is the inevitable result of being made holy by God's grace.

Peter returns again to the foundation[23] of their love: their regeneration (1:23). The new birth gave them a new likeness to a loving God and a new family, which had the characteristic and ability to love one another. Their new birth came about by means of an "imperishable" seed; like the precious blood of Jesus (1:19), that seed was rooted in the living God (1:23) and, because it was eternally effective (1:24–25a), gave them an ultimate foundation for loving one another deeply. Humans and humanly created things are like grass in that they will perish and vanish away. But the Word of God, planted in Christians, is eternal and grows in those same Christians to give them an eternal existence. This effective seed is, in fact, the sure word of God that they heard in the gospel that was preached to them (1:25b).

---

21. F. J. A. Hort, *1 Peter*, 90–91: "doing a thing not lightly and perfunctorily, but, as it were, with straining."

22. Howard Snyder, *The Problem of Wineskins*, 89–90.

23. In 1:22 and 1:23 the completeness of their conversion is emphasized by the use of the perfect tense, a tense used to denote the state of affairs.

In summary, Peter exhorts the Christians of Asia Minor to work out their salvation by building a life of ethics that is rooted in the salvation that God has given to them and is based in the holy and loving character of God. Ethics, then, is a part of theology, not something added to theology in a moment of practical urgency. Ethical decisions, in fact, are logical extensions of theology. Without solid theology, that is, a theology that reflects on the character and actions of God, there is no foundation for ethics. If one's ethics is not rooted in Christian theology, it becomes nothing more than a pluralistic option thrown into the winds of cultural changes.

GENERAL ETHICAL DIRECTIVES like those in our passage are easy to apply, but certain cultural conditions can make specific applications more difficult. For example, someone who grew up under an abusive father may find it exceedingly difficult to want to live in the "fear of the Father," just as someone who grew up hearing nothing but the threat of God's judgment may experience an understandable discomfort reading our passage. Thus, we must be aware of the context of our audience and how they will hear such directives. We may need to supplement or explain a given directive for it to gain the kind of force needed.

What is fundamental for applying general ethical directives, however, is to reflect on the *foundation* of ethics. I find television talk shows fascinating, if not a bit comical at times (not that I spend much time watching them). It is rare that one of these talk shows does not venture at some point into an ethical issue, whether it is homosexuality, abusive husbands, tattoos, losing weight, or confronting one's boss. What I find amazing is how easily these talk show hosts and their guests slide from a moral dilemma into a moral stance without any reflection on how they got there or how they can make such a decision. A standard line of reflection contends, "If it doesn't hurt anyone, then ... ," while another one suggests that ethics are based on "doing good in society." Appeals to authority, even the American Constitution, generate scorn while an appeal to special revelation (the Bible, the Koran) only begets the suggestion of fundamentalism. At their most religious moments, these hosts will strain their necks out far enough to suggest that "some old-fashioned American ideals" are just what we need in our society today. Whatever the discussion, television talk-show hosts struggle with ethical dilemmas, and their audiences are yearning for answers to some of life's most difficult problems. But where will these hosts and viewers get answers that satisfy both their sense of what is right and wrong and provide a foundation on which others can build?

Deep in the heart of television, ethical reflection is belief in the essential goodness of humans, or at least a hope that such is the case. If we dig down deeply enough or try harder or discipline our lives, so it is argued, we will find we are capable of making our world better. Then, like an explosion of a bomb in a small room, the host is interrupted with the news of ten-year-olds being shot execution-style by fellow gang members who were not much older. Belief in some kind of goodness quickly falls on deaf ears. Any theory of ethics that assumes humans are somehow inherently good and, if they are simply educated, will begin to behave in morally decent ways is about as believable as the Easter bunny—a great story but it belongs to a previous stage of development. Where then do talk hosts—and they are but representatives of their viewers—get their morals? The answer is that they base their ethics on consensus and on what makes sense to most rational people. But to suggest there are moral absolutes that apply to all people is beyond their capacities to announce.

Let's take "consensus" as a strategy for determining ethics. We must simply ask, "*Whose* consensus?" Do we take into consideration moral experts, ministers, average people, special interest groups—just whom do we ask? Are we not building a castle in the sky to think there is some consensus? And what about "rational people"? "Rational people" disagree among themselves. They cannot find any kind of unity over abortion, intervention in foreign countries, health care, welfare, or anything that has been politicized. We all agree that murder is wrong, but we refuse to prohibit the sale and use of hand guns "in the name of personal freedom." We all agree that cigarette smoking is injurious to health, both for the smoker and the one who must breathe the smoke indirectly, but we cannot come to terms morally with prohibiting the act because it breaks down a person's freedom. I have no faith in "rational people" being able to determine a code of ethics that is both respective of personal freedom and morally sensible.

Tragically, those who may be influencing our culture the most at the moral level are people who refuse to be engaged in a reflective discussion about how to make ethical decisions, for such reflection would expose the superficiality of their ethical decisions. It would also unmask the fear that each hides, namely, that there is no way to make ethical decisions binding for all apart from a belief in a final revelation or in a unique God. If human consensus breaks down and if human rationality will not get us there, then we will either be awash in a sea of relativity (fortunately for us, there is a cooperative sense of some things being good) or be blown by the same winds into the hands of a revealing God.

That's exactly where Peter is—in the hands of a revealing God, whose character and words chart the course of ethics and morality.[24] Ethics in a Christian context *begins, oddly enough, with a belief in the depravity of humans, not their goodness.* Thus, Peter says, his readers have been redeemed from a slavery to their former, empty traditions (1:18), they have been given a new life and a living hope (1:3–5), and they have been purified (1:22)—the latter two assume the opposite as a condition from which they needed deliverance: hopelessness and moral filthiness. Human beings are in need of repair, restoration, and reformation.

Peter goes on to argue that his readers have been given a new life by God, and this conviction provides the *ground of morality for Christianity.* Until we have been given God's life and have partaken of God's character (cf. 2 Peter 1:4), we have no chance of performing God's will as he wants us to. Conversion and participation in God's nature through conversion are the only true and enduring foundations for Christian ethics. John Murray, a brilliant theologian-ethicist, once concluded: "Remove from Scripture the transcendent holiness, righteousness, and truth of God and its ethic disintegrates."[25]

As we try to move the ethics of Peter into our world, then, we must carry with us the foundations he builds upon: the nature of God, the

---

24. See F. A. Schaeffer, *He Is There and He Is Not Silent,* in *The Francis A. Schaeffer Trilogy* (Westchester, Ill.: Crossway, 1990), 291–301. See also W. C. Kaiser, Jr., *Toward an Old Testament Ethics* (Grand Rapids: Zondervan, 1983), 139–51.

25. Murray, *Principles of Conduct,* 202. The entire chapter, called "The Dynamic of the Biblical Ethic," expresses in full the contentions I am making about the foundation of Christian ethics. In addition, see the many articles in C. F. H. Henry, ed., *Baker's Dictionary of Christian Ethics* (Grand Rapids: Baker, 1973).

sinfulness of humans, the need of divine revelation, and the need of salvation.[26] If we urge Peter's ethics while neglecting his foundation, we are building an edifice that will collapse. Salvation, Peter argues, is necessary in order for God's people to live like God's people in our world: "The redemptive process . . . is the only answer to the impossibility inherent in our depravity."[27] Or, as C. S. Lewis asks in his inimitable style, "What is the good of telling the ships how to steer so as to avoid collisions if, in fact, they are such crazy old tubs that they cannot be steered at all?" He continues, "You cannot make men good by law: and without good men you cannot have a good society. That is why we must go on to think of the second thing: of morality inside the individual."[28]

Accordingly, the area where this passage from 1 Peter speaks most clearly to our world is in the area of ethical systems and how to make ethical decisions. Peter's approach is theological, and the Christian who follows him will establish his or her ethical decisions on the basis of God's nature and God's Word.

OUR DISCUSSION ABOVE began to show the significance of Peter's theoretical framework for our world today. I want to continue that discussion here and then move to a related topic, the importance of living for the future and in light of that future. Living in light of God's judgment is part of the theme of anchoring ethics in God's nature and revealed Word because it involves a decision to live in light of God's holy character, which forms the foundation of his final judgment.

As much as anyone in the history of American Christendom, Thomas Jefferson (who was himself merely a brilliant spokesman for a larger worldwide trend) reduced Christianity to morals, and he founded those morals on an appreciation of classical writers, the innate goodness of humans, the Creator's implanting in humans an instinct for

---

26. Notice how C. S. Lewis, in his *Mere Christianity* (New York: Macmillan, 1952), 17–39, gets at these same points.

27. Murray, *Principles of Conduct*, 202.

28. C. S. Lewis, *Christian Behaviour* (New York: Macmillan, 1952), 72.

what is right, and the Enlightenment understanding of reason.[29] Hence, Jeffersonian morals are really a reflection of a European trend toward rational ethics. His rational, or better yet instinctive, morality became the essence of liberal Protestantism that has gripped North America for the better part of this century. The following equation expresses the mood of many Western societies: A Christian is someone who is good and loving; a loving and good person is a Christian. While biblical Christianity affirms the first, it does not necessarily affirm the second. The problem with rational morality as the definition of Christianity is that the two are not distinguished.

Our concern here, however, is not with the history of American ethics or Jeffersonian ideals. Rather, our concern is with the *foundation* of ethics. Where do we begin when we want to state a moral good?[30] To simplify greatly, ethics are either founded in ourselves (e.g., through reason, intuition, nature, moral instinct, conscience) or outside ourselves (e.g., through revelation, an established code of ethics, the Constitution). Christian orthodoxy teaches that *ethics flows from salvation* and that humans, by themselves, cannot discern the will of God—for personal salvation, for personal ethics, or for the social order. We know God's will because in his grace he has made his will known to us through his revelation, the Bible being the primary mode of this revelation. The same construction applies to our knowledge of ethics: We know what is good from what is bad because God has told us in his Word, beginning with the Mosaic legislation and climaxing in the teachings of Jesus and the apostolic testimony.

Recently I zipped home from teaching to grab a round of golf in what I thought would be one of the last nice days of the year. Rarely do golf courses let someone play alone, so I assumed I would be paired with other golfers whom I did not know. The course was empty for three holes, and I caught up to two distinguished African-American gentlemen, whom I joined for the rest of the round. We made enough light talk for me to discover that one of them was a social worker and the other a pastor. After a few holes I raised the issue of the problems

29. See N. E. Cunningham, Jr., *In Pursuit of Reason: The Life of Thomas Jefferson* (New York: Ballantine, 1987); C. B. Sanford, *The Religious Life of Thomas Jefferson* (Charlottesville, Va.: Univ. Press of Virginia, 1984), esp. 35–55.

30. See R. E. O. White, "Ethical Systems, Christian," in *Evangelical Dictionary of Theology*, ed. W. A. Elwell (Grand Rapids: Baker, 1984), 372–75.

of inner-city violence, hoping to generate an ethical conversation: "What do you think is the solution to the problems in the inner city?" Tony, the first one to speak, said, "God's Word! In one of the last Scriptures of the Old Testament [Mal. 4:6], it says that in the last days God will return the hearts of the fathers to their children. Unless hearts are made right," he went on to say, "there is no hope for the inner city." Then he made a stunning observation about our official "American policy": "All the money and programs in the world will not change people's hearts."

I agreed wholeheartedly with their solution: salvation. I also agreed that commitment to salvation as central to ethical problems does not alleviate us from seeking to help people in their socially deprived conditions. Will, the other man, said quite tersely: "Don't get me wrong. Those babies didn't choose to come into this world, and we can't choose to neglect them. We need welfare for those kids." In my judgment, these two men crystallize the testimony of God's people in the history of the church. Ethics begin with salvation, but we dare not neglect our social duties.

But what if others in society do not believe in salvation in Christ? Can we expect to stop society until it becomes Christian before we can go on profitably with ethical issues? Obviously not. But Peter knows of no foundation for proper conduct before God that does not begin with salvation and the life that comes in Christ. Precisely at this point too many Christians have compromised themselves. Ours is a pluralistic world, and this means that public discourse has to be tolerant of opposing viewpoints and alternative foundations for ethical discussions. But Christians must never pretend that the ethics of Christianity can be discovered by pure reason (as was attempted in the eighteenth and nineteenth centuries) or by legislation. The proper motive for morals comes only from God's work of grace, and a life pleasing to God finds its blueprint in the pages of the Bible. While we may have to tolerate alternate viewpoints, we must learn in our toleration not to compromise the foundation on which we stand. In our desire to be influential or to be acceptable, too frequently we have adopted the level of public discourse as the only level for ethical discussions.

Christians desire biblical ethics for society, but our society is frequently against Christian ethics. Thus, the only way we can work for

Christian ethics in society is by way of the normal means of public discourse. This requires toleration. But tolerating other views does not mean accepting them (just as the materialist does not have to accept the Christian view) or permitting them to ruin the foundation of Christian ethics. We dare not be silent about our foundation, for it is a silence that can eventually lead to erosion. So let us be political, and let us be involved; but we must avoid surrendering why we do what we do.

There is no question about the historical development of public morals in America. We now know that the need to be "nonsectarian" or "nondenominational" but still broadly Christian in our public discourse eventually led to a total breakdown of the foundation itself (biblical morality). We now find public morals at low ebb, characterized by antireligious sentiments, secularism, and blanket toleration of everyone except the one who believes in divine mandates for proper conduct. The corroding effects of pluralism have not only rusted away at public morals; indeed, evangelicalism has been assaulted by the same forces in modernity.[31] To resist this erosion, Christians must construct again the strong walls of theology and ethics both within the church and in interaction with our cultural world.

Another issue for Peter that emerges from this section concerns *living in light of and for the future,* what Peter calls *hope.* This hope is grounded in God's holiness. Peter wants believers to live in light of God's judgment, a judgment that is at the same time the Christian's hope for vindication and justice. This judgment satisfies our desire for justice.

While hope is an ethical directive, it partakes of ethics in a different way because it manifests itself not so much in behavior as in attitude and disposition. The one who lives for the future does concrete things (like living in a loving manner), but it is the orientation that leads to a system of checks and balances with love. Those who live for the future have their eyes on the horizon rather than at their feet. Because of this, they exude an attitude about this world and its brevity. We must look further at this idea of living for the future.

Peter manifests two primary emphases in the attitude of living for the future. (1) We must live in light of God's righteous judgment of our

---

31. See here esp. J. D. Hunter, *Evangelicalism: The Coming Generation* (Chicago: Univ. of Chicago Press, 1987); D. F. Wells, *No Place for Truth: Or Whatever Happened to Evangelical Theology?* (Grand Rapids: Eerdmans, 1993).

lives (cf. 1:17; 4:5, 17), and (2) we must live in the hope of the joy of final salvation (1:6—9; 2:23; 4:11, 19). These attitudes *ought to govern the entirety of our ethical behavior.* Every step we take and every move we make should be in light of what God thinks of what we are doing. This is not some form of perverse legalism, any more than my desire to please my wife, Kris, is legalism. A desire to please God is the noblest motivation in life; to reject such a desire in the name of legalism is to misunderstand our family relationship to God. This perspective on our own future ought to influence every area of life with forceful impact. I will mention three.

We ought to shape our attitude toward *materialism* in light of this future orientation in life. The Western world is a comfortable world, especially when compared to places like Zaire (racked now by a deadly virus) or the former Yugoslavia. And while it is proper and good for wealthy Christians to share with the rest of the world, they will still probably live in comfort. We need to look at this issue, however, from another angle. Material things, like large homes, extra cars, special video and computer equipment, involvement in sports entertainment that costs unreasonable amounts, boats, vacation homes, and special trips to exotic parts of the world, are all tempting. But the joy and delight we take in such things (I can get as excited as anyone about professional sports) can easily detract our attention from living before God in light of his final judgment and can steal any desire for the joy that can only come when our salvation is complete. We need in our materialistic culture a special grace from God to give us a desire for what lies beyond our days and our culture, and we need a new vision of just how great God's salvation and glory will eventually be. This vision will no doubt lead us to tone down our purchases and to rearrange our schedules so that first things are first.

Understanding our present in light of God's future will also impact *how we plan our lives.* In my judgment, far too many Christians waste too much time planning for a future, especially as it concerns insurances, investments, and retirement, and do not consider that future sufficiently enough in light of its contingency and God's providence. I do not want to sound here like some curmudgeon who believes that planning for the future is wrong, for that is neither biblical nor wise. What I am pointing to is an orientation and a *preoccupation.* Pastors who plan their ministries in light of sure benefits or profits, leaders of institutions whose plans are subjected only to the bottom line and not to God's will and his truth, and evangelists who think only in terms of the kinds of churches where profits are large are all guilty of the sin of planning without regard to God's final judgment and the beauty of final salvation. Planning for our future is wise, but being preoccupied with it may well evince a lack of faith in God's control of that future.

I have a friend who is constantly in demand to preach and teach at churches throughout the nation. He is regularly asked "what his price is." His response is always the same. "Please," he says, "give me an outline of what you need in the way of preaching, the kind of audience I will face, and the dates, and I will seek the face of God to see if this engagement is what God wants me to do because someday I will have to answer to him." Then he adds, "I will take whatever you give me because I do not preach for money. I preach to announce the good news of Christ, to serve God, and to strengthen the church." Such an attitude is one that focuses on living for the future, and it has safeguards to prevent one from making plans without regard to that future.

Finally, *our health* ought also to be subjected to God's final plans for history. Several ideas come to mind. While it is not wrong to be fit and strong, some motivations for being fit are wrong. We are not immortal, and no matter how hard we work at being fit, we will still die. Some people, however, are motivated to be fit by a fear of death. Fear of death is not a Christian emotion; joy at the prospects of fellowship with God is. We ought, rather, to desire to be fit so that we can serve God (maybe longer than otherwise) better and more energetically. This puts us right back in the lap of Peter's church. Believers in his day were suffering for their obedience to Christ, and Peter exhorts them not to worry about suffering but to live in constant expectation of God's final vindication, just as Jesus lived (2:18–25; 3:18–22). Peter shows them how they could adopt an entirely different attitude toward suffering: to trust in God, to look forward to God's final glory, and in the meantime to enjoy the fellowship with his people as a substitute for what they were losing in society because of their decisions to be Christians.

I conclude with a conversation I recently had with Lukas, my son, when he was fourteen years old—a conversation not unlike I have had with both of my children. We had been at a local sports event, and the vulgarity of the coach and his team was quite noticeable. When we got in the car to ride home, I raised this issue with my son and asked if he noticed. He said that he had heard the vulgarity. What was funny and entertaining to that team, and to some of the spectators, was sad to me. What I said to Lukas that day goes for more than just vulgarity but any moral decision we make: "You and I can talk any way we want. But we need to realize that someday we will stand before a holy God and will have to give a justification for how we have talked. That, in itself, ought to make us pause before we speak and to transform how we talk." This is living in the light of the future.

In summary, therefore, Peter's little passage of four exhortations contains strong pillars on which we can construct Christian ethics. He provides us with at least three foundations for determining whether an action is right or wrong. (1) Does it conform to the character of God? (2) Is it the natural outcome of a life that has benefited from the salvation of God? (3) Will it stand up to God's scrutiny in that final day when he ushers us into his glorious presence?

1 Peter 2:1–10

❧

THEREFORE, RID YOURSELVES of all malice and all deceit, hypocrisy, envy, and slander of every kind. ²Like newborn babies, crave pure spiritual milk, so that by it you may grow up in your salvation, ³now that you have tasted that the Lord is good.

⁴As you come to him, the living Stone—rejected by men but chosen by God and precious to him—⁵you also, like living stones, are being built into a spiritual house to be a holy priesthood, offering spiritual sacrifices acceptable to God through Jesus Christ. ⁶For in Scripture it says:

> "See, I lay a stone in Zion,
>   a chosen and precious cornerstone,
> and the one who trusts in him
>   will never be put to shame."

⁷Now to you who believe, this stone is precious. But to those who do not believe,

> "The stone the builders rejected
>   has become the capstone, "

⁸and,

> "A stone that causes men to stumble
>   and a rock that makes them fall."

They stumble because they disobey the message— which is also what they were destined for.

⁹But you are a chosen people, a royal priesthood, a holy nation, a people belonging to God, that you may declare the praises of him who called you out of darkness into his wonderful light. ¹⁰Once you were not a people, but now you are the people of God; once you had not received mercy, but now you have received mercy.

ONCE AGAIN, PETER'S style here—weaving in and out of topics, exhorting and then stating the foundation for the exhortation, and digressing to cover important ideas— prevents many readers from finding any logical sequence. This section continues what began at 1:13, where Peter drew out the practical manifestations of salvation and hope. Here we have exhortations five (2:1– 3) and six (2:4–5), along with two digressions.

The flow of the passage begins with *an exhortation to desire the word of God* (2:1–3), which derives from Peter's mention of God's preached word in 1:23–25.[1] This unit includes the exhortation itself (2:1–2a), its purpose (2:2b), and its foundation (2:3). Peter then exhorts the Christians *to build themselves into a spiritual house* (2:5), an exhortation that is prepared for by his comment that the one to whom they are coming was rejected by humans but accepted by God (2:4). This preparation leads Peter to digress in 2:6–8 for a more complete discussion of what is meant by this rejection-acceptance theme. Finally, Peter digresses even further by contrasting the rejection group (cf. 2:7b–8) with the church itself (2:9–10). The "acceptance group" (cf. 2:7a) is thus the complement of the digression in 2:9–10. And it is here, with a digression on the nature of the church, that Peter finishes the first major section of the letter.

Fifth Exhortation: Desire the Word (2:1–3)

"THEREFORE," PETER SAYS—THAT is, because his readers have been born again through the word of the living God (1:23)—they must "crave pure spiritual milk" (2:2).[2] This does not refer to having home Bible

---

1. In fact, 2:1 is a repetition of the exhortations and comments in 1:22–23, but at 2:1 the ideas are expressed in negative form. At 1:22–23 they were exhorted to "love one another deeply, from the heart," with a "sincere [brotherly] love"; here they are told to get rid of the nasty and ugly things that make love impossible. This implies that the growth of 2:2 should likely be seen as "group growth," not individual growth; furthermore, such an understanding dovetails more neatly with what is exhorted in 2:4–5, where corporate development is at issue.

2. The grammar of 2:1–3 is as follows: an introductory participle "rid yourselves of . . ." (NIV) is subordinate to the main verb "crave," which itself does not appear until 2:2. "Like newborn babies" describes *how* they are to crave; "so that by it . . ." describes the purpose of their craving and "now that . . ." (2:3) describes the foundation for their craving. Thus, "crave pure spiritual milk" provides the central exhortation of this section.

studies or personal Bible study, or to going to church and Sunday school classes, or to attending Christian colleges or seminaries. Rather, it describes the spiritual nature of their craving[3] as opposed to the former fleshly cravings (cf. 1:18; 2:11). As the "word" through which they received a new birth (1:3) was from the living and abiding God (1:23), so now the word they are to desire is spiritual.[4] "Pure spiritual milk" refers to the very things that nourish the Christian community in its growth:[5] knowledge of God, prayer, instruction in the gospel, faithful obedience, and hearing God's preached word.[6] The desire for spiritual nourishment is the desire of any church that wants to know the Lord and live in light of his will.

This desire is accompanied by learning to "rid yourselves of all malice and all deceit, hypocrisy, envy, and slander of every kind" (2:1)— problems that arise in Christian assemblies when spiritual things are not desired. In early Christian literature it was common to speak of Christians "stripping themselves" of vices and "clothing themselves" with virtues (cf. Rom. 13:12–14; Gal. 3:27; Eph. 4:22–24; Col. 3:8–12; Heb. 13:1; James 1:21).[7] This image draws a picture of bad habits that need to be eliminated and good habits that need to be developed. Peter contains only the "rid yourselves" part.

Good habits come from craving pure spiritual milk, "like newborn babies" (2:2). While some have seen here a subtle hint that the readers of 1 Peter are young, immature Christians who need to be reminded

---

3. On this term denoting intense desire, see Rom. 1:11; 2 Cor. 5:2; 9:14; Phil. 1:8; 2:26; 1 Thess. 3:6; 2 Tim. 1:4; James 4:5. See here M. Craig Barnes, *Yearning: Living Between How It Is and How It Ought To Be* (Downers Grove, Ill.: InterVarsity, 1991); Augustine, *Confessions*, 1.1.

4. Considerable academic discussion has been raised around this word "spiritual." The Greek word is not the normal (Pauline) term (*pneumatikos*) but is *logikos*. J. N. D. Kelly prefers the idea of "wordy," in the sense of "milk of the word" (*Peter and Jude*, 85), while F. J. A. Hort preferred the more classical meaning of "rational" (*1 Peter*, 100–102); the vast majority of scholars today, however, prefer "spiritual" (see, e.g., F. W. Beare, *1 Peter*, 115; L. Goppelt, *1 Peter*, 131; J. R. Michaels, *1 Peter*, 86–89).

5. See esp. J. R. Michaels, *1 Peter*, 88–89. On "milk" in early Christian literature, see L. Goppelt, *1 Peter*, 129–30.

6. To think, however, of personal Bible study is anachronistic; these Christians did not have copies of the Bible and had to rely on sermons and the local archives for such things. It makes best sense to see here the spiritual nourishment that comes to Christians in various ways. If my view of the recipients of this letter is correct in that they are socially disenfranchised, then they were likely illiterate as well.

7. On this see the discussion of E. G. Selwyn, *1 Peter*, 393–406; but see also J. R. Michaels, *1 Peter*, 83.

to desire good things, it is more likely that Peter is referring to the *manner of their desire*. Their craving for spiritual nourishment should be like the cravings of nursing children for milk. When a church yearns for spiritual nourishment, that church will not be involved in bitter disputes with hypocritical showings or deceitful communications.[8]

If you, Peter says to his readers, learn to yearn for spiritual nourishment, you will "grow up in your salvation" (2:2). Peter is not concerned here about "church growth" in a numerical sense, but about the church, regardless of its numerical strength, becoming desirous of spiritual nourishment and spiritual growth. As John Stott said at the Lausanne Conference, "We confess that we have sometimes pursued church growth at the expense of church depth, and divorced evangelism from Christian nurture."[9] This leads, not to church growth, but to stunting the growth of the church.

This spiritual growth is in the direction of "salvation," and for Peter that salvation is future (1:5, 9–10). Thus, what Peter has in mind here is essentially their "hope" and perhaps their final vindication.[10] That is, if they yearn for spiritual nourishment, they will grow into that final salvation that is being protected for them by God as they continue in their faith (1:4–5).

All of this is *founded* on the fact "that you have tasted that the Lord is good" (2:3). The psalmist exhorted his readers to "taste and see that the LORD is good" (Ps. 34:8). Peter uses this text in his argument, contending that the foundation for spiritual craving is the fact that believers have already found spiritual nourishment to be good and tasty.[11] Because the Lord himself is spiritually satisfying (again, an allusion to

---

8. The meaning of this verse needs to be distinguished from what is said by Paul in 1 Corinthians 3:2 and by the author of Hebrews at Hebrews 5:12–14. Confusion has resulted from the identity of meaning because each of these authors uses the metaphor of drinking milk. Peter has in mind the desire characteristic of an infant when wanting milk; Paul has in mind the immaturity of the believer who can have only milk, as only babies drink milk; and the author of Hebrews has in mind an idea similar to Paul's: Milk is the first kind of food Christians drink, and then they mature to the point of eating meat. There is no suggestion in 1 Peter 2 that milk is food for immature Christians; rather, Peter praises the desire of infants and prays that his readers will have that same desire for spiritual things.

9. See J. R. W. Stott, *Let the Earth Hear His Voice*, 7.

10. J. R. Michaels, *1 Peter*, 89. It is unlikely here that "salvation" means "Christian maturity" (so W. A. Grudem, *1 Peter*, 96).

11. The word translated "good" is *chrestos* and may be a play on the Greek word for Messiah (*christos*).

conversion as the foundation for ethics; cf. Matt. 11:25–30), they are to focus their lives on spiritual nourishment and growth, for it is through this kind of development that they will attain their hope of salvation.

Sixth Exhortation: Build a Spiritual House (2:4–5)

CHRISTIANS WHO TOGETHER crave for spiritual nourishment should also be fashioned as part of a spiritual house. In coming to Jesus, the one who tastes good, they will in fact build a spiritual house. In these two verses Peter raises two distinct themes, both of which are developed in what follows: (1) the twofold response to Christ in his earthly and heavenly ministries (acceptance or rejection, discussed in 2:6–8), and (2) the spiritual nature of the church (developed in 2:9–10).

Peter exhorts believers to build a spiritual house: "You also, like living stones, are being built into a spiritual house." It is preferable to translate "are being built" as "build yourselves."[12] The churches in Asia Minor must see themselves as "living stones," connected to the "living Stone" (2:4), and they must unify themselves (1:22–2:3) so that they may become a spiritual house. That is, instead of being a simple group of social outcasts, they must find their identity and cohesion in their spiritual relationship to the living Stone. In fact, Peter states that the church is a "spiritual house," that is, the temple of God. Presumably, he sees this temple as the replacement of the old temple as the dwelling place of God.

The spiritual connection of Peter's readers to the living Stone is the foundation of the spiritual house they are forming: "As you come to him, the living Stone—rejected by men but chosen by God and precious to him," you will make this connection (2:4). Peter has in mind the effects of craving pure spiritual milk; that is, their yearning for spiritual nourishment is another way of urging them to come to Christ for spiritual satisfaction.

What Peter says here of Jesus Christ is fundamental to his understanding not only of Jesus himself, but also of the Christian life. Jesus

---

12. So also C. Bigg, *Peter and Jude*, 128. The majority today understands this verb as an indicative; see, e.g., J. R. Michaels, *1 Peter*, 100. I agree with Bigg because it fits into a string of imperatives (1:13, 15, 16, 17, 22; 2:2) and would be the climax because it is the present tense. Furthermore, Peter has a custom of preparing for imperatives with participles (cf. 1:13, 15–16, 22; 2:1–2).

was rejected by human beings but chosen by God, just as his readers were being rejected by humans. Later he exhorts his readers to look beyond their present rejection and see God's final chapter of vindication as the concluding chapter of this story (see 2:18–25; 3:18–22; 4:1–6). This reflection about Christ is developed at 2:6–8.

The *impact* of their spiritual house is that are to become "a holy priesthood, offering spiritual sacrifices acceptable to God through Jesus Christ" (2:5). The metaphorical emphasis of their ministry provides both a breadth of vision and a lack of specific clarity when we try to unravel this image. Just what is a spiritual sacrifice? The wide variety of possibilities prevents us from contending that it is only one specific thing. It is probably best to see something like the list of behaviors typical of early Christian churches (e.g., 4:7–11).[13]

Digression on Christ, the Rejected-Accepted Messiah (2:6–8)

AS STATED ABOVE, these verses digress from the exhortations that form the heartbeat of our larger section (1:13–2:10). This digression concerns the themes of 2:4–5, especially as found in 2:4: the one who was rejected by human beings but who was considered precious by God. By rooting this theme in an Old Testament text (Isa. 28:16), Peter establishes that this theme was in fact predicted long ago by the prophet Isaiah.

Peter first *cites the text*:

"See, I lay a stone[14] in Zion,
    a chosen and precious[15] cornerstone,
and the one who trusts in him
    will never be put to shame."[16]

---

13. Ramsey Michaels accurately describes this as both worship and conduct; *1 Peter*, 101–2.

14. The word here is the same word in 2:4, but there "living" is attached. The "stone" or "cornerstone" of Isaiah 28:16 has become the "living stone" in its fulfillment in Christ. On this, cf. J. R. Michaels, *1 Peter*, 92 (bibliography), 103–7 (discussion).

15. These expressions were the words used in 2:4.

16. The expression "will never be put to shame" is a litotes, a deliberate understatement. Thus, "never be put to shame" could be expressed by "will find great glory."

From a section that concerns the sovereign rule of Yahweh over history in spite of appearances (Isa. 28:1–37:38), Peter draws from the first prophecy concerning Ephraim. The leaders of Israel have been given great promises, symbolized by the stone laid in Zion,[17] but they have chosen disobedience, apathy, and indulgence. The promises of God are founded in the city itself, but, as the context shows, the people do not trust in God. Therefore, God's justice will sweep them away in "his strange work" [judgment] (28:16–29). Thus, the verses Peter draws from concern the promises of God to provide a way of salvation, but this salvation is not accepted by the people.[18] What Peter sees in Isaiah is an analogous situation in the response of the contemporaries of Jesus; just as the leaders of Israel rejected God's offer in the stone laid in Zion, so people[19] in Peter's time were rejecting the one who is precious to God.

We ought to observe that Peter's quotation is only one prophetic word drawn from the context in Isaiah ("stone"), but he assumes the entirety of the context in applying it. While the words can be seen positively, clearly Peter sees in this word from Scripture a larger context that shows that the saying itself is to be understood in its former tragic sense: The Stone has been laid, but those who walk in Zion trip over it.

Peter then *applies the text* to the contemporary responses to Christ in Asia Minor and probably elsewhere (2:7–8). To those who respond in faith ("to you who believe") the Stone is "precious," just as it is "precious" to God (2:4).[20] But the positive response of believing is not developed until 2:9–10; Peter's prior concern is with those who disbelieve (2:7b–8). What he sees happening is an unfolding of two other "stone" passages: Psalm 118:22 and Isaiah 8:14. That is, the living

---

17. The expression here could have referred to the city itself (Isa. 2:2–4), to the promises inherent to the Davidic monarchy (Pss. 2:6; 118:22), or to God who is the stone himself in Zion (Isa. 8:14). What is clear is that the "stone" became a Messianic symbol (cf. Ps. 118:22; Zech. 3:9), and that is how Peter sees it.

18. On this text, cf. J. Alec Motyer, *The Prophecy of Isaiah: An Introduction & Commentary* (Downers Grove, Ill.: InterVarsity, 1993), 227–36.

19. Peter does not see the responses here exclusively in terms of how the Jewish people responded to the earthly ministry of Jesus. Rather, his scope includes how all kinds of people are responding to Jesus in his time, whether in Rome or in Asia Minor. So also J. R. Michaels, *1 Peter*, 105.

20. Another translation, preferred by many (e.g., W. A. Grudem, *1 Peter*, 104–5), is along the following line: "Therefore, to you who believe there is honor."

Stone laid in Zion is interpreted messianically in light of these two texts. From Psalm 118:22 Peter argues that Jesus has become much more than a rejected stone; he has become the "capstone."[21] From Isaiah 8:14 Peter draws from a passage where Yahweh, the Almighty, is the one to fear because he will be for both Israel and Judah a stone that causes human beings to stumble and fall in judgment. Peter finds the responses of unbelievers to Christ to be just as Israel and Judah responded to Yahweh in their history: He became a source of judgment instead of salvation.

Several observations follow from this sketch. (1) The tragedy is that those who thought Jesus was nothing more than a cause of ridicule will discover that, though they rejected him, he has become the pinnacle of God's house (1 Peter 2:7). (2) Peter clearly has in mind the responses of his contemporaries to the preaching of the word, for "they stumble because they disobey the message" (2:8b)—the "message" being the preaching of the gospel accomplished through the church and by Peter (cf. 1:12, 25; 2:9; 3:1; 4:17). (3) None of this surprises God. Those who know Scripture know that this "is also what they were destined for." God's act of appointing Jesus as the living Stone has become both honor for believers and judgment for unbelievers; this was God's design, and everything happens according to his will.[22]

Digression on the Church, the Acceptance Group (2:9–10)

PETER DIGRESSES ONE more time from his exhortations to develop an idea implicitly raised at 2:4 and mentioned at the beginning of 2:7, namely, the faith of Christians and what that faith does for them. In contrast to the unbelieving "stumblers-over-the-stone," Christians are the true people of God, who continue God's purposes that began with Abraham and Moses. There is no passage in the New Testament that more explicitly associates the Old Testament terms for Israel with the

---

21. The "cornerstone" is the first stone laid that forms the angles and foundation for the structure, whereas the "capstone" is the last stone put into a building, which becomes its climactic stone.

22. See J. R. Michaels, 1 Peter, 107; see also a more theological explanation in W. A. Grudem, 1 Peter, 107–8, and his extended essay explaining a Calvinistic view on pp. 108–10.

New Testament church than this one. Peter gives four descriptions for the church, followed by a declaration of its purpose. This, in turn, is followed by another description of the church.

Four Descriptions of the Church. Since it is not possible to do a fair analysis of each of these terms, I will offer general remarks.[23] It is important to recognize that these are Old Testament descriptions of Israel (cf. Ex. 19:6; Isa. 43:20–21), now applied to the church of Jesus Christ and giving rise to the important teaching that the church is the fulfillment and continuation of Israel. God's purposes in Israel were not frustrated by the unbelieving rejection and crucifixion of Jesus Christ; instead, that event was planned by God to be the weighty foundation stone of the new people of God, who were to emerge after that crucifixion and vindication.

I mention in passing that these four terms do not describe individual Christians; rather, they describe the church as a whole. This fundamental category is a "stumbling stone" for contemporary Western Christians, who have been taught through their culture to think in an individualistic manner.[24] Peter is not describing individual Christians here as a chosen people or a royal priesthood; rather, these are states and functions of the church. However, the function of the individual is a mirroring of the larger body, so that Christians individually enjoy the privilege of access to God (because the church is made up of people who are together the priesthood).

The Purpose of the Church. Peter cites the purpose of the church as declaring "the praises of him who called you out of darkness into his wonderful light." The church as a whole is expected to announce the good tidings of peace and joy that can be found in Christ. While some have seen here a "worship" understanding of "declare," it is more likely that this word should be seen along with the other instances of evangelism in 1 Peter (1:12, 25; 3:1; 4:17).

A Final Description of the Church. "Once you were not a people, but now you are the people of God; once you had not received mercy, but now you have received mercy." Peter appropriates the story of Hosea for the church, except that here "not a people" and "had not received mercy"

---

23. For more extensive analyses, see E. G. Selwyn, *1 Peter,* 165–68; J. N. D. Kelly, *Peter and Jude,* 95–102; L. Goppelt, *1 Peter,* 147–51; J. R. Michaels, *1 Peter,* 107–13.

24. See here esp. R. Bellah, et al., *Habits of the Heart: Individualism and Commitment in American Life* (New York: Harper & Row, 1985), esp. 142–63.

describe their pagan past, while in Hosea these phrases describe God's judgment on Israel for their disobedience.

Peter's digression ends abruptly here. This section has continued the exhortations that began at 1:13 and ends with digressions on the various responses to the preaching of the gospel: Some reject the precious living Stone (Christ), while others believe. This group of believers has become the church—in Paul's terms, the "true Israel of God" (Gal. 6:16). At 2:11, Peter begins a new section.

Bridging Contexts

BEFORE WE CAN even begin to apply Peter's exhortations and digressions to our world and churches, we need to perform surgery on our minds and hearts to see why Peter can have such a profoundly positive and exalted view of the church. It is not that Peter's churches were so much more pure, more godly, more evangelistic, more worshipful, more interrelated in fellowship, and more theological than contemporary churches. A close look at his churches, I am sure, would turn up the same kind of factors present in Pauline and modern churches: envy and jealousy, sexual immorality and perversions, insubordination and rebellion.[25] In order to appreciate Peter's perspective on the church of Christ, it is important to grasp what constituted that church: a group of sinful people who had come to Christ for salvation and who were committed to walking in obedience. *And that is no different from our churches today.*

This fact is what raises the problem: Why is it that we are so critical of the church?[26] Surely we do not need to pretend, like a little girl

---

25. See Revelation 2–3; Ignatius, *Ephesians, Magnesians, Trallians, Philadelphians, Smyrnaeans,* and his letter to *Polycarp.* Marcion, a heretic, was from Sinope in Pontus (one of the provinces mentioned in 1:1).

26. A recent spate of books about evangelicalism focuses almost entirely on what is wrong with evangelicalism and the churches. I am not arguing that we need to neglect our weaknesses and our sins; no, we must excoriate them in order to fix them. But we need also to maintain the wonderful balance of being able to criticize the weaknesses while glorying in the beauty of the bride of Christ. The books I am thinking of include D. Wells, *No Place for Truth: Or, Whatever Happened to Evangelical Theology* (Grand Rapids: Eerdmans, 1993) and *God in the Wilderness: The Reality of Truth in a World of Fading Dreams* (Grand Rapids: Eerdmans, 1994); M. Noll, *The Scandal of the Evangelical Mind* (Grand Rapids: Eerdmans, 1994); the present research seems to go back to J. Davison Hunter, *Evangelicalism: The Coming Generation* (Chicago: Univ. of Chicago Press, 1987).

coming home from class and teaching her own "make-believe" class in the quiet of her bedroom, that we have all the right credentials, skills, and knowledge that are required to go on. Nor do we need to pretend that we are dressed in holiness, righteousness, justice, and mercy. It is entirely proper for the church to turn inward to denounce its sins and shortcomings; it is proper for the theologians of the church to turn against the intellectual depravity of the church; and it is expected that prophets and preachers will point to the problems in our world. But the issue is: How often do we resonate with this theme, and how do we criticize when we do? The issue becomes even more complex when we factor in the inherent beauty of the church as the bride of Christ, as the community of grace, and as the channel through which God has chosen to express his grace in our world. When we understand the nature of the church as Peter does here in such a profound manner, then, and only then, are we licensed to proceed into critique and battle.

But before we can cross that bridge of evaluation of our own churches, we must stand on God's side and see how that church is constructed and discover its true nature. We are presently living in a (cess)pool of criticism and negativism, in which we find satisfaction in dirtying ourselves even more with criticisms and accusations of weaknesses. Of course there are weaknesses; the church is after all a community of redeemed *sinners*. Perhaps we could apply the words of C. S. Lewis to the church and world as a whole and not just to individuals within those larger communities.

> It is a serious thing to live in a society of possible gods and goddesses, to remember that the dullest and most uninteresting person you talk to may one day [in glory] be a creature which, if you saw it now, you would be strongly tempted to worship, or else a horror and a corruption such as you now meet, if at all, only in a nightmare.[27]

Lewis is saying that humans, when they are finally in the eternal state, have so much potential that, if we could see that potential now,

---

27. C. S. Lewis, *The Weight of Glory, and Other Addresses* (Grand Rapids: Eerdmans, 1965), 14–15. This little book was published in England under the title *Transposition and Other Addresses* (1949).

it would either throw us to our knees in awe or make us turn and run in fear. It is no stretch of the imagination to think this way of the church and the world. And if we can turn our thoughts this way, we can only be ashamed of our constant reprehending of the church. Some day this church will be so full of God's glory and so like the glory of Christ that we ought to pause before we start hammering away at its structures and substructures. In other words, before we get to the business of application, we need to repent from a state of critical evaluation of the church, which Christ has bought and for which God has planned a great future.

Another issue of importance before applying this passage is that we must update the images before they can be meaningful in our cultural contexts. Peter uses some images that do not resonate with most readers of the Bible in the Western world. Such terms as "living stones," "a holy priesthood," "spiritual sacrifices," "a chosen nation," and "a royal priesthood" are all difficult for us to understand, let alone to appreciate or even to jump up and down in joy for their beauty. We must sit down with some books and tools to get to the bottom of these images. Only an insensitive preacher holds these images up before modern congregations as "great images to live by." Concordances help readers find parallel expressions, commentaries (like those cited in the notes) elucidate their meaning, and dictionaries provide further information. We must use these tools if we want this text to have meaning in our world.

While we do not have the space to explain each of these terms in detail, I want to illustrate my point for one of them: "royal priesthood." Many of my readers have grown up in a country where there is no royalty, and they may well have experienced either an unchurched or low-church background. For this kind of person (I am one of them), neither "royal" nor "priesthood" has any natural reverberations as a significant religious expression.[28] To unpack its meaning, we need to know what it meant then and what analogies it might have in our world.

---

28. If my reader happens to be a Roman Catholic who has grown up under a monarchy or an Anglican who has grown up under the British royalty system, then some changes of perception would have to be made. In these cases, though the change of status may be the same (from nonroyalty to royalty) as the one described above, the ability to understand the image intuitively would be easier.

For a Jewish reader, to be a part of royalty was beyond one's natural abilities because royalty was inherited; and I suspect most Jews would have thought of the line of King David. Unless one was part of David's genealogy, being a part of royalty was unthinkable. For such people, the new-found privilege of being part of royalty would have been understood as a fantastic opportunity, however metaphorical it may have sounded. Again, the Christian gospel leveled all peoples and gave them status in God's kingdom that they would not otherwise have had. For a reader in the Roman empire, the natural connection would be with the emperor and his family. Once again, this was beyond the scope of most people's imagination and probably outside their desires. But the message of the gospel is that by believing in Jesus, these people became adopted members of the family connected with King Jesus, and they too became royalty.

But Peter adds to this notion of royalty the idea of priesthood, and here the Jewish connection is fundamentally important. Peter does not have in mind the priesthood of pagans but the inherited privilege of direct access to God.[29] The priests were from special families among the nation of Israel, who served God by mediating between the people and God. To be a priest was a privilege beyond comparison because it involved entry into the special courts and holy places of the temple in order to take human concerns before God and apply God's forgiveness.

So what we have here is a distinct calling: the dual role of having an inherited privilege of ruling God's people and of serving as mediators between God and his people. To call all members of the new family of God, a royal priesthood meant (1) to wipe away any sense of physical lineage and heritage, and (2) to grant to these same people the highest statuses that one could imagine in Judaism: kings and priests. There is simply no analogy to this in our world because we today have no concept of ruling God's people (we envision Jesus as the King of his people, the church) and because we have been raised to think that we have direct access to God through Christ's work. Nonetheless, we must imagine the incredible rise in status that would have been granted to those who perceived this image in its true Jew-

---

29. On the priesthood in the first century, see E. P. Sanders, *Judaism: Practice and Belief. 63 BCE–66 CE* (Philadelphia: Trinity Press International, 1992), 77–118, 170–89.

ish background. Precisely at this point we can make an application: To become a Christian is to be raised to the ultimate height in status because we suddenly become children of the God of the universe, and we have direct access to him because we are his children.

To aid in this perception, we should find analogies in our world that provide similarity to kings and priests in Peter's world. Thus, we might think of CEOs or office bosses or presidents of institutions or governments and compare them with office staff, menial workers, and even the unemployed. We need to challenge the imagination of Christians and ask them to visualize their being the president of their country or being related to that president, or to visualize being the most important religious figure in their culture or suddenly becoming a CEO. At this point we can suggest that this is what we have become in Christ—people with unique and enduring privileges, with a massive status change, living before the holy and sovereign God, who by his grace has made us his people forever. We have been elevated to the greatest places in God's kingdom: those who rule with Jesus and minister God's grace to others.

Another issue for us in interpreting this passage concerns our inherent individualism. Recent applications of sociological knowledge to the New Testament has clearly demonstrated that the ancient world was much less individualistic than our world.[30] While I think some of these scholars have exaggerated both contemporary individualism and ancient relational understandings (dyadism), the basic insight cannot be gainsaid: Ancients thought less individualistically than moderns.

That is to say, ancients did not think first of themselves and then of the group to which they belonged (family, church, synagogue, nation); instead, they thought first through the eyes of others and how a given fact could be processed for the group. Their "self-understanding" (to use a modern category that did not exist then as it does

---

30. This idea was presented in a small but influential monograph by H. Wheeler Robinson, which contained two essays from 1936 and 1937. The book was then revised and reissued in 1980 by Fortress Press (see *Corporate Personality in Ancient Israel*, rev. ed. [Philadelphia: Fortress, 1980]). This classic has been criticized by scholars but has withstood the test of time for many scholars. The best recent study is B. J. Malina, *The New Testament World: Insights from Cultural Anthropology*, rev. ed. (Louisville: Westminster/John Knox Press, 1993), esp. 63–89. See also J. J. Pilch and B. J. Malina, *Biblical Social Values and Their Meaning: A Handbook* (Peabody, Mass.: Hendrickson, 1993), 49–52 (under the word "Dyadism").

today) was determined by their relatedness to others. Thus, Malina has concluded that "if our sort of individualism leads us to perceive ourselves as unique because we are set apart from other unique and set-apart beings, then the first-century persons would perceive themselves as unique because they were set within other like beings within unique and distinctive groups." Such is "a person whose total self-awareness emphatically depends upon such group embeddedness."[31] The question they might ask in getting to know another person would not have been, "What do you do that makes you something?" but, "To whom are you related?"

Recently Trinity's faculty had a retreat in which one of the discussion groups concerned international students and how we, as American Western professors, can understand and teach them. Dr. Paul Hiebert made a comment that was arresting (even if it may have been a slight exaggeration) and illustrates my point. He stated that many of our African students do not like to stand out, do not always strive to get the best grade they can get, and do not like to demonstrate their knowledge by answering the teacher's questions. He suggested that this was related to their culture where *being part of the group was more fundamental than standing apart from the group*. If he is correct, and my experience with some African students confirms his observation, then we have here an illustration of how first-century Jewish and Gentile Christians would have behaved.

Simply put, most applications of our text move immediately to its *value for individual piety* and *only rarely to its value for a corporate understanding of the church and our society*. Such a context for interpretation prevents us (1) from understanding the ancient text the way it was supposed to be understood, and (2) from experiencing the nature of the church as it ought to be—a community rather than a collection of individuals.

Before we can proceed into our world, therefore, we need to admit that how we describe the *purpose of the church* has too frequently been cast in isolated, culturally conditioned categories. When the American church sees itself primarily in terms of the Republican or Democratic party, when the English church sees itself in terms of the culture created and formed at Oxbridge, when the European church sees itself in terms of the economy of a united Europe, or when the Korean

---

31. B. J. Malina, *New Testament World*, 68.

church sees itself in terms of national recovery, then we are seeing a culturally conditioned definition of the church. The church gains its identity and its purposes from the Lord and Spirit who created it. That identity and those purposes have been spelled out in the pages of the Bible, and modern cultures or subcultures in which local or national churches abide can only be dialectically related to that Bible. Culture cannot define or determine the parameters of the church, nor can it define its mission. When this happens, the church loses its bearings, begins to wobble, and eventually falls into a state of lethargy and ineffectiveness.

We are not suggesting that the specific culture in which a church dwells does not affect either its identity or purposes, for that would be foolish. But we are suggesting that culture cannot determine the mission of a church; it can only influence its directions and forms if that church wishes to remain faithful to its heritage and to its Lord. The church's mission is to exalt the Lord, evangelize the world, and edify believers. These are the kinds of missions the Bible provides for the church. But the church today can easily get sidetracked, and an apparatus for getting the church back on its rails is what reformation is all about.

Our text addresses this issue because Peter makes several statements that are sweeping and directly relevant to the entire history of the church. Thus, the church is to grow into salvation (2:3), is to be a spiritual house that offers to God spiritual sacrifices (2:5), and is to declare the virtues of God (2:9). While these are not the only missions given to the church, the church is not the church if it is not performing these particular missions. Culture, however, has within it the capacity to substitute its own goals for the goals of the church, and we must learn to discern what God has called the church and churches to do in the present world.

WE BEGIN BY observing that one of Peter's major concerns in this letter can be broadly labeled "the relationship of the church to the state," though he did not think in those terms. This text provides some important grist for the mill if we want to produce healthy ideas for a living church. In particular, it seems that Peter sees the relationship of the church to society in rather "sectarian" terms. That is, he sees the primary business of the church to be concerned with itself, its own identity, and its own formation, not in terms of how it can either counter or enhance the state. The primary mission of the church is to grow as a spiritual community and to declare the virtues of God. Peter does not deny that Christians should be involved in society, nor does he insist (as nearly all sectarian movements do) that they must insulate themselves from the world's values by separating from the world. Nonetheless, his concern is inward, and in that sense, he reflects what is seen today by sociologists and others as a "sectarian approach" to life.[32]

It just so happens that Peter's and our worlds dramatically differ in this regard. That means we must be careful of importing a world (which does not exist for modern Westerners) rather than importing theological direction for the church. The entire sweep of the Bible teaches that Christians in non-Christian environments are not to be worried so much about changing their environments as they are to remain faithful in whatever kind of environment they find themselves. In fact, the New Testament is unified on this point: Christian teaching concerns Christian theology and behavior, not social institutions and how they might be changed. Accordingly, the tasks of the church are transnational and universal, not culturally restricted. Thus, the mission of the church as defined by Peter here helps to form, and together with the rest of the New Testament does form, the foundation of church's mission everywhere and in all ages.

In other words, Peter's agenda here of *spiritual formation* and *evangelistic outreach* identifies the preeminent purpose of the church in society. Just how that might be done differs from culture to culture. Peter's churches, for example, would probably not have held massive rallies in the city square, but that is no reason why Western churches cannot do so. In addition, Peter's comments are also restrictive in that they define the primary tasks of the church. From day one the church of Christ was involved in spiritual formation and evangelistic outreach. In fact, one might contend that these are the two primary human-

---

32. In our next text, 2:11–12, I will look closely at how one modern sociological theory would apply to 1 Peter.

oriented missions of the church, alongside the primary task of bringing glory to God through corporate and individual worship.[33]

What this means is that other tasks are to be seen either as subordinate to these goals or a means of accomplishing them. In applying
this passage to our culture, therefore, we should begin with a fruitful
analysis of the purpose of the church and of local churches in terms
of what Peter brings to the fore is: spiritual formation (2:2, 5) and
evangelism (2:7–8, 9).[34] He envisions a spiritually formed, evangelistic people. As Richard Foster has said, "Superficiality is the curse of our
age. The doctrine of instant satisfaction is a primary spiritual problem. The desperate need today is not for a greater number of intelli-
gent people, or gifted people, but for *deep people*."[35]

How are we to accomplish these purposes? I will make suggestions,
largely the conventions of Christian wisdom, for both purposes. First,
how are we to develop spiritual formation? It begins with our theology, as
David Wells has amply demonstrated.[36] We must understand that true
spirituality is neither just an experience nor a technique but a relationship of obedience and trust to the one and only living God, the
Father of Jesus Christ, that Jesus Christ is the Son of the living God,
and that he has sent the Holy Spirit to guide and nurture us in our spiritual formation. Until we understand theology (and let this overwhelm
our ideas and practices), we will not develop true spiritual formation.
All true Christian development is the result of knowing God the Father,

---

33. That "worship" is not to be restricted exclusively to "ecstasy" or "praises of song" or
"moments of awe," however, has been powerfully brought out by D. Peterson, *Engaging
With God: A Biblical Theology of Worship* (Grand Rapids: Eerdmans, 1992).

34. A constant factor in applying the Bible to our world is the restriction that any particular application creates. Thus, in applying this passage to the issue of the church's mission, I do not want to suggest that other applications are not permissible. Space limitations
require a focus; sermons are even more focused. I mention a few others: (1) the true nature
of church growth (cf. 2:1–3, 5), (2) desiring what is healthy (2:1–3), (3) the problem of
disbelief (2:4–8), and (4) the nature of the church (2:9–10). Each of these could have been
explored in this Contemporary Significance section.

35. Richard Foster, *Celebration of Discipline: The Path to Spiritual Growth* (San Francisco:
Harper San Francisco, 1988), 1.

36. Wells's two books, *No Place for Truth* and *God in the Wilderness*, are strenuous (if not stri-
dent) essays on the fundamental importance theology plays in the health (or sickness) of
the church. Many writers today, such as J. I. Packer, D. Bloesch, and J. R. W. Stott, are making the same points, though Wells reserves more room for interacting with modern sociological analyses.

participating in the work of the Son, and submitting to the guidance of the Holy Spirit.

Perhaps the greatest obstacle to spiritual development today is that people are too busy. "In contemporary society our Adversary majors in three things: noise, hurry, and crowds. If he can keep us engaged in 'muchness' and 'manyness,' he will rest satisfied. . . . Hurry is not *of* the Devil; it *is* the Devil."[37] In the development of spiritual maturity in our churches, we need to ask for time and for focus so that the noise of modern society can be eliminated to hear the glorious tones of God's Word. This is best done in the context of a community.

It follows, then, that we will seek for Christian fellowship in the church of Jesus Christ and will find a special place for our Christian brothers and sisters. We will find a special bond with them and will nurture those friendships in the context of a local church. We will receive instruction and rebuke, as well as fellowship and guidance, from fellow Christians. We will find the contribution (our giftedness) we can make to that fellowship, and we will be thankful to God for what he permits and enables us to do. We will dedicate ourselves to praying for one another and about important items together.

It also follows that we will find a place for personal devotion, including the regular reading of the Bible and prayer, because through these disciplines we come to know God and his will. We will delight in the knowledge of God and will want to learn what is true about ourselves in light of that knowledge. In short, for spiritual formation to take place, we will desire a deepening of our understanding of God's will and his work in this world (a theological and cosmic view of reality), will foster spiritual fellowship with other Christians, and will devote ourselves to time-honored disciplines.[38]

To develop spiritual formation does not involve any special experience (such as speaking in tongues, experiencing a miracle, or acquiring an education), nor does it necessarily involve any special techniques. Techniques often are "post-event" reflections on what we did prior to a special experience. But more often it was not the technique that brought on the event; rather, it was an event produced by

---

37. R. Foster, *Celebration of Discipline*, 13.

38. Important reading can be found in D. Bonhoeffer, *Life Together*, trans. J. W. Doberstein (San Francisco: Harper & Row, 1954); R. Foster, *Celebration of Discipline*.

God that we were privileged to experience because we were waiting on God, who was ready to give. To think that by repeating certain words we will meet God in a deeper way is a Christian version of magic. God comes to us in powerful ways when he wants. As with Narnia, so with God: It was not in the Pevensie children's power to make the wardrobe itself turn into a gateway into Narnia. Sometimes, yes; sometimes, no. It was all of Aslan, and when Aslan wanted them there, they got there. So it is with our experience of God: Sometimes certain "techniques" lead us to God; sometimes not. It is all of God and his Spirit.

How can we develop an evangelistic outreach ministry in our churches today? Once again, it begins with theology. We need to understand that bringing people to himself is God's great design, which makes heaven resound with praise (Luke 15). This design finds its power and effectiveness through the Holy Spirit, whose mission is to convict and convert (John 16:8–11).[39] Evangelism always has as its subject the work God has done for humans in Jesus Christ, in his life, his teachings, his death, and his resurrection. Christian evangelism takes people beyond a belief in God to a trust in the cross of Christ and his resurrection. First Peter demonstrates this admirably: Peter tells his readers that they are to be Christian in their behavior because they have been redeemed by the blood of Christ (1:18–19), and that the cross is the essential model of Christian behavior (2:21–25). Further, he hopes to instill in his readers a hope grounded in the resurrection of Christ (1:3).

Evangelism runs aground when it roots itself in shabby and superficial theology; apart from a grasp of God's holiness, which unmasks the sinfulness of humans, and apart from the love of God shown to people in the Cross and Resurrection, there is no basis for Christians declaring that they know the truth. And apart from the conviction that conversion takes place through the work of the Holy Spirit, Christians will resort to techniques and manipulations. But once we are standing on the greatness of the Trinity (Father, Son, and Spirit), Christians can fervently declare the truth of the gospel and trust in God to bring conversion about.[40]

---

39. See D. F. Wells, *God the Evangelist: How the Holy Spirit Works to Bring Men and Women to Faith* (Grand Rapids: Eerdmans, 1987), esp. xi–xvi, 1–15, 28–47.

40. The greatest evangelist of this century is Billy Graham. His ministry is testimony both to the effectiveness of the gospel of Christ crucified and to the (usual) subordinate role

But in saying that theology is the foundation, we dare not forget the important role the church plays in the preaching of the gospel. Emphasis needs to be given to two dimensions here: the gospel creates the church, and then to the church is given the task of preaching the gospel.

> The gospel is the message of Christ's salvation; the church is its most important corporate expression. The truth about Christ and his death, therefore, should find tangible expression in the church. Thus the gospel that created the church should also be modeled by the church.[41]

Methods and techniques are important for evangelism as long as they are subordinate to and in the context of trusting God to do the work and the Spirit to convert people. Whether one is trained to evangelize through the use of tracts or uses a technique like that of a well-known evangelist does not matter as much as the person who is evangelizing. Good methods in the hands of poor evangelists can be damaging, just as poor methods in the hands of good evangelists can get the task done. I am firmly convinced that mature Christians do not need "methods or techniques" any more than experienced carpenters need directions on how to operate a saw or a drill. Experienced evangelists trust in God, discern through the Spirit the person they are evangelizing, and know (like Jesus) how to adapt the message to the person and situation.

Let me express these concerns about the church's mission to evangelize in a more educational manner. (1) What the local church needs to do in training evangelists is to instruct its members fully in the basics of the gospel, discerning that those who are evangelizing are genuine Christians and adequately educated in the message itself.[42] I have been

---

techniques play in his preaching of the gospel. For a candid assessment, read the brilliant biography of W. Martin, *A Prophet with Honor: The Billy Graham Story* (New York: William Morrow, 1991).

41. D. F. Wells, *God the Evangelist*, 54.

42. I do not mean to suggest that young Christians cannot evangelize, for it is often the newest Christians who are most vibrant about their faith and who therefore share it most completely. Such personal testimony evangelism is vital, but it needs to be baptized into a more complete mode of operation if it is to last and to minister beyond the immediate circle of friends. And in this context, a good tract can be useful because it focuses the attention of the audience on a set of statements and away from the personal opinion of the evangelist.

with young Christians who have evangelized and who have offered some of the most (theologically) incredible arguments in their zeal to convert others.

(2) We need to instruct our churches and evangelists so that they have a profound grasp of our world and its culture, from its materialism to its cultural diversity. I am not saying that evangelists have to be psychologists, sociologists, and philosophers, but the learned insights from each of these disciplines will help the evangelist in understanding his or her audience. A sensitive evangelist may perceive that a person is in the clutches of some materialistic philosophy and so will expound on the message of the Bible concerning the temporality of riches and this world. Understanding people, sometimes called sympathy or empathy, forms the heart of solid evangelism. But ultimately what we are talking about is spiritual discernment—discernment of what a particular person needs to hear as we preach the gospel to him or her.

(3) Finally, as we educate our churches in evangelism, we must give the priority of our focus to prayer and spiritual direction. We must emphasize that it since it is God's work, we must be in tune with God; since it is the Spirit who convicts, we must depend on the Spirit; and since it is the cross of the Son, we must focus on the glorious achievements of Christ.

1 Peter 2:11–12

DEAR FRIENDS, I urge you, as aliens and strangers in the world, to abstain from sinful desires, which war against your soul. [12]Live such good lives among the pagans that, though they accuse you of doing wrong, they may see your good deeds and glorify God on the day he visits us.

Original Meaning

THIS IS THE pivotal passage in 1 Peter. Some have found in it the summing up of what has gone before and the thematic statement of the ethical exhortations to follow. It is probably an overstatement to see this as a summary of the letter up to here, though the expression "aliens and strangers" undoubtedly captures what has gone on before with respect to the exhortations. Accordingly, although 2:11–12 does not summarize the theology of 1:3–12, it does recapitulate the social status of believers and infers from that basis the nature of the Christian life in society.

The thematic summary of these verses is organized as follows: (1) the present condition of Peter's audience (2:11a), (2) an exhortation to good behavior (2:11b), and (3) the purpose of the good behavior (2:12).[1] Furthermore, these verses play a critical role in what follows: Christians should live exceptional lives in the midst of suffering because such behavior brings glory to God. These themes emerge regularly (though each does not appear evenly) in what follows. In fact, these two verses are a thematic summary of what is expounded in particular situations that Christians encounter: (1) in their relationship to government (2:13–17), (2) in their relationship to masters (2:18–25), (3) in their relationship to their non-Christian husbands (3:1–6), (4) in their relationship to their wives (3:7), and (5) in their relationship to the Christian family of God (3:8–12). The theme of suffering is then

---

1. The first clause of 2:12 is a resumption of 2:11b but in a positive form: Abstaining from fleshly lusts (negative) becomes having good conduct (positive).

developed in 3:13–4:6, after which an exhortation to the family of God finishes off the exhortations (4:7–11).

The Condition of the Believers (2:11a)

PETER'S EXHORTATION TO believers to abstain from sin and live a virtuous life is grounded in the nature of their existence as "aliens and strangers."[2] As developed in the introduction and at 1:1, 17, I agree with those who maintain that Peter has in mind here the *social location* of the believers. That is, this description does not refer to their "pilgrimage from this life to the next" but to their particular social status as people without rights and without a permanent residence in the Roman empire. They are, literally, "guests and temporary residents."[3] There is little evidence to guide us through the issue of whether their social location was determined by their pre-conversion status or by their conversion, which (presumably) drove them out of a previously better social status. It might be argued, however much by silence, that since the letter presents no evidence that they had previously been of a higher status and are now of a lower status, it is more likely that their social location obtained prior to their conversion.[4] At any rate, they are now socially excluded from privilege and power, and we are on good grounds when we argue that this exclusion was made worse by their conversion to this new religious sect that was sweeping across Asia Minor and the Roman empire.

Peter's point is this: Those who are on the low end of the social scale need to be particularly exemplary in their behavior because for the smallest of matters, injustice can be meted out to them with no recourse to justice or to power. Therefore, Peter emphasizes that these socially

---

2. The NIV adds "in the world," but neither is this in the text nor does it permit the reader to determine on his or her own whether the description is metaphorical or literal (see the discussion at 1:1–2).

3. J. R. Michaels argues that this expression is one more piece of evidence suggesting that Peter was attempting to describe the church in the terms of Israel (*1 Peter*, 116). He appeals here to Psalm 39:12. It might be observed that if (1) Peter is alluding to this passage (which is by no means clear to me) and (2) if this passage is to be understood as a refuge status, then the meaning of the terms here are social, describing the persecuted status of the believers. On this interpretation of the psalm, see H.-J. Kraus, *Psalms 1–59: A Commentary*, trans. H. C. Oswald (Minneapolis: Augsburg, 1988), 419.

4. It is possible that 1 Peter 4:4 indicates a change in social status; however, it is by no means clear that such is the case.

excluded Christians should provide no basis whatsoever for those above them and against them to persecute them or accuse of improper behavior. In addition, Peter wants them to live an exemplary life to provide an attractive alternative to the pagan way of life (cf. 2:12; 3:1). Such a life may even lead some to cast their lot with this Jewish Messiah, Jesus Christ.

The Exhortation to Good Behavior (2:11b)

PETER'S EXHORTATION TAKES a negative form in this verse; in the resumption in 2:12a, it takes on a positive form. Such a repetition allows him to state the same point from two angles. The prohibition reflects the typical Pauline theme of the war between the flesh and the spirit (cf. Rom. 8:1–14; Gal. 5:16–25). Christians are to abstain from "sinful desires" because those desires "war against your soul." "Soul" here has the same meaning that Paul has when he uses "spirit" to refer to that dimension of people that relates to God.[5] Thus, Peter urges his readers to deny themselves the temporary pleasures of indulging in physical, sinful passions because those impulses prevent them from living a spiritual life. Abstaining from fleshly passions, then, is the negative dimension of living a holy and obedient life.

The Purpose of Their Good Behavior (2:12)

PETER NOW MENTIONS the problems for his readers in such concrete fashion that this letter becomes a virtual mirror of the living conditions of the Christians in Asia Minor. If they live godly, blameless lives in their hostile environment, then even if the pagans accuse of them doing bad things, they will be able to see the good behavior of the Christians, and that very behavior will become a source of judgment against the unbelieving world.[6]

---

5. J. R. Michaels, however, concludes that the term here is equivalent to "life" (see *1 Peter*, 116–17). He goes on to suggest that Peter has in mind such things as "comfort, self-protection, and self-gratification" (117).

6. Bruce Winter, in his *Seek the Welfare of the City: Christians as Benefactors and Citizens* (FCGRW 1; Grand Rapids: Eerdmans, 1994), sees these acts of goodness as acts of benefaction given for the civic good so as to enable the citizens to see that Christians are good people and supportive of society.

In verse 12, Peter first repeats the ethical exhortation of 2:11b but in positive form, forming the *foundation* (2:12a): "Live such good lives among the pagans...." Reputation was a dainty thing as much in the first century as it is now; a bad reputation ruined a person's chances in life. Early Christians were suspect, so they developed an ethic of blamelessness and reputation to give the hostile forces of society no ground for their evil workings.[7] Peter develops this "good life" by addressing the issues of submitting to the government, living honorably and industriously before masters, loving one's spouse, and living harmoniously with one another (2:13–3:12).

Peter situates this ethic of reputation in a specific *problem* (2:12b):[8] "though they accuse you of doing wrong." The Christians of Asia Minor, in spite of living good lives, were apparently unjustly being accused of wrongdoing. Peter brings this theme up several times: Foolish men have said ignorant things (2:15), slaves were being mistreated (2:18–21), spouses were probably turning against one another (3:1–7), and believers were being insulted unfairly and persecuted (3:9, 13–17; 4:12–16). Peter urges his readers to live circumspectly and honorably when these accusations are lodged against them and to refrain from insulting their unjust accusers.[9]

Repeating himself, Peter offers once again the *alternative* (2:12c): "that ... they may see your good deeds"; but this time he adds the *result*, that the opponents will "glorify God on the day he visits us" (2:12d). While it is clear what "glorify God" means, the issue here is what "on the day he visits us" means.[10] The ambiguity of the expression has led interpreters to two main options: (1) the day of their conversion, which was stimulated by the good works of the Christians, or (2) the judgment day, which involved judgment against unbelievers and

---

7. For New Testament references to the theme of reputation and good behavior, see Matt. 5:16; 1 Cor. 10:32; 2 Cor. 1:12; Col. 4:5; 1 Thess. 4:12; 1 Tim. 3:7; 5:14; 6:1; Titus 2:5, 8, 10. See C. Spicq, "ἀναστροφή," in *Theological Lexicon*, 1.111–14; G. Ebel, "Walk," *NIDNTT*, 3:933–35.

8. Peter's language is exact. Literally it reads: "in *the very thing* [in which] they accuse you as evildoers, they, by observing your good deeds, may glorify God...." That is, the very thing they use as a pretext of bad behavior is turned against them on the day of God's visiting vindication. See J. N. D. Kelly, *Peter and Jude*, 105; J. R. Michaels, *1 Peter*, 117.

9. See Origen, *Against Celsus*, 6.14–15, for an early example of some unjust accusations.

10. Literally, the Greek expression can be translated as "on the day of visitation" and is probably a quotation of Isaiah 10:3, where it is clearly a day of judgment.

led them to realize that they were wrong in accusing believers unjustly (Isa. 10:3; see also Ex. 32:34; Jer. 6:15; 10:15; 11:23).[11]

While it is true that Peter does see the fruit of good works to be conversion (3:1), the more normal response of unbelievers to the good behavior of believers is not conversion. Rather, Peter foresees judgment coming on the unbelieving world (cf. 2:15, 23; 3:9–12; 4:5, 17). At 3:16, which shows some striking parallels to this verse, the important phrase is "put to shame," which clearly refers to judgment (Pss. 40:14; 69:4–7, 19–20; 83:16–18; Rom. 9:33; 1 Cor. 1:27).[12] In conclusion, while there is some evidence favoring the notion that Peter sees conversions of pagans taking place as a result of the good behavior of the Christians, it is more likely that he has the final day of judgment in view here, the day on which God will vindicate the good behavior of Christians and will drive the hostile accusers to see that they were wrong.

BECAUSE THE TWO options for interpreting the intended audience ("aliens and strangers") are so different—one describing the Christian life as a pilgrimage on earth, the other describing the social status of believers who need to learn how to live in a difficult world—a serious issue for application presents itself. What do we do when we think there is more than one reasonable interpretation of a passage? Another example of this issue is 2:12, where a reference either to salvation or judgment can be argued. What do we do when more than one view is possible? Do we apply both?

First, we need to see if either of the options is found elsewhere in the Bible or in Christian theology. If it is, we are safe (theologically but not necessarily exegetically) in applying either view. If we conclude that one of the options is not taught elsewhere and there is considerable doubt about it being the view that is actually being taught in the passage under consideration, we should exercise caution. As for our dis-

---

11. Scholars are divided as to which of these is the proper interpretation: for *salvation* one can find J. N. D. Kelly, *Peter and Jude*, 106–7; L. Goppelt, *1 Peter*, 159–60; W. A. Grudem, *1 Peter*, 116–17; for *vindication and judgment* one can find F. J. A. Hort, *1 Peter*, 137–38; W. C. van Unnik, "The Teaching of Good Works in 1 Peter," *NTS* 1 (1954): 92–110; P. Davids, *1 Peter*, 97.

12. See H.-G. Link, "Shame, Respect," *NIDNTT*, 3:562–64.

cussion of 2:12, the Bible clearly teaches that Christian behavior leads both to others becoming Christians (this is also the witness of countless Christians throughout the history of the church) and to a criterion for final judgment (cf. Matt. 25:31–46). Thus, we would be within the realm of truth to take either view, even if we were eventually to discover that we interpreted the passage incorrectly. Yet we should always strive to interpret a passage accurately and apply the view that is most accurate as we perceive the evidence.

Second, it is in my judgment *always unwise* to pretend that any passage has two distinctly different meanings. At times (though rarely), an author may intentionally write in such a way to give a double entendre, but this is usually not what is going on when we hear someone make two different applications for a single passage. When double entendre does occur and is consciously intended by the author, then two meanings are implied. But when it is not intended, we need to find one meaning.

What, however, do we do when there are at least two meanings possible and we are unable to decide? This calls for some cautious statements in our search for the intended meaning.[13] If we are undecided, we ought to say we are undecided, which is far better than being sure of two or more meanings. This takes place when an interpreter offers one meaning and applies it, then turns around and says, "Or the passage could mean this, in which case the application would be so and so." This can lead Christian listeners to think solid, precise thinking is unimportant, and all that we need is to get within "shooting distance" and offer alternatives. Authors write in order to communicate; surely distance of time makes biblical communication and interpretation more difficult, but we cannot escape into some kind of interpretive model where anything goes. We must hunt for the author's meaning, and, as R. H. Stein has said, "There is one meaning to a text, that meaning consciously willed by the author. . . ."[14] This means that we

---

13. The standard study of this is E. D. Hirsch, Jr., *Validity in Interpretation* (New Haven: Yale Univ. Press, 1967); see also his *The Aims of Interpretation* (Chicago: Univ. of Chicago Press, 1976); W. Klein, C. L. Blomberg, R. L. Hubbard, Jr., *Introduction to Biblical Interpretation* (Dallas: Word, 1993), 117–51; G. R. Osborne, *The Hermeneutical Spiral: A Comprehensive Introduction to Biblical Interpretation* (Downers Grove, Ill.: InterVarsity, 1991), 366–415; R. Stein, *Playing by the Rules: A Basic Guide to Interpreting the Bible* (Grand Rapids: Baker, 1994), 17–36 (fo an excellent, easy-to-understand explanation of the various issues involved).

14. R. H. Stein, *Playing by the Rules*, 36.

should have as our goal the single meaning of the passage when we begin interpreting and when we apply that one meaning.

However, arguing for one meaning does not exclude that an author may have intended a double entendre. In our passage, if one could establish that the meaning is truly a double entendre, then we could instruct and apply both senses (salvation and judgment). But I know of no interpreter of 1 Peter 2:12 who argues for this. Thus, we must either choose one or the other, or state that we are unable to decide. But we should not argue for both, especially when they are mutually exclusive.

My experience with interpretation leads me to think that most of the time individual interpreters can come to a more committed view. A little more time, a little more effort, and a little more careful exegesis will often lead the interpreter to greater confidence in one view over the other. I fear that too often the feeble interpretation of more than one view is caused by the interpreter's not having enough time to work through the evidence carefully, in which case we need to examine whether we are giving ourselves adequate time to study the Bible. We ought also to ask if we are being responsible to our task of preaching and teaching if we are not giving ourselves sufficient time to sift through the evidence carefully and come to solid conclusions.

One of the most fruitful areas of modern interpretation of the Bible is taking place as readers are experimenting with other disciplines of the liberal arts in order to give themselves a more well-rounded perspective on the context of the Bible and how to bring that text into our world.[15] Classically, interpreters have been trained in language, philosophy, and theology; but contemporary experience demonstrates that life is more complex than these disciplines (though I do not want to depreciate or minimize their priority for interpreters of the Bible). Thus, scholars today are using literary theories, sociology, and psychology to augment their linguistic, philosophical, and theological approaches. Scholars are also using the more complex theories of understanding how authors work (narrative theories) and how readers read (reader-oriented theories). I would like to offer here one example of how a modern sociological model might be used fruitfully for understanding 1 Peter.

---

15. For a brief survey, see Klein, Blomberg, Hubbard, *Biblical Interpretation*, 427–57.

The theory I propose to use is that of B. J. Siegel.[16] This theory concerns itself with understanding a "religious sect" by seeing how a religious movement protects itself in a hostile environment. Few of my readers would contest that Peter's letter is intended for a group of churches that find themselves in a hostile environment, and most will forgive us for using the term *sect* in its sociological sense.[17] What these kinds of models do is to give us new lenses to see information that was left unnoticed or to see old information in a new light. When we apply the model of Siegel, several items from 1 Peter gain a clarity and focus that would not have been seen without this model. The only necessary assumption to make in applying this model to our text is a simple one: Groups essentially behave in a similar manner when stress is encountered.[18] We emphasize *"similar* manner," for the word "identical" is inappropriate and too deterministic. Groups do adapt themselves in similar manners but not in identical manners.[19]

---

16. B. J. Siegel, "Defensive Structuring and Environmental Stress," *AJS* 76 (1970): 11–32. For surveys of how scholars are adapting sociology to the study of the New Testament, see C. Osiek, *What Are They Saying About the Social Setting of the New Testament?* (New York: Paulist, 1984); B. Holmberg, *Sociology and the New Testament: An Appraisal* (Minneapolis: Fortress, 1990); H. C. Kee, *Knowing the Truth: A Sociological Approach to New Testament Interptation* (Minneapolis: Fortress, 1989); for a briefer introduction, see T. E. Schmidt, "Sociology and New Testament Exegesis," in *Introducing New Testament Interpretation*, ed. S. McKnight (GNTE 1; Grand Rapids: Baker, 1989), 115–32.

17. *Sect* has normally been used theologically for groups that are no longer orthodox. I use *sect* here more in the sense of a "break-off religious group"; I do not intend any kind of negative evaluation with the term. In this sense, the Christian church is a *sect* of Judaism.

18. Siegel's theory itself emerges from both his own reading and his observation of various kinds of groups, including religious groups. A recent book that used Siegel's model profitably for learning about the Amish society is D. B. Kraybill, *The Riddle of Amish Culture* (Baltimore: The John Hopkins Univ. Press, 1989), 18–20.

19. I must warn the reader that each point being made in this section could be easily illustrated with many examples, both from early Christian literature and from modern social groups. Space prohibits such documentation, but it would be useful for teachers to ask students in a class to find evidence for each of these points in various New Testament books. I taught a class at Trinity ("Sociological Approaches to the New Testament"), in which students were assigned different books of the New Testament and asked to report to the class their findings of "defensive structuring." Each presentation generated engaging discussions and, on the whole, appreciation both for Siegel's model and for what such theories can do for the interpreter. In my discussion here, I have benefited from the discussion of the papers of three of my students (Curt Coddington, Tim Freeman, and Thomas Fode).

It goes without saying that criticisms could be offered of Siegel's model, including how the evidence itself of our letter at times counters minor aspects of the model. This section

The Theory of Siegel. Siegel's essential theory describes the adaptation techniques that specific groups use when they perceive stress or a threat to their existence. That is, they structure themselves to form a defense and so to preserve their distinctiveness. He outlines four typical strategies: (1) Such groups demonstrate authoritarian control over members by developing an elite group of leaders; (2) they have a high rate of endogamy (marry only members of the group); (3) they cultivate cultural identity symbols; and (4) they educate the youth associated with the group to control various desires.[20] Thus, when a group feels stress over against outside groups (as Peter's churches did), they will use that stress to motivate the group to defend itself against invasion, corruption, and dissolution. In this way, the group solidifies its identity and so preserves its life.

Let us now compare this model to the evidence in 1 Peter. (1) There can be no doubt about *environmental stress* for the churches of 1 Peter. They were encountering various trials[21] (1:6), they were experiencing verbal attacks (2:12, 23), the slaves were finding their masters to be ornery (2:18), and wives were finding that their husbands were unbelieving (3:1–6). In short, they were being persecuted (3:13–17; 4:1–6, 12–19). We can infer that the churches would have responded to this threat in a way that would preserve their identity and cultivate their continued existence. To accomplish these purposes is why Peter wrote this letter.

(2) We need also to look at the various *adaptive strategies.* (a) I will begin with the fourth strategy, *early socialization*, since there is no evidence for it in 1 Peter. However, it is likely that the Christians of

---

of my commentary, however, is only an example of how we might appreciate certain kinds of models, not a full-scale analysis of the model of Siegel.

20. According to this model, the early church as a whole would fit into the scheme of defensive structuring. Strong leadership is common throughout the New Testament (Pastorals); as with ancient Israel, the early churches surely taught that Christians ought to marry in the faith (1 Cor. 7); they clearly cultivated cultural symbols (language understandings, rituals, etc.); and they also can be seen as educating their youth in the "ways of the Lord." To the degree that such features are present in a given document is the same degree to which we could infer the presence of a threat to that community's identity and existence.

21. Peter interprets their stress as a testing from God, thereby providing for the believers a perception of what is going on that fits into their general perception of reality and permits them to deal with the stress in a cognitive manner that allows them to carry on in joy (cf. 1:7).

Peter's churches were educating their youth in the values and teachings of the early Christian movement, not only because such an interest is found in the Bible (beginning with Deut. 6), but also because such a theory makes sense. What we can learn, however, from making this assumption is that such educational activity has a social angle and purpose; in part, we educate our children in the truths of our faith because we are preparing them for dealing with a world that does not embrace that faith. Thus, while there is no evidence in the text that such education was going on in Asia Minor, we can readily assume it. Furthermore, we can assume that the letter itself is part of that very education.

(b) Peter does have a concern with strong *leadership* (strategy 1). His letter is a prime example. He addresses them as "apostle" (1:1; cf. 2 Peter 1:15–21; 3:15–17) and frequently uses the imperative mood to tell them what to do. But he is also concerned with leaders in the churches and the important role they play in socializing their flocks into the truths of Christian theology and the practices enjoined by the gospel. He commands the local pastors to take care of their congregations (5:2) and the young men of the churches to submit to them (5:5). Siegel's theory invites us to see the social nature of leadership and the role it plays in preserving doctrine and practice, especially when the community itself is under threat of persecution and dissolution.

(c) It is clear that *marriage of Christians* is of no concern in this letter, though we could guess that it was an issue. Clearly such a concern is found in the Bible (Ezra, Nehemiah), and we know that intermarriage was a significant issue in Judaism.[22] We can reasonably infer that Peter would have encouraged Christians to marry other Christians, if only to avoid the problem of unbelieving spouses (1 Peter 3:1). In my judgment, we are justified in inferring this, as long as we caution that such is only an informed inference. In light of the history of Judaism and the nature of this issue in the other parts of early Christianity (cf. 2 Cor. 6:14–18), I cannot imagine that such an issue did not arise for the fathers, mothers, and prospective wives and husbands in Peter's churches, in order for the community to survive in the face of serious

---

22. See V. P. Hamilton, "Marriage (OT)," *ABD*, 4:559–569, esp. 563–65; S. J. D. Cohen, "From the Bible to the Talmud: The Prohibition of Intermarriage," *HAR* 7 (1983): 23–39; S. McKnight, *A Light Among the Gentiles: Jewish Missionary Activity in the Second Temple Period* (Minneapolis: Fortress, 1991), 23–24.

opposition. What we have here is sound historical judgment informed by sociological theory.

(d) The most obvious feature of the model found throughout 1 Peter is the *development of cultural symbols*, where "cultural" means that which gave the early Christian groups their identity and where "symbols" is understood in its broader sense of linguistic, ideological, and physical expressions of beliefs and values. The entire letter is Peter's attempt to keep the group cohesive by providing theological clarifications and ethical exhortations that give the group some foundations for understanding their stress in such a way that it becomes explicable in an otherwise baffling series of events. Persecution, Peter says, occurs within God's sovereignty and is used by God to develop their faith (1:7). The persecutors are unbelievers who are simply continuing what happened to Jesus. The believers should understand that God has given them a new inheritance, and they are to trust in God's mercy as they endure their present stress. Such ideas as the unity and glory of the church, the nature of salvation in Christ, the exhortation to love and holiness are each cultural symbols of what Peter is trying to tell these churches. Even his inculcation of a distinctive dress for women (3:1–6) is part of his design to give the churches a foundation for identifying and defending themselves over against a persecuting culture.

The most obvious cultural symbol that Peter provides his readers is a new term of identity: they are "aliens and strangers." This identity-forming expression provides a way of understanding both their social location and the spiritual basis for that location. Society may see them as excluded, but Peter appropriates these terms of censure for a new category of the spiritually gifted. What was then a term of criticism becomes a badge of merit. Because they are the church (a symbol) and although they are socially excluded (a symbol), they can live holy lives (a symbol) in the midst of tribulation as they look forward to the day of judgment (a symbol).

Sociological models like Siegel's, of course, are not perfect, but they do provide students of the Bible with another avenue on which to travel as they seek to understand the fullness of God's Word and its relationship to its original world and our world. Sociologists seek to examine the everyday realities of our lives and then describe that behavior in a way that helps us understand that reality. When models like these are applied to the ancient world and the New Testament, they can at times shed light on features of the text that would not otherwise have been noted or observed. Siegel's model helps us to see the ethics of Peter and his exhortations to leaders in a new way. When our observations find confirmation in other evidence in the early church, we are on much safer grounds for inferring such for 1 Peter.[23] Learning about Peter's world in turn helps us find analogies for application in our world.

In sum, Siegel's theory about defensive structuring illuminates the fundamental principles Peter urges in 2:11–12. His exhortations are for his readers to live holy lives, to avoid entangling themselves in difficult situations, and to live in such a way that others will join the church. These principles (or symbolic structures), in other words, are a part of a strategy for coping with a society that is hostile to one's beliefs and associations. Peter's strategy, then, is both theological (it is God's will) and sociological (it will enable us to cope and survive). As the commentary proceeds, I will occasionally glance back at this sociological model of interpretation or assume some of the insights gained here.

PETER'S ESSENTIAL MESSAGE here is: Live holy lives in the midst of secular chaos, and let God take care of the final results. Put differently, Peter is calling the churches in Asia Minor to a lifestyle radically different from the surrounding culture as part of their strategy for pleasing God and coping with their environment. This call to holiness is no different today; indeed, it may even be more important today, for the contemporary Western church is more under the influence of the modern culture than most of us realize. What we need is a breath of fresh air to fill us with the aroma of holiness, justice, and righteousness. David Wells, in his recent book *God in the Wilderness*, calls the church to precisely this by saying,

> The choice for God now has to become one in which the church begins to form itself, by his grace and truth, into an outcropping of counter-cultural spirituality. It must first recover the sense of antithesis between Christ and culture and then find ways to

---

23. When no evidence can be found in the ancient world, we are probably better off thinking that such an idea was not a part of that ancient reality.

sustain that antithesis. . . . It must give up self-cultivation for self-surrender, entertainment for worship, intuition for truth, slick marketing for authentic witness, success for faithfulness, power for humility, a God bought on cheap terms for the God who calls us to costly obedience. It must, in short, be willing to do God's business on God's terms.[24]

These are categories for Peter as well: self-surrender (2:11), worship (2:4–5), truth (1:22), authentic witness (2:12), faithfulness (1:6–7), humility (2:13–3:7), and a God who calls us to costly obedience (1:15–17). What Peter wants from his churches (and what God wants from his people!) is a heart focused on him, a behavior focused on love and obedience, and a lifestyle impeccable in the sight of non-Christians.

This is precisely how religion, the Christian faith in particular, ought to function in this country. Religion is neither a prop for politics nor a sanctification of governmental wishes. Instead, it is a separate voice, a voice in the wilderness, an alternative society to the prevailing culture and status quo. In his book *The Culture of Disbelief*, Stephen Carter writes that a "religion is, at its heart, a way of denying the authority of the rest of the world; it is a way of saying to fellow human beings and to the state those fellow humans have erected, 'No, I will *not* accede to your will.'"[25] This statement, by a brilliant lawyer-social critic, comes from a book that seeks to demonstrate how American law and politics have trivialized the deservedly prominent place religious faith actually plays in the lives of countless Americans. One of his main points is that Christians must let their faith stand up and keep themselves from succumbing to social pressure. They must speak their mind—the mind of religious faith. Only in so speaking will they as Christians perform their proper function in our current political situation.

The church, Peter says, is a countercultural alternative to society and culture. Church history shows countless examples of the church operating in precisely this manner.[26] In general in the early church,

---

24. D. F. Wells, *God in the Wilderness*, 223.

25. S. L. Carter, *The Culture of Disbelief: How American Law and Politics Trivialize Religious Devotion* (New York: Doubleday [Anchor Books], 1994), 41.

26. See here W. Barclay, *Educational Ideals in the Ancient World* (Grand Rapids: Baker, 1974 [reprint edition of 1959 edition]), 192–233. Barclay's chapter, however, is an extensive

Christians felt the ambivalence of "life in this world"; while they knew they had to live among pagans, they also knew their lives were but a preliminary to an eternal state that held them responsible for a holy and loving life. Second Clement 6:3–5 states:

> This world and the next are two enemies. The one urges to adultery and corruption, avarice and deceit; the other bids farewell to these things. We cannot therefore be the friends of both; and it behooves us, by renouncing the one, to make sure of the other. Let us reckon that it is better to hate things present, since they are trifling and transient and corruptible; and to love those which are to come, as being good and incorruptible.[27]

This early Christian attitude did not lead to withdrawal into conventicles or to insulating the church from the world. It led instead into a robust conscience of addressing the world with a countercultural message that, while the bulk of Christians were simplistic in their intellectual endeavors, developed into a brilliant tradition of apologists who answered pagans on their own terms—men like Athenagoras, Jerome, and Augustine. Through careful education and exacting analyses of pagan thought, early Christians apologists "spoiled the Egyptians" and their knowledge for the sake of Christ.[28]

But how will this work out today? First, we need to recognize that the forces working today to enculturate the mandates and truth of the gospel and to swallow holiness are *not as overtly physical as they were in Peter's day*. But the threat to the church is not to be minimized. While Peter's churches could spot those opposed to them because they had seen such people beat on Christians physically, we must have discernment to perceive the same kind of pressure today on the church and on Christian living. In particular, we have the forces of modernization, privatization, and secularization. These forces war against our souls as other forces warred against the souls of the Christians in Asia

---

documentation of the pilgrimage theme in early Christian literature (in which category I do not place 1 Peter); I draw from it only to illustrate the countercultural dimension of the church.

27. Translation from Barclay, *Educational Ideals in the Ancient World*, 193.

28. See also *The Epistle to Diognetus* and *A Plea for the Christians* by Athenagoras for further early Christian evidence. For a good study, see R. M. Grant, *Greek Apologists of the Second Century* (Philadelphia: Westminster, 1988).

Minor. Why, for example, do so many Christians think that the essence of Christian living is to be disciplined and efficient? While such ideas are not absent in the Bible, they are hardly held up as core values. Do we not hold them up so high today because they reflect what we have found effective in our capitalistic society? Culture influences us more than we will ever know.

Second, we need to learn what holiness means in *all areas of life*. Inasmuch as the government, employer-employee relations, and the wife-husband relationship will occupy our attention in the next sections, we can leave these topics to the side. Peter is calling his people to a lifestyle that begins and ends with the theme of holiness, and we need to realize that holiness is not just a call to read the Bible daily, to pray daily, to be faithful attendees of church, to be tithers, or to follow any other Christian virtues that have become the essence of Christian living. Holiness is a thirst, a drive to know God in his fullness and an unashamed commitment to obey God whatever it costs and wherever we are. It begins in the morning, directs our path during the day, and leads us to confession and praise in the evening.

Just as Peter's call to holy living was a symbol for the identity of the churches, so today holy living ought to be a characteristic symbol of what identifies a Christian. This includes holiness and righteousness in sexual practices, in the words we utter and do not utter, in economic decisions, in recreational pursuits, in vocational direction, and in theological decisions. It includes doing things that contribute to personal holiness, such as Bible reading, prayer, fellowship with other Christians, and the evangelization of our world.

Third, the Church needs *to call all of its members to a life of holiness*, to a life that denies itself any indulgence in the passions of the flesh and demonstrates to the world that God is at work in the church. Thus, holiness has both a negative and a positive dimension. It means avoiding sin *and* actively performing acts of goodness and love. Avoidance of sin, like the cult of separationism that sometimes swallowed fundamentalism, is only one part of the biblical notion of holiness; the other part is positive behavior that demonstrates the goodness and glory of God. But this demand must be asked of people from the beginning of their Christian lives; it is not a tacked-on doctrine asked of those who have progressed in the faith for years. We are asking the church to attack sin in society (e.g., fighting casual sex, drugs, alcohol, discrimination against the poor and disenfranchised, institutionalized gambling), and we are also asking the church to live in such a way that others take notice of the Christian's good behavior.

Recently, a student-pastor of mine entered my office to talk about some details of class. Before long we were chatting about concerns he had regarding pastoring. He related to me how he had grown up in a conservative wing of evangelicalism and had gone through the (now nearly incredible) days of worrying about how long men's hair ought to be and whether or not women ought to wear slacks to church. I told him I too remembered those days. He then began talking about the massive difficulty he was having speaking about holiness in his church because, he said, "you can hardly raise any ethical standards today without being accused of being a legalist." This problem is not simple, nor is it only found in a few churches. Whether churches have survived the scary days of nearly indescribable lists of good and bad behavior or whether they have entered the modern scene through the doors of Protestant liberalism, many today find no way of appropriating and instituting legitimate Christian ethical standards without feeling guilty about legalism and excessive meddling in others people's lives. The legalism of the previous decades has now led us to a liberty that feels almost neurotic about boundaries.

In my judgment, we live in a perfect setting for proclaiming the biblical message of holiness, a holiness that sometimes has only a few sharp lines but which always carries its powerful influence on every kind of behavior. We need to have committees in our churches that address the issues of how to live a holy life in our pluralistic culture, on how to live righteously when those around us seem to have few moral standards. Grass roots movements need to grow in the church, carrying with them the seeds of holy living. Sunday school teachers, especially of adult classes, need to ask their classes what it means to live a holy life in the business world, in the real estate world, in the world of skilled labor, in the world of factories and farming, in the professional world of psychology and sociology, and in the world of teaching. We need to ask Christians to evaluate the media, especially television, in light of the Christian demand for holiness.

This means at the level of evangelism that evangelists need to carry the message of conversion in their packet with the message of redemption; they need to tote the message of the cost of following Jesus along with the message of his comfort; they need to rally behind the message of God's holiness as well as his loving-kindness. At the level of education the church must urge its members to live holy lives day in and day out. We must emphasize that Christians are different and will often be unaccepted by society. Holiness is for all and is to be found in all areas of life.

Most importantly, Christianity's countercultural message needs to address the issue of self-indulgence. Our culture is preoccupied with the desire to "express oneself" and to "live one's own life." The church offers a message to "deny oneself" and to "live God's pattern for one's life." Only when the Christian message about self-denial is heard will the grace of God be heard in its fullness, and only when the holiness of God is displayed will his grace be clearest.

Our text speaks, perhaps as much as any text, about Christians in society. The Christian is the one who is countercultural because he or she is out of step with trends and passions in culture. It is not this way because we are trying to be odd; we are odd because we are trying to be godly. Again, countercultural living is not the goal of the Christian; rather, countercultural living is the result of following Jesus Christ. Sometimes, in fact, this countercultural life is even out of step with the local churches where Christians are supposed to find their home and their patriots. Martin Luther found the gospel of justification by faith to be radically countercultural to his own church, the Roman Catholic Church, just as John Wesley met opposition when he began to preach his message in England. And so today, when Christians preach a gospel of radical grace and holiness, they can find themselves unappreciated and rejected. But because of their desire to please a holy God, they will seek to leave behind no traces of sin and to be free of accusations.

After class recently, after I had delivered a lecture on the ethics of Jesus, a student came to me to share an interview he heard with a well-known American preacher (whose name must go unmentioned). The interviewer had contended that some of this preacher's message was contrary to the message of the Bible on self-denial. To which the preacher said, "If I preached that, the people in my church would be mad as hell." (Those are the words the student used for this preacher's comments.) When the interviewer said that these concepts were still in the Bible, the preacher responded: "Just because it is in the Bible does not mean I have to preach it." Here is a classic example of the culturalconditionedness of some modern preaching. It is a message based on what will get results—and of course, results are judged by acceptance. But the message of Peter and the faithful witnesses we find in the pages of the Bible do not bring a message that seeks to find acceptance. It is a message that goes contrary to culture because it is consistent with God, his holy character, and his holy will for holy living. God is contrary to culture because culture is created and sustained by sinful human beings. Would it not be good if Christians should be accused only for a thoroughly holy life and an inflexibly loving approach?

The first task, I contend, for Christians in society is to live before God in love and holiness in such a way that culture sees the radical difference between the two worlds. We must leave no room for accusations against us for the way we live. To live in holiness and love will mean adopting a countercultural life when that culture opts for a way less than God's will. It may involve some kind of social exclusion and suffering, for that is what happens to faithful Christians in faithless contexts. Like Peter's churches, we may become "aliens and strangers." But Peter's letter provides a means of coping with this kind of stress—a message that permits us to structure ourselves against that culture in a healthy, God-pleasing way.

1 Peter 2:13–17

S UBMIT YOURSELVES FOR the Lord's sake to every
authority instituted among men: whether to the
king, as the supreme authority, ¹⁴or to governors,
who are sent by him to punish those who do wrong and
to commend those who do right. ¹⁵For it is God's will
that by doing good you should silence the ignorant talk
of foolish men. ¹⁶Live as free men, but do not use your
freedom as a cover-up for evil; live as servants of God.
¹⁷Show proper respect to everyone: Love the brotherhood of believers, fear God, honor the king.

Original Meaning

PETER'S COMMENTS ABOUT the Christian communities' relationship to the Roman emperor
and to local governors is his first application
of the principle, enunciated in 2:11–12, of
living a holy life regardless of the response they find in their social setting. He will go on to apply the same principle to slaves' relationship
to their masters (2:18–25) and to the relationship of husbands and
wives (3:1–7), before turning to general remarks of the church community itself (3:8–12). In all of this, Peter keeps in view the important
impact holy living has on those who observe believers and the value
lifestyle has for maintaining good relations with society at large.

This passage expresses a common form of early Christian ethical
instruction, known as "Household Codes" (such instructions are also
found, in one form or another, at Eph. 5:22–6:9; Col. 3:18–4:1; Titus
2:1–10; 1 Tim. 2:8–15; 6:1–2). This form of instruction addresses specific "classes" of people in the church and provides for them specific
kinds of ethical direction. Scholars have disputed the origin of this
form (other than from the obvious need to instruct certain kinds of people with role-related behavior) and have come to little consensus,
other than that both the Greco-Roman and Jewish worlds expressed
concerns in a similar manner. As will become evident in the Bridging
Contexts section, study of one "Code" (e.g., 1 Peter 2:11–3:12) in

comparison to similar codes (e.g., Eph. 5:22–6:9 and Col. 3:18–4:1) can yield penetrating insights for understanding specific codes and for applying them to Christian living today.

Peter's code is concerned with the themes of Christians' avoiding sin and living a holy life, in the context of being persecuted by those who may end up admitting to God that such behavior is pleasing to him. The specific topic of this section is the relationship of the churches to governing authorities. Peter begins with an exhortation of submission (2:13–14), explains why believers should be doing good, includes a pattern of submission (2:15), cites a condition for submission (2:16), and then repeats his exhortation in both general and specific categories (2:17).

We begin with Peter's *exhortation to submit to the governing authorities* (2:13–14). Whatever "submit" means, it is important for us to recall that such submission is a form of abstaining from fleshly desires and of good behavior that will influence those observing. This connection of "submission" to 2:11–12 is the natural implication of understanding 2:13–17 as an application of the principles found in those thematic verses.

The word "submit" is a compound verb from the Greek words *hypo* (meaning "under") and *tasso* (meaning "to order, place, appoint"). While it is often inaccurate to determine meaning from the roots of a word,[1] the roots here do give an adequate determination of the meaning of the verb: "to order oneself under, or according to, a given relationship," or "to live according to the governmental order."[2] Clearly here the notion of "submitting" to the government is secondary to obeying God (1:2, 14, 22) and to doing his will (2:15), because this group of subjects (the church) is "free" (2:16).[3] That is, *even though* the Christians

---

1. See the discussion of D. A. Carson, *Exegetical Fallacies* (Grand Rapids: Baker, 1984), 26–32; D. L. Bock, "New Testament Word Analysis," in *Introducing New Testament Interpretation*, ed. S. McKnight (GNTE 1; Grand Rapids: Baker, 1989), 97–113.

2. A useful overview of the discussion of the term may be found in L. Goppelt, *1 Peter*, 174–76; see also G. Delling, "τάσσω," TDNT, 8:27–48 ("acquiescence in a divinely willed order," p. 43). See also L. Goppelt, *Theology of the New Testament. Volume 2: The Variety and Unity of the Apostolic Witness to Christ*, trans. J. E. Alsup; ed. J. Roloff (Grand Rapids: Eerdman 1982), 168–71.

3. Michaels, *1 Peter*, 124, therefore suggests that the translation "defer to" or "respect" is more appropriate. I like his suggestion because his translation reveals that the relationship to the government is not the same kind of submission required of the Christian in his or

are "aliens and strangers" (2:11), they are to live in the order that God has ordained.

Furthermore, for Peter and the entire church, "submit" does not imply total obedience, for the Israelites and the early Christians participated in civil disobedience when the demands of society overrode the demands of the Lord (e.g., Ex. 1:17; Dan. 3:13–18; Acts 4:18–20; Heb. 11:23).[4] Wolfgang Schrage has expressed it well: "They are free with respect to the authorities, and *normally* this freedom manifests itself in respect and loyalty, submission and honor."[5]

Finally, the word "submit" is carried forward in the different kinds of submission found in the master-slave relationship (2:18) and in the wife-husband relationship (3:1, 5; cf. 3:22; 5:5). The exhortation to husbands to live honorably with their wives (3:7) as well the church's need to live together in love (3:8–12) are related to this notion of "live under the order." Thus, as L. Goppelt states, "New Testament social ethics ... began with the directive that those called to faith ought to enlist themselves in the social orders in which they found themselves and to conduct themselves in accord with their 'rules for playing the game' (cf. 1 Cor. 7:17, 20, 24)."[6]

Peter exhorts the believers to live in submission "to every authority instituted among men." What he has in mind is either the "institution" itself (government as a human arrangement or, as in Rom. 13:1–7, as a divinely appointed human arrangement) or the person so instituted.[7] The odd combination of "creation" and "human"[8] leads one to

---

her relationship to God. That the submission here is rooted in a voluntary choice is crucial to understanding Peter's exhortation. Also, his grounding of the exhortation in a desire to please, and be influential for, God adds special insights into the way the early Christians perceived their relationship to the state and its governing power.

4. For a sketch of the ancient evidence, see D. Daube, *Civil Disobedience in Antiquity* (Edinburgh: Univ. Press, 1972).

5. W. Schrage, *The Ethics of the New Testament*, trans. D. E. Green (Philadelphia: Fortress, 1988), 278 (italics added).

6. L. Goppelt, *Theology*, 2:170.

7. For those who contend that the translation should be something on the order of "to every human institution," see E. G. Selwyn, *1 Peter*, 172; F. W. Beare, *1 Peter*, 141. For the view that it refers to humans as created by God, see L. Goppelt, *1 Peter*, 182–83; J. R. Michaels, *1 Peter*, 124.

8. Literally, the text reads "to every human creation." F. W. Beare, *1 Peter*, 141, strenuously argues that the expression describes *only* human institutions and does not suggest at all that a "divinely ordained" human institution is in view. He is correct grammatically; however, both the combination of "creation" and "human" as well as the biblical view of

suspect that Peter sees the institution of government as supervised and appointed by God at some level. His exhortation, then, is that Christians, in spite of their relative freedom, are nevertheless to live according to every sort[9] of governmental order. The alternative is chaos. To be sure, an excluded minority is tempted to chaotic rebellion, but Peter exhorts believers to good conduct that honors God. He is following Jesus here, who exhorted his disciples to be peacemakers (Matt. 5:9).

Christians are not to submit to the governmental authorities because of the native authority of government or because governmental officials are particularly charismatic. Rather, they are to submit "for the Lord's[10] sake." As has been seen in 2:12, such an idea includes the impact of observers seeing the justice and holiness of God in their behavior and giving praise to the Lord (cf. 2:15 and 3:1, where proper behavior leads to an opportunity to speak of the grace of God; 3:15–16). Alternatively, "for the Lord's sake" could (but less likely) refer to the example of Jesus (2:18–25).

Peter specifies two kinds of human institutions under which the Christians should order their lives: the emperor ("whether to the king, as the supreme authority") and the local governor. If the early dating of 1 Peter is correct (early 60s), then the emperor to whom Peter is referring is none other than the rascal Nero. Hort tartly remarks that "there could be few rulers indeed whose claims on loyalty would be sustained by less personal merit" than Nero.[11] Such a setting, which seems reasonable not only for 1 Peter but for much of early Christian teaching, has significant implications for the Christian attitude to the state,

---

God's sovereign control of all government leads me to see more than human institutions in this expression. In addition, the passive voice in "are sent" (2:14) suggests divine sending. That divinely *ordained* can be misinterpreted has been shown by J. H. Yoder, *The Politics of Jesus* (2d ed.; Grand Rapids: Eerdmans, 1994), 193–211, though I cannot agree with him in all details.

9. The Greek word is *pas* and refers to the various kinds of governmental authorities. W. A. Grudem, because he sees 2:13 as a heading not only for 2:13–17, but also for 2:18–3:7, sees the word "all" as encompassing a much wider audience (*1 Peter*, 118–19). But Peter mentions both emperor and governor; thus, the term "all" refers to governmental authorities at all their various levels.

10. Debate here is over whether this refers to the Father (J. N. D. Kelly, *Peter and Jude*, 109) or the Son (L. Goppelt, *1 Peter*, 183–85). Since 2:15 is likely a comment on this clause, "Lord" here probably refers to the Father.

11. F. J. A. Hort, *1 Peter*, 141. On Nero, see M. Grant, *Nero: Emperor in Revolt* (New York: American Heritage Press, 1970); M. T. Griffin, "Nero," *ADB*, 4:1076–81.

for it demonstrates that Christians are expected to be good citizens even in extreme situations.

The local governor is one who has been "sent by him [the emperor] to punish those who do wrong and to commend those who do right." That is, the local governor has derived authority and exercises it in a moral direction. Governors had more responsibilities than these two concerns (obviously), but Peter's concern is with the need for Christians to be good people so that the judicial arm of the governor is not raised over the churches. They must remember not only that their governor has authority to punish, but also that he can honor them for their good deeds. Thus, "What starts off, then, as apparently a lesson in political passivity culminates in an injunction to take an active role in society."[12]

A second part of Peter's discussion of the relationship to the state concerns the *explanation for doing good* (2:15): "For it is[13] God's will that by doing good you should silence the ignorant talk of foolish men." The opening word, "For,"[14] can be interpreted as introducing the cause of their submission: They should submit to the various levels of governing authorities *because* in so doing their behavior will silence their accusing ignorance. More likely it introduces an explanation of 2:14: "for, as for this doing good business, it is God's will that in doing good. . . ." The good conduct exhorted in 2:12 provides an opportunity for Christians to be approved by the governors, whose task it is to approve of good behavior. Furthermore, their good behavior "should silence the ignorant talk of foolish men" in that it will both demonstrate

---

12. I. H. Marshall, *1 Peter*, 84. However, we must keep in mind that Peter is not talking here about mass demonstrations or political agitation for representation in power. This was well beyond the reach of those who were socially excluded, the "aliens and strangers." But the research of B. W. Winter suggests that the Christians of Asia Minor may well have had within their number those who were capable of donating large sums of money or were able to exercise powerful influence for the good of society; see his *Seek the Welfare of the City: Christians as Benefactors and Citizens* (FCGRW 1; Grand Rapids: Eerdmans, 1994).

13. The original text has "thus" (*houtos*) here and it points forward: "For it is [thus] God's will that by doing good. . . ." "Thus" is to be understood as "For it is thus, that is, in doing good, that one does God's will." Some recent grammarians, however, contend that "thus" is the predicate of "is" and should be translated "For the will of God is thus, in doing good to silence. . . ." See, e.g., BDF 434 (1).

14. The Greek word is *hoti*, used for introducing both a cause ("for" or "because") and an explanation ("that is"). For the former, see J. N. D. Kelly, *Peter and Jude*, 110; for the latter, see J. R. Michaels, *1 Peter*, 127; P. Davids, *1 Peter*, 101.

in their eyes the good behavior of this socially excluded group and thereby prevent the development of persecution. In addition, their behavior will provide God with an objective measure for assessing them at the final judgment (2:12).

Just what does Peter have had in mind here in his idea of *doing good?* If Bruce Winter is correct, he may have in mind the large donations Christians made to the good of society in the form of *benefactions.* He describes them as follows:

> Benefactions included supplying grain in times of necessity by diverting the grain-carrying ships to the city, forcing down the price by selling it in the market below the asking rate, erecting public buildings or adorning old buildings with marble revetments such as in Corinth, refurbishing the theatre, widening roads, helping in the construction of public utilities, going on embassies to gain privileges for the city, and helping in the city in times of civil upheaval.[15]

While it is naive to think that Christians will always be saved from social pressure or outright persecution just because they live holy lives, it is not naive to think that such behavior will sometimes have the desired affect on their opponents so that they will back off their foolish accusations and baseless persecutions.[16]

Next, Peter adds a *condition for submitting to the authorities* (2:16). These socially excluded Christians are to submit to the authorities (2:13), not only because they are driven to it by their social location, but also because they are ultimately free from the jurisdiction of these authorities. Christians live under the governing order as free people, not as

---

15. B. W. Winter, *Seeking the Welfare of the City,* 37. The weakness of Winter's view is that nowhere else in 1 Peter does Peter speak of the Christians of Asia Minor doing things for the civic good. And here the text is ambiguous because Peter may be appealing to the dual nature of public offices: They do good to the good and they punish those who do things that are evil. Thus, Peter may be generalizing rather than speaking of some specific benefaction institution in Asia Minor. I am not contesting the institution itself, but only whether Peter is speaking of it specifically in this text as a description of the behavior of the churches.

16. J. R. Michaels, *1 Peter,* 132: "The most conspicuous feature of this section is its optimism. . . . Under normal circumstances loyalty to God and loyalty to the empire will not come into conflict." We might emphasize the word "normal" and then suggest that little did Peter know what was to come for the Church. Not only would the Church go through some terrible times but tyrannous regimes would develop, regimes that have only been recently toppled, that would make "normal circumstances" exceedingly rare.

its slaves,[17] for they are slaves of God, not Caesar. But they are not to use this freedom from human authorities as an excuse[18] for living in chaos and insubordination. That kind of life will only hurt the church and will give ample justification to the persecuting powers that now threaten them. What we must realize is that it was this passionate temptation to break free from the governing authorities that forced Peter to make these remarks.

The key here is the Christian perception that those who were followers of Jesus Christ were, like their master, independent of and free from the ruling governmental powers.[19] But that freedom and liberty were not to be used negatively, either to create political chaos or moral irresponsibility. While the Pauline letters emphasize freedom from the law, sin, and evil powers, Peter's emphasis is a development of the statement of Jesus that the sons of the kingdom are free (Matt. 17:26). Christians ought to *choose* to be orderly.

This theme emerged from a Jewish strand of thought that developed, quite naturally, when the people of the Land found themselves in subjection to foreign powers.[20] While such a condition may have come about as a result of sin and punishment, true members of the covenant knew that their ultimate allegiance was only to the God of the covenant. Consequently, while submission was required, it was not the relationship that sustained and protected them. They were servants of God alone. This theme became a natural setting for understanding early Christian persecution, and Peter's words here are to be interpreted in that setting.

---

17. There has been some debate over the meaning of "as"; the NIV adds "*Live* as free men" to clarify the problem. In so doing, the translators suggest that "as free men" modifies 2:15. But 2:15 is a parenthetical remark, and the nominative case of "free men" in 2:16 makes a connection to the accusative in 2:15 difficult. Rather, 2:16 picks up the theme of 2:13 ("submit") and adds a condition of Christians for that submission. Nor can I agree with J. R. Michaels when he connects the "as" clauses of 2:16 with the subject of 2:17 (*1 Peter*, 128).

18. See the remarks of J. R. Michaels, *1 Peter*, 129.

19. On freedom in the early church, see J. H. Yoder, *The Politics of Jesus*, 162–92, where he discusses the early Christian development of "revolutionary subordination." See also W. Schrage, *Ethics*, 277–78; E. Käsemann, *Jesus Means Freedom* (Philadelphia: Fortress, 1969); H. Schlier, "ἐλεύθερος," *TDNT*, 2:487–502.

20. See the brilliant exposition of this theme with respect to the Zealots in M. Hengel, *The Zealots: Investigations into the Jewish Freedom Movement in the Period from Herod I until 70 A.D.* (Edinburgh: T. & T. Clark, 1989).

To be sure, the early Christians did not see their persecution and social exclusion as a result of sin, but they did find analogies for understanding in previous Jewish experience. The governing authorities were there and had to be obeyed (to a certain degree), but such allegiance was secondary to their submission to the Lord. Far from an endorsement of Roman authority, Peter's perspective was one that put Neronic authority in its place. "They are free with respect to the authorities, and normally this freedom manifests itself in respect and loyalty, submission and honor."[21] In the words of Goppelt, when Christians perceived this and lived in the freedom to serve God, they "broke through to God's will for preservation in terms of the original and ultimate destiny of man."[22] But it is especially the words of Martin Luther that have crystallized Peter's point the best: "A Christian is a perfectly free lord of all, subject to none. A Christian is a perfectly dutiful servant of all, subject to all."[23]

Finally, Peter *repeats his exhortation* (2:17), doing so in both general and specific terms. Beginning with a general command to "show proper respect to everyone," Peter then details three specific manifestations of this "proper respect."[24] Their holy living, their abstinence from fleshly inspired passions, is to be manifested in respect for all people, whether that means the church, God, or the emperor. Such conduct is thus orderly (under the order of the day) and will prevent the gospel from disrepute and stave off some of the persecution that may be imminent.

In sum, Peter's first application of the principle of holy living in the midst of persecution concerns how Christians ought to relate to governing authorities. Here for the first time he addresses the issue of the church and the state. But this theme is critical to the entire letter

---

21. W. Schrage, *Ethics*, 278.

22. L. Goppelt, *Theology of the New Testament. Volume 2: The Variety and Unity of the Apostolic Witness to Christ*, trans. J. E. Alsup; ed. J. Roloff (Grand Rapids: Eerdmans, 1982), 173.

23. See in J. Dillenberger, *Martin Luther: Selections from His Writings* (Garden City, N.Y.: Doubleday [Anchor], 1961), 53. See also Luther's timely exposition of political freedom in his *Peter and Jude*, 120–22.

24. The first command is aorist; the other three are present. The first is the categorical command, the general one; the other three express the action as ongoing behavior within that holistic command. See S. Porter, *Verbal Aspect in the Greek of the New Testament, with Reference to Tense and Mood* (SBG 1; New York: Peter Lang, 1989), 360. But see also J. R. Michaels, *1 Peter*, 129–30, who sees the aorist command as programmatic for the other three.

because it was this tense relationship that formed the context for everything he wrote to these beleaguered churches. It took him some time to get down to specific behaviors because he first had to establish his theological points. In spite of a tyrant for an emperor, Peter exhorts Christians to live under the orders of the day, as free men, for the sake of the Lord and their security. Such an angle on the Christian's relationship to the state has many implications for Christian living in our world.

THE IMPLICATIONS OF this passage cannot be brought to the fore until we examine how the ethics taught here were to be lived out in the first-century world and how that same kind of ethics can be manifested in our world. This is not as simple a matter as one might think. For example, we might simply consider the difference between an ancient "noncitizen" and a modern citizen, or we might think of the emperor and his modern analogs. Are a Roman emperor and our country's leader equivalent positions in society? Most of my readers can hardly maintain that, for the Roman emperor was far more dictatorial and more of a tyrant than any Western leader can possibly be (with tragic exceptions). Thus, the American president's hands are tied by the American body politic; he can only get done what his people (through their representatives in Washington, D.C.) permit. The same can be said in comparing the emperor with a British prime minister, the queen of England, or the German chancellor.

What is more germane to our discussion, then, is what such a difference makes for the notion of submitting to governing authorities. In other words, is submission more in order for a Christian to a Roman emperor (where the alternative, from disagreement to revolt, put one's life in immediate jeopardy) than for a Christian voting citizen to the American president or the Canadian prime minister? This is not only an academic query, for it hits at the essence of what it means to apply the Bible to our world. While it may be fairly easy to apply the injunction to "show proper respect to everyone," since any kind of cultural condition seems to be transcended here, it is not so easy to contend that "submitting to your specific leader's political agenda" is a necessary or even a natural extension of the principle of submitting to the Roman emperor. In the Untied States, for example, Christians seem divided over every election; this division has an impact on what submission means for the next four years, in that some like it and some do not.

Furthermore, the more important issue is whether noncitizens in the Roman empire had any options. Did noncitizens, which is precisely what these Christians were, have any choice but to submit? Of course not. Too often almost every kind of public "nonsubmission" met with some kind of immediate punishment. Any strategy other than compliance (submission) was foolish. Thus, in bringing this text into our context, we are dealing with light years of changes.

The issue then becomes: Is the commandment to submit so culturally specific that its application to our world is completely different? In that case, do we have to find "noncitizen aliens" in our world for a comparable group for whom this injunction might apply? Or do we simply have to admit that "submission" is only a general principle (Christians should be good citizens and not chaotic rabble-rousers) and that in specific situations the Western citizen (United States, France, Germany, Italy, Great Britain, Bahamas, etc.) makes up his or her mind on how to respond to a given bit of legislation? In this latter case, "submission" can legally involve civil disobedience[25] as well as overt opposition to the government as part of what it means to live "within and under the order" as duly established in a country's institutionalized laws.

An example here clearly puts the issue into context. The book of Stephen L. Carter, *The Culture of Disbelief*, is a provocative treatise that challenges American society and its legal procedures with respect to how "religionists"[26] have been treated in public discourse and legal

---

25. On this, see J. B. Anderson, "Civil Disobedience," in C. F. H. Henry, ed., *Dictionary of Christian Ethics* (Grand Rapids: Baker, 1973), 104–5; M. L. King, Jr., "Love, Law, and Civil Disobedience," in J. M. Washington, ed., *A Testament of Hope: The Essential Writings of Martin Luther King, Jr.* (San Francisco: Harper & Row, 1986), 43–53. This latter essay demonstrates theology in action at a critical crossroads in the history of American interracial relations.

26. Carter uses this term throughout his book for a group of people who adhere to some religious belief that prompts them to act in a specific way. Carter himself is a theologically alert, socially sensitive Episcopalian, who is also the William Nelson Cromwell Professor of Law at Yale University. See *The Culture of Disbelief: How American Law and Politics Trivialize Religious Devotion* (New York: Doubleday [Anchor Books], 1994).

decisions. At one level this book is an obvious act of insubordination and lack of submission to the "order that exists," which he frequently labels as "liberal"; at another this book functions as a truly American way of protesting against the orders that be. It is irenic while critical. But had Carter written his book under Nero, directly challenging the essence of political power and process (which Carter's book does do), it may well have been seen as a lack of submission and therefore condemned by the Petrine commandment (not to mention what Nero would have done!). What we see here, then, is a change of circumstances that leads to a change of how we are to apply the Petrine injunction. So the questions we asked in the preceding paragraphs are important as we seek to apply this text to our world.

To answer these kinds of questions involves more than simple yes and no answers. It requires an awareness of the relations of Roman citizens and noncitizens to the emperor and a solid grasp of what relationship such groups have to our specific form of government. Such issues are not simple, but neither are they so beyond our reach that we should despair of trying to resolve them. Instead, we recognize that application is in some sense immediate for many people, and we seek to be as faithful to the will and revelation of God as we can.

In my judgment, the change of circumstances that can be found in moving from a Roman emperor like Nero to life under a British prime minister or an American president is so cataclysmic that major changes in the ethical directives must also be made. That is, "living under the order" no longer means "submission" in the way it did in the first century. What we do now is to live decently and as good citizens, but we can still be good citizens in vehement protests and civil disobedience in a way that was completely outside the capacity for first-century citizens (and noncitizens). We ought to respect our leaders, but we do not for a minute think we have to obey their every wish—out of a fear of serious punishment.

Another feature of interpreting and applying our specific text is to see it in its larger, early Christian context—the so-called *Household Codes* that were the normal context for instructing the churches in how they were to live within the order of the society.[27] The standard

---

27. The best survey I know of is R. P. Martin's "Haustafeln," in *NIDNTT*, 3:928–932. See also L. Goppelt, *1 Peter*, 162–79; D. Balch, *Let Wives Be Submissive: The Domestic Code in 1 Peter*

hypothesis is that as the church settled in (if an expression like that can be used for the churches addressed by 1 Peter!), leaders found it necessary to instruct members on how to live within the normal social categories. That is, for example, how should Christian wives behave, and how are a Christian's children to conduct themselves? The early Christian teachers fell back on the instructions typical in Diaspora Judaism, instructions rooted in the "Two Ways" tradition and containing specific injunctions for various stations in life (master, slave, husband, wife, etc.). It is then inferred that the early Christian "Household Codes" reflect those ethics (cf. Eph. 5:22–6:9; Col. 3:18–4:1).[28]

This is a reasonable hypothesis, though the parallel evidence from Judaism is not as strong as some have proposed. Nonetheless, this hypothesis helps us understand what Peter and Paul were doing. Like other early Christian pastor-teachers, they were providing their churches with a set of principles by which believers could live as Christians in a non-Christian world. To recall our discussion at 2:11–12, Peter was providing some "defensive structuring" for his churches so they could cope with the pressures of the outside world.

Furthermore, a comparison of Peter's concerns with those of Paul reveals some interesting emphases for Peter that help us discern the intent of his instructions. (1) Peter includes a special section on the relationship to the emperor and the government (2:13–17). This relationship appears particularly important for Peter and his churches (probably because of the [sudden] rise of tension in Nero's regime over the Christians), and so he includes it first.[29] (2) While each of the early Christian household codes that survives in the New Testament emphasizes "reciprocal submission," only Peter gives special emphasis to the motivation of doing so: in order to please God and to have a special impact upon one's society (2:12; 3:1). (3) Peter apparently sees

---

(Chico, Calif.: Scholars, 1981); W. D. Davies, *Paul and Rabbinic Judaism: Some Rabbinic Elements in Pauline Theology*, 4th ed. (Philadelphia: Fortress, 1980), 121–36.

28. Thus, an early Christian document, the *Didache*, 4:9–11, contains instructions for parents about educating their children, for masters about treatment of their slaves, and for slaves about submitting to their masters. That is, the ethics were both crosscultural and tailored to meet the contexts at hand.

29. Such concerns can be found in Paul as well, but they do not find their way into his household codes, probably because they were not as critical to his churches' concerns (cf. Rom. 13:1–7; 1 Tim. 2:1–3; Titus 3:1–3, 8). A nice chart of the issues can be found in E. G. Selwyn, *1 Peter*, 427. See also L. Goppelt, *1 Peter*, 164–65.

such a lifestyle as especially important for those who are second-class citizens, that is, for those who are socially excluded (2:11). (4) It may be a clue to Peter's churches that he addresses slaves (2:18—25) rather than masters (as does Paul; but cf. Eph. 6:9; Col. 4:1; Philemon) and that he addresses wives so much more completely than husbands. This suggests that Peter's churches were composed mainly of slaves and women, with few (if any) masters and only a few believing husbands. In other words, Peter's "emphasis throughout is on those points at which the Christian community faces outward to confront Roman society."[30]

Accordingly, when reading Peter's household code, we are to understand that his concern to instruct in ethics is dominated by his social concern with how Christians are to live within the Roman empire when that empire in part turned against them. These are not timeless exhortations but timely words of advice for a community under serious threat. This is not to say that Peter's advice is *merely* advice; rather, it is to say that Peter is concerned with a special context for Christian living, and *this context must be considered before one begins to apply it to our world*. In particular, this context means that the first angle we pursue is the one that concerns Christian living in a modern society, rather than personal ethics.

Extending this observation, I also contend that we should not apply this text simply to our world when our world is completely different. As I will argue when I get to 3:1—6, a Christian woman's response to, and toleration of, her unbelieving husband (whom she is trying to win over to faith) is considerably different than the Christian wife's response, toleration, and expectations of a believing, godly husband. That is, these texts were generated within a specific concern of living under pressure in an unbelieving world and concerned the entire problem of the Christian in society. They are much less interested in personal ethics in a neutral or positive context, though they do have some things to say in those contexts as well.

A final observation here, though difficult to demonstrate, concerns Peter's reason for including such material. It can be easily established that his ideas here are typical. Why, then, did he have to state that Christians needed to submit to the order of the day if his audience

---

30. J. R. Michaels, *1 Peter*, 122.

already assumed that? Many have argued that he had to do so because the early Christians found, like never before, a freedom in Christ that led them to think they were an entirely free group. That is, the freedom they found in the church inevitably led them to think in terms of a social revolution that was neither workable nor wise. Thus, Peter urged them to remain good citizens even if they sensed a mind-boggling freedom.

I contend that such a conjecture, though hard to prove as a predominant sense on the part of the church, has foundations. In particular, it seems to be precisely what Peter is battling against in our section. While believers are free (2:16), he says, they must also be respectable citizens, since this is God's will and is the only way they will be able to win outsiders to the gospel. One must take this point into consideration before applying the notion of submission to our world. That is, submission is not some blanket commandment but is a principle, *particularly* for those who sense their freedom in Christ and who think social revolution is what God wants.

IN WHAT FOLLOWS I assume that, in light of the differences between our world and the world of 1 Peter, submission, while it remains a fundamental principle for Christian living in society, can now be understood to include obedience, protest, and at times even civil disobedience. What do I mean by this? The Christian is to be obedient to the structures of society and to live within those structures, but such obedience at times may involve a justifiable disobedience that remains within that governmental structure. As when Stephen Carter protests the liberal tendencies to trivialize religious devotion in law and politics in America, so also Christians at times must speak out against the government. But this has to be done in a way that remains submissive in the sense that Christians protest in ways permitted by society.

To be specific, Christians may protest at abortion clinics (and the Constitution gives them that right), but they may not protest in a way contrary to the policies governing such behavior (as when a self-proclaimed justice freak murders a doctor as a form of protest). Civil disobedience remains a right within the governmental policies of most

Western democracies as legitimate social behavior. Some acts of civil disobedience are even perceived by society as a "good thing," enabling the Christian to be both "insubordinate" yet within the parameters of "good behavior."

In fact, a good many of modern conventions of social expectation were originally established as law (in the United States) through the actions of those who acted in some kind of civil disobedience. One can think of women's suffrage and rights to vote, of the elimination of many barriers to racial equality, and of the compulsory education of children. The impulse of these movements was largely the result of Christian disappointment and actions.

Take the example of Martin Luther King, Jr., whose actions have recently been imitated by the Christian conservative right. We need only consider one of his speeches, perhaps his greatest: "I Have a Dream." Delivered before the Lincoln Memorial on August 28, 1963, this speech electrified the American public, solidified support for the civil rights movement, and helped change American (and Western) society for the good. But my focus here is not on civic pride and change but on the anchoring that King gave to his speech: From front to back it was a biblically based vendetta against injustice and a plea for justice, so that society would be better.

But his mechanism for getting this material out was a massive act of civil disobedience in the face of a government that had turned its moral head away from the entrenched racial inequality that stood against that government's own Constitution, guaranteeing equal rights to all. In disobeying, King acted both biblically (he eschewed violence) and counterculturally, while he sought to establish biblical values in society. While it may be true that today such an overt appeal to biblical themes and verses would be accused by the left as imposing religion on the state,[31] it is nonetheless a part of our history that the civil rights movement was inspired, in part, by a biblically grounded sense of justice and love.

I would contend that such activity is permitted by Peter, though he never had such activity in mind (nor could he have). Peter demands

---

31. And usually in the name of the separation of the church and state. But the Constitution never prohibits the church from seeking to work its values into society, and the state cannot bar such activity. See here Stephen A. Carter, *Culture of Disbelief*, esp. 105–210.

that believers live holy lives and that such lives involve orderly activity with respect to the emperor and local authorities. Peter preaches submission in order to prevent the government from turning against the church as well as to encourage others to follow Christ through the church. And as long as church members live within the order of society and do not live recklessly outside of that society's standards, and as long as the government does not turn against them for this kind of action, then social acts of civil disobedience will be perceived as "citizen-like behavior." In this sense, actions of this sort will not harm the cause of the gospel.

On the other hand, while some may justify the bombing of abortion clinics as a tragic mistake born in a moment of "holy impatience," I find such actions to be what Peter prohibits here. He wants actions conducive to others seeing the glory of God, and I find it impossible (even ridiculous) to think that non-Christians will see the glory of God in such atrocious actions.

But what happens when the government demands something that a Christian, in good conscience, cannot give? Sometimes Christians find that they must disobey, and on such occasions they must suffer the consequences, for the sake of God, in the light of God's will, and in order to bring the message of God's kingdom to others. I use here what is certainly a controversial example, partly because noncontroversial examples do not exist for this kind of disobedience. I also take this example because I am unclear myself where Christians ought to stand and what they ought to do. The example concerns *protesting nuclear weapons facilities*. It is a fact that within the church universal many Christians are pacifist or at least against the notion of a nuclear war being possibly just. It is for this group that I speak, confessing that while I sympathize with their stance, I am unable to answer all of my own objections to their position.

In 1987, Jim Wallis, founder and director of the Sojourners Community in Washington, D.C., edited and published a book on the recent developments in Christian conscience over social issues.[32] One of the chapters, recorded by Jim Douglass, concerns the actions of numerous Christians who protested the so-called "White Train," a

---

32. J. Wallis, ed., *The Rise of Christian Conscience: The Emergence of a Dramatic Renewal Movement in Today's Church* (San Francisco: Harper & Row, 1987).

freight train that arrived at the Trident submarine base in Bangor, Washington.[33] This train carried nuclear materials; if the group prevented it from moving, they would be able to prevent some of the worldwide build-up of nuclear weapons as well as witness to the peace call of the gospel. The community statement adopted by the Agape Community, which sought through nonviolent means to monitor and resist the nuclear train, was as follows: "We believe the spiritual force capable of both changing us and stopping the arms race is that of *agape*: the love of God operating in the human heart."[34]

After months of garnering forces and devising plans, the Agape Community began a series of vigils to protest the White Train. Some were arrested for getting too close to the train (an understandable law), others for kneeling on the tracks to prevent the train's progress (another understandable law), and others for sitting in front of the gates at the Bangor plant (again, understandable). The story is a moving testimony to the faith and vigilance of a group of Christians who believed that nuclear build-up destroys lives. Christians who sit by, without at least reflecting on the morality of this kind of governmental activity, are not fulfilling their duty to live according to God's will. And it just may be that many Christians sit idly by, without reflection, because they refuse to live first for the kingdom and instead choose first to live according to their social agenda. Whatever one thinks of nuclear pacifism, the work of these Christians represents in my mind a clear example of civil disobedience, with serious consequences, for the sake of the gospel.[35]

So far I have focused on the "disobedience" side of submission. What about the "obedience" side? First, I reiterate that many social organizations and many "goods" of our society are the result of Christian activity and of Christian obedience to governmental authorities. As a rule, Christians today are good citizens, and I know of few accusations today that Christians are prone to being bad citizens. While the first-century Christians may have keenly felt the temptation to

---

33. J. Douglass, "The Nuclear Train Campaign: Tracking and Resisting the Train," in J. Wallis, *The Rise of Christian Conscience*, 62–71.

34. Ibid., 64.

35. In a note from one of my editors, Frank Thielman, I was informed that Jim Douglass's story continues along other lines now in Birmingham, where he operates a halfway house ministry to victims of AIDS.

turn the tables over and pursue a revolution, that is hardly the accusation made against Christians in the Western world today.

Second, Christians ought to be known for their respect and even-handed work in governmental and political actions. Sadly, this is not how they are always known today. Many Christians who are candid about their faith and political action are also known for being obstreperous in their political action. Too often the Christian right is disrespectful of the left. I have heard far too many nasty, even unchristian, remarks about political parties in power that differ with the Christian right wing. And I suppose that the same kind of remarks are made about politicians of the other variety by those on the opposite side. We must remember that Peter's remarks were in the context of showing respect for *all* people, regardless of their partisan politics (2:17). I regret my connections with both sides of this moral flaw: We as Christians ought to be known for our respect of the government, even when we disagree.

I call to our attention once again the work of Stephen Carter, who as a moderate liberal (I think that description fits his platform) is praised for his evenhandedness, irenicism, and respect. His approach ought to characterize all Christian political activity.[36] In fact, we ought to recall that Peter's remarks for respect came out of a situation very unlike ours: His churches were being hounded at times because of their faith. To be respectful in that context only puts our lack of respect toward governmental authority and process in bolder relief.

Third, our motivation for political activity needs to be set in the context of our mission as a church. Too often political activity by Christians seems to have so little Christian motivation that it betrays what we are all about. Our first task is to glorify God by bringing the good news of the gospel of the kingdom to bear on our world. If our political activity is not drenched in that motivation and is instead only slightly stained (work as hard as possible to appear nonreligious and acceptable) by the message of the kingdom, then we are denying the purpose of our existence. Peter motivated the churches to good actions in their world so that they would declare forth the good news of God and demonstrate his goodness and glory, in the hope that others would

---

36. See the numerous blurbs for his book in the frontispiece to the 1994 paperback edition, blurbs coming from both sides of the issues he addresses.

want to become Christians. He did not exhort them to do good for some altruistic motive. Far too often Christians are involved, or at least get involved, to protect their own investments or to accumulate more power for themselves. These are not worthy motives for those of us who claim to follow Jesus Christ and the pattern of the apostles.

In saying this, however, I do not want to sound like I think every action has to have an evangelistic motive. Sometimes our decisions are made on the basis of what we think it means to be good citizens. We do not vote to witness; we vote because we care and because that it is what it means to be a citizen. There is a time for the Christian to "practice random acts of kindness," and there is a time to witness. My concern is that, no matter what we do, we do all in the context of offering ourselves to God and in the context of attempting to bring glory to him.

Finally, Peter shows us that the Christian's relationship to the government is ultimately not a final relationship. Christian are free because they have been redeemed. The state's authority over the them is secondary, and their submission to the state is secondary to their submission to the Lord. Christians are to be good citizens because they are obedient to the Lord, not good Christians because they are obedient to the state.

Jonathan Edwards, long forgotten for his university presidency and his brilliant philosophical analysis, is mostly remembered for his famous sermon entitled "Sinners in the Hands of an Angry God." In the midst of a busy intellectual life, Edwards fashioned a theory for the relationship of the Christian to public life. Gerald R. McDermott, professor of religion at Roanoke College (Salem, Virginia), summarizes six points of Edwards' theology of public life for the Christian.[37] In my judgment, Edwards clearly perceived how we are to operate today—a perception also consistent with Petrine teaching. His six points are as follows:

(1) Christians have a responsibility to society beyond the walls of the church. Christians must break through the tendency to isolationism that has at times characterized the church.

(2) Christians should not hesitate to join forces with non-Christians in the public square to work toward common moral goals. While I generally agree with Edwards here, we must also keep in mind the

---

37. Gerald R. McDermott, "What Jonathan Edwards Can Teach Us About Politics," *CT* 38/8 (1994): 32–35.

need to establish our principles and to refuse to compromise in areas that are fundamental to Christian truth. But cooperation is critical and isolationism is to be avoided.

(3) Christians should support their governments but be ready to criticize them when the occasion demands. Once again, we find here the cautious respect that Peter invites but also the willingness to speak against policies when conscience demands.

(4) Christians should remember that politics is comparatively unimportant in the long run. Many Western Christians have gotten off the path at this point. The Christian's responsibility is first to his Master, the Lord Jesus Christ, and then, and only then, to his government. Too many have confused the two responsibilities. Peter looked forward to a day when Jesus Christ would return, and he knew at that time the Roman empire would dissolve into the kingdom of God and that final kingdom would not tolerate geographical or power distinctions. No matter how much we respect our government, we should respect the church even more.

(5) Christians should beware of national pride. In the history of the church there has never been a truly Christian nation. Until that does occur (and we have reason to doubt that it ever will), we are obliged to put our pride on the back burner and put our trust in the kingdom of God, which transcends national borders. I have taught with people from New Zealand, Canada, the Netherlands, and Great Britain; we have students who come from every corner of the globe. In such a context, to focus on national pride would be an affront to others' consciences. The gospel of Christ levels us all into an international community of those who follow Christ, and that church deserves our allegiance. I believe in the "holy, catholic church," and in so confessing I confess also that national pride is secondary.

(6) Christians should care for the poor. Such a point cannot be dismissed lightly, for it reveals an attitude of mercy toward those in need and encompasses more than financial help on bad days. It means that Christians ought to help, and ought to want to help, those who are in need, whatever those needs are. Furthermore, they ought to extend this desire into a plan for the government to help. If God is a God of compassion and mercy, then Christians ought to reveal that compassion and mercy to those they meet. Moreover, Christians ought to work for compassion and mercy to be written into the fabric of their society.

Jonathan Edwards died in 1758, over two hundred years ago. Although his ideas need adjustment because of changes (just as Peter's ideas do), we can see in him a thoroughly biblical approach to the way Christians should live in society. Edwards himself was a sterling example of such a life, and, happily, many who follow his teachings have been noble witnesses to Christian citizenship. Christians who live in today's world will need special insight, drawn from Peter and others, if they are to live before God faithfully and draw others to him.

Yet we should always remember that at times, the believing citizen and noncitizen may be able neither to obey nor to disobey. Instead, suffering is the only option, if indeed that can be called an option. The Christian is called to follow Jesus, and Jesus himself knew that his path was one that led to the cross. Those who follow him sometimes end up with him at the Golgotha of their own suffering. Peter's next section incorporates suffering as one potential risk for Christians who live obediently in an alien society.

1 Peter 2:18–25

SLAVES, SUBMIT YOURSELVES to your masters with all respect, not only to those who are good and considerate, but also to those who are harsh. ¹⁹For it is commendable if a man bears up under the pain of unjust suffering because he is conscious of God. ²⁰But how is it to your credit if you receive a beating for doing wrong and endure it? But if you suffer for doing good and you endure it, this is commendable before God. ²¹To this you were called, because Christ suffered for you, leaving you an example, that you should follow in his steps.

> ²²"He committed no sin,
>   and no deceit was found in his mouth."

²³When they hurled their insults at him, he did not retaliate; when he suffered, he made no threats. Instead, he entrusted himself to him who judges justly. ²⁴He himself bore our sins in his body on the tree, so that we might die to sins and live for righteousness; by his wounds you have been healed. ²⁵For you were like sheep going astray, but now you have returned to the Shepherd and Overseer of your souls.

Original Meaning

SLAVES ARE PETER'S second target group. They also must apply the principle of holy living to their situation. In effect, they are to live as holy Christians in spite of the strong temptation to break free from their low station in life. Peter exhorts them to be good and obedient workers, even when their masters are cruel and despotic, thereby testifying to God's grace; they are to give no occasion to slander this fledgling movement. If they act rebelliously—no doubt a temptation for those set free by Christ—they will ruin their opportunity to worship in freedom and will probably crush any hope of reaching their society with the good news of Jesus.

Peter begins with a straightforward *exhortation* to "submit" (i.e., "live under the order"; 2:18). This is followed by a double statement of the *motivation* slaves should have in their submission: to conduct their lives in a way consistent with the desire to have God's approval (2:19–20). Undergirding both the exhortation and its motivation is the *foundation*: Slaves are to please God by submitting to their masters *because of the example of Jesus* (2:21–25). Peter's statement of this foundation is extensive, and one is left wondering, when he completes his thoughts at 2:25, whether he has even left the topic; this concern is well-placed because Peter digresses from Jesus' death as an example to his death as a substitution at 2:24–25. But digressions characterize Peter's style, as much as tidy writing marks the style of modern-day theologians.

The Exhortation (2:18)

PETER EXHORTS SLAVES[1] to submit[2] to their masters, even if they are scurrilous and petulant. It goes without saying that it is easy to work for masters who are kind, beneficent, and generous; but it is hard to have the same disposition to those who are nasty, irascible, and capricious. Yet, Peter insists, Christian slaves should be obedient to all masters, regardless of their personal characteristics. The principles enunciated at 2:11–12 now become critical: The slaves are to be, like the social members of 2:13–17, obedient because it is God's will (cf. 2:19–20) and because through such obedience they will both witness to God's grace and provide him with a measuring stick for their opponents at the judgment.

The issue here for us, though only occasionally an issue in the earliest churches, is the *nature of slavery* in the ancient world.[3] We want to

---

1. "Slaves" translates *oiketai*, a term frequently used for the "household servant."

2. This translates, in imperatival form, a participle. This participle applies the imperative of 2:13 to a new station, the slaves, and its mood is drawn from that original imperative. However, both the imperative of 2:13 and the participle of 2:18 are to be seen as derived from the exhortation to the holy and sin-avoiding conduct of 2:11–12.

3. The single best survey is S. S. Bartchy, "Slavery (Greco-Roman)," *ABD*, 6:65–73 (with extensive bibliography). (In this article, the subtitle is "New Testament" but the header is "Greco-Roman"; I use the latter.) In the paragraphs that follow I depend heavily on Bartchy and refer the reader to him for more details and information. See also E. Ferguson, *Backgrounds of Early Christianity*, 2d ed. (Grand Rapids: Eerdmans, 1993), 56–59. A wide-ranging study is F. M. Snowden, Jr., *Blacks in Antiquity: Ethiopians in the Greco-Roman Experience* (Cambridge, Mass.: Harvard, 1990).

avoid doing here what we will discuss in the next two sections, but we do need to describe what slavery was like in the first century so that we will know whom these verses address in our modern world. In fact, while this commentary series emphasizes the changes needed as we move from an ancient text to the modern world, there is also the need at times for a change when we move to understand the ancient world. The New World slavery that was institutionalized in the United States, especially known to the American public through the TV series *Roots*,[4] differed dramatically from first-century slavery. I will mention more about this in the Bridging Contexts section, but for now we must bracket off modern conceptions of slavery as practiced in the United States for nearly two centuries, in order to learn what slavery was like in the Roman empire.

Slavery was a diverse institution in the ancient world, altering itself from one culture to another. Yet the Roman and Greek worlds anchored their entire economic system in this institution. Some have estimated that one-third of the population in urban areas was slave population. In both worlds, especially the Roman world (which is our interest for 1 Peter), slavery was not usually a permanent condition of life. Rather, it was a temporary condition on the path toward freedom. Many ancient people voluntarily chose to be slaves of a Roman citizen so that, upon being granted manumission as a result either of good behavior or adequate savings, they could become full Roman citizens.[5] In fact, it is entirely possible that one reason Peter (and Paul) urged Christian slaves to be submissive and obedient was that by living obediently, they could be set free (if the slaves even wanted freedom; cf. 1 Cor. 7:21).

To be a slave was not to be assigned to a specific, especially low-class, station in life. Slaves had the status and power that was connected with their masters; if their master was powerful, they indirectly inherited that power too. Thus, it was desirable at times to be a slave. While most slaves of the New Testament documents were born that way (because their mothers were slaves), many chose slavery over the vagabond existence of finding odd jobs.[6] The tasks characterizing

---

4. Based on Alex Haley, *Roots: The Saga of an American Family* (New York: Dell, 1976).

5. S. S. Bartchy, "Slavery (Greco-Roman)," 70–72 (Bartchy sketches this material with details).

6. Bartchy (ibid., 67) lists several motives for choosing slavery, including the desire to become a Roman citizen after being set free and the hope that large debts could be paid off.

slavery were immensely diverse, and we must avoid the notion that all slaves were manual labor servants. "Doctors, teachers, writers, accountants, agents, bailiffs, overseers, secretaries, and sea-captains" all comprised the slave population.[7]

Slavery was deeply entrenched in the patriarchal system of antiquity. Household heads (fathers) had immense power (*patria potestas*) over their charges, including the power to sell into slavery. Sometimes slaves converted to Christianity with their masters, but other times they converted on their own (as in 1 Peter 2:18—25). It is no wonder that Peter exhorts them in the context of household regulations; this is even more clear for Paul (Eph. 6:5—9; Col. 3:22—4:1). But this power of the father was sometimes abused; some slaves were both physically abused and sexually available to their masters (Seneca, *Epistle* 47).

The idea of slavery as the foundation of the Roman economy needs to be stressed, and this foundation may well lie at the heart of early Christian exhortations to remain submissive to masters. If it is true that slavery was the central labor force of the Roman economy, it follows that if Christians became known for opposing the institution, the Roman authorities would immediately, and perhaps even irreparably, damage the movement. Put differently, it was important to the survival of Christianity for its slaves to be good slaves. Since this was the case, one motive for Peter's exhortation would have been the desire to survive as a movement.

Peter's exhortation to live under the order as slaves emerges, then, from this economic context. He reminds them that they are to do this "with all respect," or "with deep respect."[8] He insists that they are to show the same "deep respect" even to "those who are harsh." Peter wants the Christian slave community to manifest a kind of behavior that transcends the norm of society and demonstrates its supernatural origins. In so doing, the economy will not be threatened, and the Christians will be seen favorably.

---

7. K. Hopkins, as quoted by S. S. Bartchy, ibid., 69.

8. This expression has been debated. Is it fear/respect of men or of God? The majority sees here a religious basis for respect (thus, J. N. D. Kelly, *Peter and Jude*, 116; J. R. Michaels, *1 Peter*, 138).

The Motivation (2:19–20)

"FOR IT IS commendable" translates an expression that describes whether or not one pleases someone. In this case, it concerns pleasing God.[9] The same expression stands at the beginning and end of these two verses, forming what is called an "inclusio"—a literary device that ties a section together and is used to give emphasis to this expression.[10] What pleases God—if one is going to suffer—is suffering for doing good; God is displeased when his people suffer because they have acted in some rebellious or sinful manner. It is of God, Peter argues, for his people to endure suffering in spite of, or even because of, doing good. Thus, Christian slaves are to submit to their masters as part of their holy conduct (2:11–12). If they suffer in a submissive condition, then it is God's will for them to experience the suffering; if they suffer for insubordination, then they are acting outside of God's will for his people.

The Foundation (2:21–25)

PETER PROCEEDS TO contend that suffering is the slaves' calling from God (2:21) and, adding a new feature, suggests that call to suffer is rooted in following Jesus. Jesus also suffered, and his pattern of life is to become their pattern. Peter's insight here is immensely important, though it was not easy for Peter himself to grasp this idea. We should pause here to reflect on Peter's own experience with the cross of Jesus. The first time he heard of the cross he met it with a stiff rebuke (Mark 8:31–33); the second time, in the Passion week, he hid from Jesus (14:66–72). Then a change occurred. His subsequent repentance and restoration led him to a complete about-face with respect to the cross, and he found it not only to be a healing instrument (2:24–25), but the *paradigm for Christian existence.* Presumably that change occurred at Pentecost (Acts 2) with the Spirit's endowment in his life, completely

---

9. The Greek term behind "for it is commendable" is *charis,* usually translated "grace." But, as J. R. Michaels notes, "'Grace' refers here not to that which God gives freely . . . but to that which counts with God or that with which God is pleased" (*1 Peter,* 139).

10. When the same expression (or, more subjectively, the same idea) both begins and ends a unit, if the intervening features are also in repeated in reverse order, as they essentially are here, it is called a chiasm. On this, see N. W. Lund, *Chiasmus in the New Testament: A Study in the Form and Function of Chiastic Structures* (Peabody, Mass.: Hendrickson, 1992 [reprint of 1942 edition with a new preface]).

reversing in his mind the significance of the cross. What was formerly a stumbling block became the cornerstone of his theology.

After stating the general pattern he finds in the life of Jesus (2:21), Peter states the condition of Jesus' life (its perfection; 2:22), records the opposition he encountered and the response he showed (2:23), explains the benefits of that life and death (2:24), and then applies that entire work of Jesus to the lives of his readers (2:25). Here is an early Christian interpretation of Christ's life that is, at the same time, an exercise in the explanation of the essence of the Christian life. This little section, in other words, is a glimpse into a Christian worldview of the first century—a world not at all like our world because of the predominance of suffering in the early church, but a worldview that retains its significance for Christian living.

The suffering of Christ created a *general pattern*[11] that believers were to follow.[12] The reason his suffering is such a noteworthy example for Peter's teaching is because of the *condition of perfection that Jesus achieved* (2:22–23). That is, Jesus exemplified someone who suffered for doing good; he was perfect and yet suffered. Thus, Christian slaves should take this example as a paradigm for their lifestyle. They are to live holy lives and submit in obedience, even to petulant taskmasters; in so living they are following Jesus, who *responded distinctively to opposition* (2:23). When he was slandered, he did not retaliate with sharp barbs, nor did he threaten those under whose hand he suffered; instead, he entrusted his case to the God who judges justly and waited for God's vindication. The slaves, therefore, are also to respond kindly and not retaliate.

At this point Peter reflects on aspects of the life of Jesus that are not integrated into the pattern of imitation he has been explaining. That is, he digresses to discuss the *benefits* of Christ's suffering and death as a vicarious atonement ("He himself bore our sins in his body on the tree," 2:24),[13] giving those who trust in him the opportunity both to

---

11. The Greek term for "pattern" (*hypogrammos*) was used for the wax tablet on which children wrote in order to "learn their letters." Patterns were impressed in the wax so that children could learn to shape their letters properly. For further details, see J. R. Michaels, *1 Peter,* 144.

12. A second image lies behind the word "steps" (2:21), that of walking behind someone in the footprints left by them; on this, see L. Goppelt, *1 Peter,* 204–5.

13. A marvelous study of the vicarious nature of the atonement can be found in J. R. W. Stott, *The Cross of Christ* (Downers Grove, Ill.: InterVarsity, 1986), 133–63 (on the "Self-Sub-

"die to sins and live for righteousness" (cf. 2:11–12).[14] In other words, Peter fastens the conduct he wants from his readers to the work of Christ on the cross. Then he gives his final *application* (2:25): His readers were at one time (cf. 1:18–19) wandering like lost sheep, but they have now returned to the Shepherd and guardian of their souls, Jesus Christ.

A MODERN AMERICAN can hardly read this text without thinking immediately of the development of the horrible institution of slavery in the so-called New World. I do not want to make light of that institution, nor do I want to deny that this text was used over and over as justification for its evils. Even if I argue below that the ancient institution of slavery and the "modern" one are significantly different, I do not want to suggest that I would defend any form of slavery.

Put differently, African-Americans read this text in a radically different way than American whites who have never seen such an institution in their lifetime. The only semblance of the enslavement of African-Americans I have seen was a neighbor's small statues at the curb in the front of their house. These small statues consisted of two black men who held out their hands, with steel rings in them; riders were to tie their horses to them, depicting (I suppose) the slave's work of receiving horses and taking them to the barn. My father often expressed disgust with these statues, though most people did not care enough to do something about them. (Once, however, I noticed someone had painted their faces white.)

Even if most of us have never seen a real situation of slavery, modern African-Americans have the previous two centuries etched so deeply into their consciousness that it becomes impossible for them to hear the word "slave" without thinking of that wretched period of American history. But why bemoan a period of history that is so far remote from normal experience today? Not only because it has

---

stitution of God"); for a more analytical presentation, see J. I. Packer, "What Did the Cross Achieve? The Logic of Penal Substitution," *TynBul* 25 (1974): 3–45.

14. See here J. R. Michaels, *1 Peter*, 148–49; a parallel is surely 1 Peter 2:11–12, where both renunciation of sin and living in holiness is the heart of the exhortation.

consequences to this day (one cannot but believe that many of the problems African-Americans experience today are the long-term effects of slavery), but because before we can bring this text into our day and find analogies, we must deal with at least two dimensions of this problem.

First, African-Americans read their experiences of oppression as reenactments of the biblical descriptions of slavery.[15] No matter how hard whites try to distance themselves from this experience, and no matter how thoroughly (and accurately) they argue that ancient slavery was not like modern slavery, African-Americans will still hear this text in modern tones. To be sure, some will transcend the modern institution to appreciate the original context, but even that act (and I would see it as generally the result of God's forgiving grace) betrays the horror itself. Until we understand this, we have no business speaking of this text in our modern world.

Second, we must disabuse ourselves of how this text has been used to justify slavery and shed that concept of slavery as part of what Peter was saying. In other words, we must understand what slavery was then and what slavery was like in the New World, observe the radical differences, and then apply what is significant to our own context.

The conclusions of Scott Bartchy are fundamentally important here:[16]

> Central features that distinguish 1st century slavery from that later practiced in the New World are the following: racial factors played no role; education was greatly encouraged (some slaves were better educated than their owners) and enhanced a slave's value; many slaves carried out sensitive and highly responsible social functions; slaves could own property (including other slaves!); their religious and cultural traditions were the same as those of the freeborn; no laws prohibited public assembly of slaves; and (perhaps above all) the majority of urban and domestic slaves could legitimately anticipate being emancipated by the age of 30.

Here we have some important historical conclusions that disabuse us of the modern concept of slavery where humans were owned (for life!),

---

15. Negro spirituals are noted by this sense of reenactment.
16. S. S. Bartchy, "Slavery (Greco-Roman)," 66.

where children and wives were far too frequently abused both physically and sexually, where ownership was prohibited, and where (most of all) any sense of equality or equal rights were surrendered on an altar of thinking that Africans were both morally and constitutionally inferior. However hard it is for us to think of slavery without thinking of modern abuses, we must learn to penetrate behind this period of history back into the first century if we are to make 1 Peter relevant to our world.[17]

This raises one more critical issue: Is slavery, as an institution, immoral in itself? This question takes us well beyond the text we have, but it is worth pausing for a few reflections.[18] The question is important, and, of course, moderns will immediately contend that slavery is immoral. I agree, especially if the meaning of slavery is like what was practiced in the New World. But if slavery is defined as it was in the ancient world, then I do not believe it would be considered necessarily immoral, no matter how hard it is for us to think in such a category. Yet in light of the ease with which the ancient institution led to abuse, I still think we are far wiser contending that the ancient institution was morally inferior, if not downright immoral in itself.[19] I agree, then,

---

17. I am not saying that abuses did not take place in antiquity; abuses were present. On this see, e.g., Seneca, *Epistle* 47.

18. For a survey of the issues, see M. J. Adler, *The Great Ideas: A Syntopicon of Great Books of the Western World* (Chicago: Encyclopaedia Britannica, 1952), 2:774–790. Surely this topic deserves more than I can offer here. Among the important writings on the topic, the following are included: T. Harry Williams, ed., *Selected Writings and Speeches of Abraham Lincoln* (Putney, Vt.: Hendricks House, 1980), xxiv–xxxii; J. M. Washington, ed., *A Testament of Hope: The Essential Writings of Martin Luther King, Jr.* (San Francisco: Harper & Row, 1986), 85–90 ("The Current Crisis in Race Relations"), 117–25 ("The Ethical Demands for Integration"); M. L. King, Jr., *Why We Can't Wait* (New York: Penguin [Mentor], 1964); Jesse L. Jackson, *Straight From the Heart*, ed. R. D. Hatch and F. E. Watkins (Philadelphia: Fortress, 1987), 87–90 ("*Brown* Twenty-Five Years Later"). A necessary reading for this topic is the gripping story of John Howard Griffin who, in the autumn of 1959, had his skin darkened so he could live the experience of the southern black, and live it he did. See his *Black Like Me* (updated ed.; New York: Penguin [Signet], 1976). I first read this book when I was fourteen, during the turbulent times of the civil rights movement; I was delighted that my daughter, Laura, took the same interest in this book during high school.

19. I make these cautions only because I am sure there were situations that were voluntary, that were good, or that were far better than some other condition. In that sense, slavery was not "as immoral as it was in the New World." Furthermore, it is clear that biblical revelation modified and improved the conditions of slavery if it did not at times also condemn it. On this, see A. A. Rupprecht, "Slavery," in C. F. H. Henry, *Dictionary of Christian Ethics* (Grand Rapids: Baker, 1973), 626–27.

with those who argue that slavery is itself a morally inferior human institution that diverges from God's will for society.

Slavery is therefore immoral unless some kind of voluntary submission is involved—in which case I would prefer not to call it slavery. The earliest Christian tradition recognizes, at times, the inferior nature of which I am speaking (cf. 1 Tim. 1:10). Some scholars believe that Peter is arguing that just as Christians in society did not have to resort to their freedom in Christ, and just as women did not have to appeal to the same freedom to opt out of their marriage, so also slaves may very well have sensed the same freedom to opt out of their human bondage. This implies that the freedom of the gospel itself led to the undoing of the institution.[20] Tragically, that trumpet call of freedom was held down while others appealed to the same texts as legitimizing slavery in the plan of God.[21]

If slavery is immoral, or at least morally inferior, how do we apply this text to our world? First, we could simply dismiss this passage as irrelevant because it is outmoded or reflects an inferior cultural system. But this would be to operate on an unfair basis, that ancient slavery and modern slavery are identical. Too much of our passage is valuable for our day and has proven so in the course of church history. Appealing to the example of Jesus as the paradigm for enduring injustice is hardly irrelevant, and slavery for Peter was in fact different from slavery for the New World. Or, second, we could subtract the bad elements of slavery and find analogies to what remains—some kind of servile employment or social injustices. That is, we can dismiss slavery as an evil institution but still find situations in which Christians are being mistreated unjustly and find in this passage both an exhortation to endure and a consolation for sufferers.

It is customary to find in this passage "advice for the employed." I believe such a custom is reasonable and consistent with Petrine teaching in light of the broad kinds of activities that slaves performed in the

---

20. In fact, the entire sweep of the biblical message is involved in the development of this freedom; on all of this, see M. A. Dandemayev, "Slavery (ANE)" and "Slavery (OT)," *ADB*, 6:58—65, where the treatment of slaves by Israel is contrasted with treatment elsewhere in the Near East. I contend that this general kindness was developed even further under the influence of the early Christian gospel.

21. For a brief survey of the treatment of slaves in the early church, see A. A. Rupprecht, "Attitudes on Slavery among the Church Fathers," in *New Dimensions in New Testament Study*, ed. R. N. Longenecker and M. C. Tenney (Grand Rapids: Zondervan, 1974), 261—77.

ancient world (teaching, selling, farming, etc.) and those same employ-
ment-type of activities that are done today. Whatever we think of the
ancient institution of slavery, slaves were in some kind of employment
relationship with their masters. This was how they "made a living." In
our day, Christians frequently find themselves employed by non-
Christian bosses who themselves are at times unjustified in their treatment of Christians. In such situations, Peter's message here is especially
relevant. But we must remember that the situations are hardly identical. Employment in free-market capitalism or socialism is difficult to
compare to first-century slavery, even though there might be similar features. The principle of living "under the order" does not apply directly
to employment, but it at least moves in this direction, and we are wise
in applying this text to the conditions of employment in our world.

Once again, it is helpful for us to broaden our understanding of
Peter's comments here by comparing them to similar teachings in Paul,
to his *household regulations*. In so doing, we gain a wider perspective of
the early church's perceptions of Christian slaves. Paul also exhorts
Christian slaves to be obedient (Eph. 6:5–8; Col. 3:22–25), but he
emphasizes the importance of motive. They are not to be obedient in
order to gain human approval; instead, they are to be obedient because
they want to honor the Lord through obedience. They are to look to
the reward they will gain from the Lord, not the reward they might
gain from their masters. In living this way, they can also be evangelistic (1 Tim. 6:1; Titus 2:9–10). Furthermore, Paul threatens slaves with
a warning about doing evil because it will bring punishment (Col.
3:25); this, too, is similar to Peter's orientation.

In addition, Paul instructs masters (Eph. 6:1; Col. 4:1), urging them
to be kind and just in their treatment of slaves. He buttresses this with
the warning that they, too, have a Master, God, who will evaluate
them on the basis of how they have treated others. Peter, on the other
hand, does not exhort masters. Is this because there were no masters
in the Christian churches to whom he wrote? If so, we have further
confirmation that the churches of Asia Minor were comprised of lower
social elements (see comments at 1:1; 2:11). While I think such an
inference is reasonable, I am not persuaded that an argument from
silence ought to lead us to any sure conclusions.

We can infer from the presence of slaves in the early Christian
household codes that many slaves became Christians and that their

behavior was potentially problematic. They had to be exhorted to obedience both because they sensed a new-found freedom in the church and because it was important to the success of the gospel that they be "orderly." Such a concern in the early churches is, in my judgment, a clear reflection that the gospel created a new order of society, whether or not the earliest churches were able to work this new order out in a consistent manner. While they may not have done so in all its ramifications, as only time and situations can do, it remains true that the gospel itself created a people of God with a special identity, and this new condition led, because of the growth of the church, to social changes.

IF THIS TEXT can be brought forward into our day to the world of employer-employee relations and to how Christians are to conduct themselves in such conditions, then we need to ask what the significance of this text is in our capitalistic society. Two angles can be used. The first draws its energy from the kind of interpretation and application we have outlined in the previous two sections, that of reordering the concept of submission so that it is consistent with the "order of our day," namely, actions and behaviors consistent with a worker's contract with his employer.

If the early Christian slaves had little option but to submit, then that part of Peter's exhortation is rooted in a social condition that no longer applies to the employed in today's world, a world preoccupied (often to its own peril) with personal rights. That is, if Peter urges slaves to submit because disobedience brings disrepute to the gospel, then a logical application today would be in the direction of living under working conditions that are according to the order of the day. If it is indeed contractually sound for an employee to protest a certain kind of working condition (e.g., racial discrimination), then it is acceptable *for a Christian* to protest such a practice and still stay within the order of submission to his or her employer. One has to believe that the progress we have achieved since the first century in the realm of personal and civil rights has altered what we expect as characteristics of submission.

I. Howard Marshall, in his stimulating commentary on 1 Peter, has proposed several guidelines for Christian employees who are considering such "submission" in our modern world.[22] (1) All of our social rela-tionships should find a behavior that is driven by a desire to do God's will. (2) Our conduct ought to be consistent with the obligations we assume in our relationship to that person and job. (3) Our conduct ought to be determined by that relationship, not by what we think of the personal traits of the employer. (4) When we disregard our rela-tional contract with its obligations, we do disservice to the gospel. (5) If we suffer as a result of our obligations, such suffering is both commendable and Christian; it is not unchristian to suffer!

As an example of the importance of living according to the agree-ment and obligations of one's employment, I recall a conversation with Laura (my daughter) about her place of employment. This job occa-sionally required work on Sunday mornings. We informed Laura (who still was young enough to need our permission) that she could take this employment, but *only* if it meant an *occasional* Sunday morning. She cleared this with her employer, and the employer agreed. We did not think it was wise for us to lay down some law (e.g., one time in six Sun-days) because the need would be determined by her employer. But we did leave open the warning that if it became too regular, she would have to terminate her employment and find something less intrusive into Christian order. In other words, it is important for Christians to live reliably within their employer's expectations, but if those expec-tations become too intrusive into the needs of the Christian life, that kind of employment should give way to a higher calling.

I mentioned above the occasional need for Christians to oppose their employer while working "under the order" of our society. But is that the only way? And, more importantly, is this the Christian way? A second kind of application draws more deeply on the example of Christ, namely, on the value and effects of suffering. In a world driven by litigation (which is itself driven by the desire to sustain personal rights), it is hard for us today to see that sometimes it is best not to assert our rights but to endure some kind of social pressure. That is, it might be best for a Christian man to endure the shame of not being promoted or getting a raise, or of a Christian woman of not asserting her equality or fighting for equal pay, *because of the gospel!*

---

22. I. H. Marshall, *1 Peter*, 89–90, 97–98.

The assertion of rights, of course, is not always wrong; but we have become dominated by such assertions. Yet the way of Jesus was not the way of assertion; it was the way of self-denial and of suffering, by which he came to inherit the greatest glory of all—the right hand of God (Phil. 2:5–11). This profound example is the one Peter uses to root his exhortations; we need to do the same. A cruciform understanding of the Christian life is the one thing that is easiest to discern in this passage, though it may be the one item contemporary society resists the most.

The suffering of Christ is a *paradigm of Christian existence*. What Peter finds in his churches is a consistent pattern of suffering, injustice, and social exclusion. Yet he exhorts his churches to submit, *even under such conditions*. And, more importantly, he grounds his exhortation to endure injustice *in the very life of Jesus*. Now it might be argued that Peter had no other alternative because the churches, comprised as they were of the socially excluded, had no chance to pursue the righting of the wrongs. This could be the case; however, we need to examine ourselves to see if we prefer this view so that we can make our life easier and avoid the cruciform nature of Christian living.

Because of his understanding of the Christian life, Peter has found a situation to which the Christian message can especially speak, namely, a situation of injustice. Peter's call to Christian slaves is to follow Jesus, endure injustice, and find their identity in God's acceptance and his final vindication of what is right. While I would not say this is the proven method for every imaginable situation in today's world,[23] I am convinced that churches today need to hear the message about the *cruciform nature of Christian existence*, especially since our litigant society is wasting far too much of its energy in defending personal rights. Recently I heard of legal suits over apples dropping in one's yard from a neighbor's tree, of neighbors tearing down a "neighbor's" wooden fence because it was partly in the first group's lawn (but less than a few inches)—and the mess goes on. In such a society it is fundamental

---

23. For instance, one would be wrong to argue that African-Americans should have continued in their "unequal" state in order to show forth the gospel more. At times, though we have no guidelines that will make each situation clear, it is important to protest peacefully; at times it is important to protest in more intrusive ways; at times it is important to surrender and wait for God's time.

for Christians to sound forth a different message—that of Jesus Christ, who suffered injustice in order to testify to God's grace.

How can we do this? (1) In the business world Christians should not be known for their assertiveness as much as for their industriousness, their work ethic, their kindness, their loyalty, their fairness, and their honesty. While they clearly will want to improve their "station in life" and will seek raises and promotions, there is no need for those desires to deafen the sound of Christian virtues.

(2) In our personal lives we need to suppress the desire to be noticed. Whether we are tempted to give money so our name might be placed on a brick at some conspicuous location, whether we are tempted to assert our child's ability within the hearing of teachers, or whether we are tempted to trumpet our daughter's swimming talents— whatever our temptations here, we need to learn from the example of Jesus who, though in the form of God and though equal with God, did not grasp for that same glory, but took on himself the very limitations of humanity so that he might accomplish his task (Phil. 2:6–11). While it may be difficult to give firm rules on this kind of "self-denial," I am deeply suspicious that we confront this kind of decision far more frequently than we care to admit. I am also convinced that the example of Christ in his self-denying role plays far too little a role in our decision-making. Instead, we have become too much like our litigant world even to see our assertive sinfulness. But the Christian life, as exemplified here by Peter, is a life that is shaped by the cross.

(3) Another area of life where we need to let the pattern of the cross infiltrate is that of personal finances, especially for those who live in an affluent country. It is a tragic irony that on the very coins we use to assert our control over others, to accumulate goods, and to stockpile material possessions is written, "IN GOD WE TRUST." This is the one area where we are more trusting in ourselves than in God, and yet it is here that we inscribe our national debt to God. A cruciform lifestyle with respect to possessions is found in persons who do not find their greatest pleasures in shopping, who are not motivated to buy more things when they get their paycheck, and who are not using the credit cards well beyond their limits. This cruciform lifestyle is found in families who have consciously decided not to buy a bigger and more prestigious house so that others might stand in awe of a home with six bedrooms, three garage doors, a sauna in the master bedroom, and a

putting green in the back lawn.[24] It is found, instead, in the lives of those who inconspicuously choose to follow Jesus in every adventure and share their possessions.

It might be argued that such a cruciform nature for Christian existence will not work! This sad charge is also tied into secular values. What does "work" actually mean? Surely we are not concerned with whether or not the practice of Christian giving will prohibit us from buying a sportier boat or a newer coat for winter. It may not work— in the short run. But the way of suffering *is the divinely intended manner of bringing the greatest victory of God into the world.* What really works is what works with God, and what works with God is the cross! The cross is a sterling example that, while we may be considered fools and conquered in this world's eyes, we are considered victors with God. We may be considered poor in our society, but with God we are considered rich.

And this divinely willed manner of victory, a victory achieved less through self-assertiveness than through self-denial, is the paradigm for how we are to deal with others and with God. It has been said that no marriage vow would ever be broken if each partner lived a cruciform existence, that is, if each lived for the other and surrendered their wills to the other. This is not some utopian ideal. A married partner who seeks to live for the other, who seeks the happiness of the other, and who learns to say no to personal wants and wishes is living a cruciform existence. Such a pattern of life is not inherently selfish; rather, it is other-directed and fulfilled in serving the other. This is a true imitation of Jesus.

In addition, if church members learn to give themselves in self-sacrificing surrender to one another, church splits will not occur. When the vote does not go according to the pastor's plans, when the choir does not get behind a certain special service, when the pastor speaks on topics that you or I would not choose, or when others are elevated to positions of leadership we might want—in all of these, individual

---

24. See especially R. J. Sider, *Rich Christians in an Age of Hunger,* rev. ed. (Downers Grove, Ill.: InterVarsity, 1984); R. J. Sider, ed., *Living More Simply: Biblical Principles and Practical Models* (Downers Grove, Ill.: InterVarsity, 1980); W. W. Wells, *The Agony of Affluence* (Grand Rapids: Zondervan, 1989); see also R. G. Clouse, ed., *Wealth and Poverty: Four Christian Views of Economics* (Downers Grove, Ill.: InterVarsity, 1984); C. M. Gay, *With Liberty and Justice for Whom? The Recent Evangelical Debate over Capitalism* (Grand Rapids: Eerdmans, 1991).

Christians are often confronted with the option of cruciform living. Either we choose selfishness, and grumble and divide, or we choose cruciform living by conceding God's will to other people and plans. Cruciform living also refuses to bring up a past decision (the "I told you so" approach) when it appears to have been misguided. I have heard people grouse for years about a pastor who was called. In so doing, they continue to express a selfishness and lack of cruciform living.

This very recipe of self-surrender is the precise formula Peter uses for those who treat Christians unjustly; this model is not just for the voluntary relationship and for the marital relationship. It governs especially the relationship of the Christian to injustice. In the words of Ronald Sider, who in his survey of the place of the cross in Christian living, argued that following Jesus did not necessarily mean acquiescence to injustices:

> But it does mean that if they [the Christians] obey the biblical command to follow Christ's example, they will refuse to regard oppressors as enemies to be reviled and hated. Rather, precisely as they remember that Christ died for their sins while they were still enemies of God, they will imitate God's unfathomable love for enemies incarnated in His Son's cross.[25]

As one looks through 1 Peter 2:11–3:12, one gains the impression that the "orderly behavior" the apostle enjoins on his churches is an orderly behavior anchored in the cross of Christ. It is not just a piece of pragmatic advice: Live orderly and you will not cause troubles for the church. Nor is it a piece of power: Live orderly or God will punish you. Rather, it is a piece of Christian theology: Live orderly because that is how Jesus himself lived and that is the kind of behavior God wills. Such a theological basis gives rise to its benefits, for in this way of living we will be able to further the gospel the most.

This text has great significance for our world today. While there are times when the Christian ought to assert himself or herself or when Christians ought to fight for their rights, there is another way—the way of suffering that follows the life of Jesus. This path of suffering injustice is not for the feeble or the weak-kneed; it is for those who are willing to pick up their cross daily and follow Jesus.

---

25. Ronald J. Sider, *Christ and Violence* (Scottdale, Pa.: Herald, 1979), 38.

1 Peter 3:1–7

✌

WIVES, IN THE same way be submissive to your husbands so that, if any of them do not believe the word, they may be won over without words by the behavior of their wives, ²when they see the purity and reverence of your lives. ³Your beauty should not come from outward adornment, such as braided hair and the wearing of gold jewelry and fine clothes. ⁴Instead, it should be that of your inner self, the unfading beauty of a gentle and quiet spirit, which is of great worth in God's sight. ⁵For this is the way the holy women of the past who put their hope in God used to make themselves beautiful. They were submissive to their own husbands, ⁶like Sarah, who obeyed Abraham and called him her master. You are her daughters if you do what is right and do not give way to fear.

⁷Husbands, in the same way be considerate as you live with your wives, and treat them with respect as the weaker partner and as heirs with you of the gracious gift of life, so that nothing will hinder your prayers.

PETER'S PRINCIPLE OF denying sin and conducting oneself in holiness (2:11–12), with its important manifestation in society of living "under the order" (2:13), is now applied to a third group: wives and husbands (3:1–7). His emphasis on the wives (3:1–6), like his emphasis both on governmental authority (2:13–17) and slaves (2:18–25), probably emerges from the presence of a large number of women whose husbands were not yet Christians. Because Peter spent most of his time addressing women does not mean today that men need to be addressed only briefly.

Peter's address to wives begins with the exhortation to "be submissive" (3:1a) and follows with the reason: so they can win them to faith on the basis of their good behavior (3:1b–2). His reason is developed further in 3:3–4 as he delves into the kind of clothing Christian women should be known for. Following this Peter gives examples (3:5–6) of the kind of behavior mentioned in 3:1b–2. Christian husbands come next: They are exhorted to live with their wives knowledgeably and considerately (3:7ab) so that their prayers will be heard (3:7c).

Exhortation to Wives (3:1–6)

The Exhortation to Submit (3:1–2). As with the other units in this section,[1] the exhortation to submit in 3:1a is part of a larger pattern: living a holy life before unbelievers with the hope that such conduct will have a positive impact on them. The exhortation to "be submissive" draws its energy from 2:13. Christian women, like Christian slaves, when they find themselves with a non-Christian husband, are to partake of the same ethic that Christians ought always to have: Live under all the orders of the day (2:13).

As with 2:18–25 on slaves, so with this passage—we must beware of the problem of hearing a passage today in a way that was never intended. To begin with, because of the dominance of men in the history of the church and the patriarchal-hierarchical nature of culture in the greater part of the world, we must admit that great abuses have taken place and have led many to see in this passage some kind of moral subjugation of women by men.[2] While I do not want to pretend that "submission" did not really mean some kind of respectful deference to authority, neither should we go to the other extreme and think this text says nothing about the relationship of wives to husbands. Parallels with the relationship of the Christians to Roman authority and slaves to their masters have to be recognized: Peter sees an importance in wives "living under the order of their husbands." Our problem here is with the fundamental abuse this text has created in the hands of too many men who have forced their wives against their wills.

Accordingly, to begin with this text is to begin with a problem: We will never hear this text the way it was intended to be read, nor will

---

1. Peter begins with "in the same way" so he can connect the exhortation of submission to the exhortations to slaves (2:18) and to those under governmental authority (2:13). Thus, all three exhortations are drawn into the same imperative at 2:13, revealing that Peter sees each of these injunctions as part of the kind of orderliness that ought to be characteristic of the Christian community as it lives a holy life (2:12) in society. In this way, the Christian community can have an enduring impact upon society.

2. See the citations of evidence in G. L. Martin, *Counseling for Family Violence and Abuse* (Resources for Christian Counseling 6; Waco, Tex.: Word, 1987), 22–26.

we able to bring this text into our world, until we confess the abuses it has been made to serve. Many women do not hear this text in any other way than how it has been practiced by abusive men. Until we learn to understand how women have heard this text, we will never learn what our interpretations are leading people to do. This means that the place to begin is with the ancient world.

What was it like for women in the ancient world?[3] There are two dimensions to the answer to this question: (1) The women Peter addresses are in Asia Minor where, it may be supposed, a Greco-Roman attitude toward women prevailed; (2) yet some of his converts presumably had a Jewish background, where a different attitude dominated.

In Jewish perspective, while women were respected and protected in the laws, they were treated as inferior in most every way to men. In the words of Ben Witherington, III,

> The dominant impression left by our early Jewish sources is of a very patriarchal society that limited women's roles and functions to the home, and severely restricted: (1) their rights of inheritance, (2) their choice of relationships, (3) their ability to pursue a religious education or fully participate in the synagogue, and (4) their freedom of movement.[4]

---

3. In what follows, I will follow the outlines of Ben Witherington's and Craig Keener's research; furthermore, it will not be possible here to document each point being made with references to the ancient world since these texts are largely inaccessible to most readers of this commentary. Further discussions and documentation of evidence can be found in the sources mentioned in the notes.

The literature on this is so vast I can but record a few books that have become influential on my thinking: B. Witherington, III, *Women in the Ministry of Jesus: A Study of Jesus' Attitudes to Women and Their Roles as Reflected in His Earthly Life* (SSNTMS 51; Cambridge: Cambridge Univ. Press, 1987), esp. 1–10; *Women in the Earliest Churches* (SSNTMS 59; Cambridge: Cambridge Univ. Press, 1991), esp. 1–23; "Women (New Testament)," *ABD*, 6:957–61; J. B. Hurley, *Man and Woman in Biblical Perspective: A Study in Role Relationships and Authority* (Leicester, Eng.: Inter-Varsity, 1981), esp. 20–78; R. A. Tucker and W. L. Liefeld, *Daughters of the Church: Women and Ministry from New Testament Times to the Present* (Grand Rapids: Zondervan, 1987); C. S. Keener, *Paul, Women, and Wives: Marriage and Women's Ministry in the Letters of Paul* (Peabody, Mass.: Hendrickson, 1992)—while this book is devoted to Paul, each of the pertinent issues in 1 Peter are directly addressed. For the broader debate, I like A. Mickels ed., *Women, Authority and the Bible* (Downers Grove, Ill.: InterVarsity, 1986).

4. Ben Witherington, III, "Women (New Testament)," 958.

While it would be wrong to think that everything was bad for women in the Jewish world, it would not be wrong to think that their world was highly restrictive, patriarchal, and clearly debilitating to the development of their gifts.

Women in the Greco-Roman world, on the other hand, were in most cases better off. But what women could or could not do depended on location and culture. Wives of citizens in Athens, for example, had about as much freedom as Jewish women in Palestine (though for different reasons), while women in Asia Minor had much more opportunity to pursue their own interests. Women there "engaged in private businesses, served in public offices, and had prominent roles in various religious cults."5 They were even able to vote and hold public office. Roman society in particular—and we can assume that over time such attitudes influenced Asia Minor—allowed more property rights for women, permitted greater leverage for women in marriage and divorce situations, and encouraged more education for women.

What all of this means for our text is simple: Peter is urging the women of the Asia Minor churches to live a life that is respectable in society so that they will be able to maintain a good reputation for the gospel. If women in Asia Minor had considerably more freedom than women under the influence of Jewish customs, then we must interpret Peter's words in the former context. That will mean that "submission" here probably does not refer to the same kind of restrictions in society that such a concept meant in Palestine. Furthermore, it makes his injunction a more pragmatic one.6 That is, Peter wants wives to submit *because of the influence* (3:1b–2) they can exert on their non-Christian husbands. This is entirely consistent with his agenda at 2:11–12, that Christians live such holy lives so that nothing can be lodged against the gospel because of their behavior. Any insults they receive must be the result of injustice.

Accordingly, Peter's injunction to Christian wives is that they conduct their lives so as to win7 their husbands to the Christian faith "without words."8 That is, "in certain cases the eloquent silence of

---

5. Ibid.

6. So also L. Goppelt, *1 Peter*, 218.

7. This term, "won over," is used frequently to describe success in missionary activity (Matt. 18:15; 1 Cor. 9:19–22; 1 Peter 3:1).

8. Several words echo 1 Peter 2:11–12 here: "conduct" (2:12) and "when they see" (2:12).

Christian deportment is its most effective vehicle."[9] As we saw above, Asia Minor permitted freedoms to women, including some kind of religious freedom; however, most scholars are agreed that when a woman struck out on her own and joined a religion different from her husband's, that could be seen as an act of insubordination.[10] Far from making what was probably a difficult situation worse, Peter exhorts these women to be especially circumspect. Thus, as Wolfgang Schrage contends, "the author ... expects missionary success from Christian life, lived in the power of the Word and representing its reality—not with a zeal for conversion, but in the knowledge that one's life is a form of proclamation, which can affirm or deny the authenticity of the gospel."[11]

Development of the Reason (3:3–4). Having mentioned that women ought to have a life that is noted by "purity and reverence," Peter develops this lifestyle issue further by delving into the matter of appearance. He contrasts external beauty with internal beauty. Every culture has its own ideas of external beauty for women. Today, for example, the "ideal woman" is tall and thin, shapely, dressed in the latest of fashions (which change by seasons), and full of zest and confidence. For Peter's day, the image was that of the woman with "braided hair," who wore "gold jewelry and fine clothes"[12]—comments that might indicate some of Peter's churches contained women of wealth and standing.[13] Peter's critique here joins a long list of ancient writers who chastised women for their concern with appearance,[14] including Paul (1 Tim. 2:9–10). Some have suggested that Peter's comments here actually prohibit Christian women of all ages from braiding their hair and wearing jewelry and fancy clothing,[15] but the majority see a comparison of values: External appearance is relatively unimportant, but internal virtue is the prime pursuit of life.[16] Yet this interpretation ought not to

---

9. J. N. D. Kelly, *Peter and Jude*, 128.

10. L. Goppelt, *1 Peter*, 219; J. R. Michaels, *1 Peter*, 157.

11. W. Schrage, *The Ethics of the New Testament*, trans. D. E. Green (Philadelphia: Fortress, 1988), 274.

12. A survey can be found in D. R. Edwards, "Dress and Ornamentation," *ADB*, 2:232–38.

13. E.g., J. N. D. Kelly, *Peter and Jude*, 129.

14. See J. R. Michaels, *1 Peter*, 159, who gives extensive quotations of this material.

15. Thus, in the early church, Clement of Alexandria has an extensive discussion of Christian attire in his *The Instructor* 3.11.

16. See L. Goppelt, *1 Peter*, 220–21; J. R. Michaels, *1 Peter*, 160.

lead to the view that Christian women can dress as they like; rather, Peter urges them to regard their external appearance as a secondary matter to personal beauty and to dissociate themselves from the cultural trend of that day to adorn themselves so as to attract attention.

The virtues Peter praises are "the unfading[17] beauty of a gentle and quiet spirit, which is of great worth in God's sight." The "quiet spirit" Peter enjoins here is that Christian wives avoid a cantankerous grumbling that would prevent a non-Christian husband from seeing God's grace and goodness in her behavior.[18] This expression, however, is not a virtue assigned in the early churches exclusively to women: in fact, this "nonviolent disposition" was characteristic of the early church in general and is but one example of "living under the order" of the day.[19] Such a beauty emerges from "your inner self," the hidden person, a person who has been transformed from the inside out by God's Spirit.[20] Such virtues are pleasing to God and have a powerful impact on unbelieving husbands.[21]

Examples of Good Behavior (3:5−6). Peter now legitimates his instructions to Christian wives about their good behavior by appealing to "the holy women of the past." What is noticeable here is that Peter extends the instruction to include women who had believing husbands, showing that his instructions to submit are not just some pragmatic expedient.[22]

Exhortation to Husbands (3:7)

HAVING ADDRESSED THE wives of unbelieving husbands, Peter now addresses Christian husbands. He assumes that their wives are Christians too, so his exhortation to them moves in a different direction. Inasmuch as his exhortation to them to "be considerate" borrows its force from the verb of 2:13,[23] it is best to see here a specific kind of

---

17. No doubt a contrast to the effects of aging on women's external appearance.

18. L. Goppelt, *1 Peter*, 222−23.

19. See here the lucid explanation of J. R. Michaels, *1 Peter*, 161−62.

20. L. Goppelt, *1 Peter*, 221−22.

21. See here the dramatic account of St. Augustine in describing his mother's behavior and how it led her husband to faith (*Confessions*, 9.19−22[IX]).

22. J. B. Hurley, *Man and Woman*, 153.

23. The grammar of 2:13−3:12 is such that the imperative of 2:13 ("submit") governs the participial imperatives of 2:18; 3:1, and 3:7. Thus, each of these latter three are specific applications of the general command for Christians "to be orderly."

"living under the order" for husbands, a kind of submission,[24] yet distinct from it.[25] The order for Christian husbands is one of being considerate—literally, of "living with one's wife knowledgeably."[26] The verb *synoikeo* ("living together") was especially used for sexual relations between husband and wife (Deut. 22:13; 24:1; 25:5), and that is no doubt the intended meaning here, though obviously not limited to that.[27] The Christian man, Peter says, is neither demanding nor selfish in his sexual and marital relations; he is instead considerate, sensitive, and serving.

The reason the Christian husband must be especially considerate in these relations is because his wife is "the weaker partner."[28] This expression has given rise to two major interpretations: physical weakness, and spiritual weakness. Inasmuch as the preponderance of evidence in the ancient world uses identical or similar language when describing a woman's physical condition, it is almost certain that Peter has in mind a wife's physical capacities.[29]

Peter largely repeats himself in the second clause of 3:7: Christian men are to "treat [your wives] with respect," inasmuch as they are "heirs with you of the gracious gift of life." Here again Peter participates in the early Christian tendency to elevate the position of women in society; they are seen as *fellow* heirs.[30] Twice in this verse he forms a compound verb in his incorporation of women into the lives of husbands: "living together" and "fellow heirs." In respecting their wives, these men and their wives will gain a hearing with God, and their prayers will be answered (cf. Matt. 5:21–26; 6:12, 14–15; 18:19–35; 1 Cor. 11:17–34; James 4:3).

---

24. P. Davids, *1 Peter*, 121–22.

25. That Peter changes expressions here (from *hypotasso* to *synoikeo kata gnosin*), after using "submission" for all (2:13), slaves (2:18), and wives (3:1), shows that he does not think the husband's relationship to his wife is one of submissiveness. Rather, within the larger framework of orderliness, Peter sees the husband's behavior as one of showing consideration and respect.

26. Literally, it reads, "Husbands, likewise, dwelling with [your wives] according to knowledge. . . ."

27. J. N. D. Kelly, *Peter and Jude*, 132; J. R. Michaels, *1 Peter*, 167–68.

28. There is some dispute whether "weaker partner" goes with "dwelling together" (Goppelt) or with "treating with respect" (NIV, NRSV); the word order favors "dwelling together."

29. J. N. D. Kelly, *Peter and Jude*, 133; P. Davids, *1 Peter*, 122–23; for a view that the weakness here may be more than physical, see W. A. Grudem, *1 Peter*, 143–44.

30. "Heirs with you" (NIV) translates a special word for Peter, *sygkleronomos*, or "fellow heir."

Bridging Contexts

SOME THINGS ABOUT men and women apparently do not change: Just as men in the ancient world had a tendency to be demanding, both sexually and emotionally, so also today; and just as women had a tendency to desire compliments for appearance, so also today. Furthermore, although great strides have been made in the development of physical strength through today's culture of physical training, it remains a fact of physical nature that women are physically weaker than men. And it also remains a tragic fact that men love to assert their strength and overpower women. In these traits of human nature, there is little change.

But many other features about men and women have changed since the first century, most notably in society's perception of how the marriage relationship is to work itself out. Just arguing that the term "submission" (or translating it "living under/according to the order," in order to take modern sensitivities into consideration) is a legitimate word to describe the relationship of a wife to her husband can make many readers hyperventilate. But it is in such a context that we must apply this text today.[31] I am aware that some women appreciate this term today and dutifully submit to the authority of their husbands; but I am also aware that this is not the case with the majority. Some interpreters might want to spend time castigating the majority as living with less than God's will. But I will not, because I believe times have changed, the culture has changed, and it is ours to relate the gospel to our modern world.

How, then, do we bring this matter into our day? First, as with the meaning of the term at 2:13 and 2:18, I do not believe "submission" here means always "living under the order of one's husband." It is obvious that the Christian woman who is married to a non-Christian man should not deny the Lord or refuse to associate with other Christians for the sake of submitting to her husband; such would be to make her husband tantamount to God. And note how Abraham at times was instructed to act (Gen. 21:10–13). No matter how one understands this category, there are times for "civil disobedience" for the Christian wife. Just as civil

---

31. An example of a more traditional, but highly sensitive, view of what submission means today can be found in Joyce Huggett, *Two Into One? Relating in Christian Marriage* (Leicester, Eng.: Inter-Varsity, 1981), 40–52.

disobedience is necessary at times for the Christian in society (2:13–17), and just as it is at times necessary for the worker to buck heads with his or her boss, so it is sometimes necessary for the wife to take umbrage with her husband, whether he is a Christian or not.

Second, if we have understood the ancient context properly, Peter is saying that Christians have an obligation to live "under the order," whatever order that may be, so as to maintain a credible witness. Living "under the order" always involves some kind of submissiveness. If this is the case, we have to examine carefully what the "orders" are today, so that we will know what kind of behavior is expected. There is little doubt that the "orders" have changed from a hierarchical to more of an egalitarian view; if this is the case, then changes of "living under the order" will follow.

To be sure, Peter justifies this orderliness on the basis of other godly women behaving in this manner (3:5–6) and not just on the basis of an expediency. In addition, we must also be prepared to admit that those "older women" lived in the same kind of environment. On the other hand, we must admit that they did so as one covenant member to another, not as a believer to an unbeliever so as to be a witness to God's grace. Furthermore, in the wider sweep of the New Testament, Paul's justification of submission is anchored in other themes (for example, Christ's relationship to the church, creation).[32] However, I am still of the view that both Peter's and Paul's prescriptions for a culturally relevant dress here are firmly anchored into a specific period of history and that the views of that culture helped shape each of their minds. Our culture has changed so dramatically that we have to think through this issue to discern how we are to apply such teachings to our world. To think that a one-to-one correspondence obtains for today would be a tragic (and completely unworkable) mistake.

One specific point we can make is that the principle of living for the sake of the gospel is transcultural. Thus, it would be wrong for a Christian woman to give the wrong impression of the nature of the gospel to her unbelieving spouse (and vice versa) by acting in a manner inconsistent with their marriage contract. This is where Peter's

---

32. In the previous sections we compared Peter's teaching to Paul's teachings in the "household regulations" sections of Paul's letters. The same can be done here; what emerges is a Petrine emphasis on the evangelistic impact of submission and the absence of a rooting of the idea of submission in either Christology or Creation.

focus is—with how believing wives relate to their unbelieving husbands. The wives must be beyond reproach, loving, and serving—so much so that their husbands will be won to the faith by their behavior. Christian women ought to be concerned with the kinds of obligations that are perceived by our society and with what is assumed in the marriage contract. For the sake of the gospel, these conventions ought not to be flaunted. Just as a mother who does not take proper care of her children receives deserved criticism in our culture, so also does the woman who shows no respect for her husband.

Furthermore, it is my firm conviction that we have placed the wrong emphasis on the word "submission"; we have also been preoccupied with "what we can do" and "what our rights are," whereas the biblical injunction is that the wife ought to give her life to her husband, "to serve and cherish him," and the husband ought to lay down his life for his wife.[33] Thus, when the Christian wife is seeking to love her husband with her whole being and the husband is seeking to love his wife with his whole being, the issue of submission never emerges. If the Christian husband resorts to demanding sexual satisfaction, he is not considering his wife's needs; if the Christian woman refuses to go along with her husband, she may not be considering her husband's needs. In each of these cases, to apply the "doctrine of submission" is to focus entirely on the wrong thing. The focus of biblical marriage is on love and service of one another.

In Cloud and Townsend's insightful book *Boundaries*, they come to the following conclusion:

> We have never seen a "submission problem" that did not have a controlling husband at its root. When the wife begins to set clear boundaries, the lack of Christlikeness in a controlling husband becomes evident because the wife is no longer enabling his

---

33. In my judgment, this is where the focus of W. A. Grudem's article on the meaning of submission goes astray; while Grudem clearly has good points about the meaning of submission, that conversation too one-sidedly focuses on the wrong item. Submission ought to be enveloped always by the biblical meaning of loving service to one another. See his "Wives Like Sarah, and the Husbands Who Honor Them: 1 Peter 3:1–7," in *Recovering Biblical Manhood and Womanhood: A Response to Evangelical Feminism*, ed. J. Piper and W. A. Grudem (Wheaton, Ill.: Crossway, 1991), 194–208. I am not saying that Grudem does not realize this context; the approach, however, typifies the concern: What submission means can only be understood by asking the question of what love means. His discussion does not do that.

immature behavior. She is confronting the truth and setting biblical limits on hurtful behavior. Often, when the wife sets boundaries, the husband begins to grow up.[34]

What these two authors are saying is that focusing on submission is
almost surely an indicator that one's priorities are messed up. Husbands too frequently resort to demanding submission when they are
unable to "get their way"; that indicates selfishness, not loving and
devoted service to one's wife (which is the way Christ loved the
church). What the husband ought to be saying to himself is, "Why do
I have to use force to get this done?" Often he has decided that his own
desires and ideas have to be fulfilled and that his wife's do not matter.
Such behavior is not loving. Marriages that are full of love, respect, and
honor rarely, I believe, need to resort to the issue of submission.

Perhaps discussing an issue in my relationship to Kris, my wife, will
illuminate what Cloud and Townsend mean by *boundaries* and how they
work themselves out in the issue of submission. I am a spontaneous
type; my wife is not. I have learned over the years that major decisions
around our home require time because Kris needs to process such decisions for a while. Often time will cure my "spontaneous urges"; on
other occasions it will enable Kris to make the decision the way she
likes to make them. Rarely do we disagree if time has been given for
the decision; we do, however, disagree if I demand some spontaneous
decision with significant implications for our life together.

One of my students illustrates this perfectly. He told me, rather
humorously, that he had an old Volkswagen that had been sitting in
our seminary parking lot, rusting and rotting there for two years.
"Why?" I asked. He responded, "Because my wife was not ready to
part with her dear old VW." He also told me that she was now ready
to "cut the cord." I appreciated his sensitivity to her boundary line:
She simply was not ready to make that decision, and he was respectful of that view. Someone might argue that she should have been submissive; I think my student was right and was "living with his wife
considerately." Had he pushed forward in the name of submission, he
may have done irreparable harm to his marriage. Good for him!

---

34. H. Cloud and J. Townsend, *Boundaries: When to Say Yes, When to Say No, To Take Control of Your Life* (Grand Rapids: Zondervan, 1992), 161–62. The entire chapter "Boundaries
and Your Spouse" is directly relevant to our observations here.

Before bringing this text into our modern world, we must also address the issue of how such a practice (submission) is to be understood within a larger unfolding theme in the Bible, namely, the equality of the sexes in Christ (Gal. 3:28). Few will squabble with me when I contend that the Bible sowed the seeds that eventually grew into the doctrine of the total inappropriateness of slavery, even if the Bible itself permitted and accommodated itself to such a practice in the ancient world. I maintain likewise that the biblical notion of equality has given rise to the modern notion of the equality of all people, and in particular, to the equality of the sexes in the church.

After surveying briefly the teaching that submission is rooted in the fall of humans into sin and that Paul teaches the equality of the sexes in Christ, I. H. Marshall concludes that "this teaching clearly shows that the effects of the Fall are undone in the new creation that is manifested in the church."[35] And K. R. Snodgrass, at the end of an exposition of Galatians 3:28, concludes: "If God has poured out his Spirit on both the sons and the daughters (Acts 2:17ff.), it will not do for us to erect a modern-day 'court of women' for our churches."[36]

I agree with this approach in the main: The seeds of equality have grown so high that the earlier plants of hierarchy are not as visible. This is why I. H. Marshall can argue that "the command here [1 Peter 3:1] may be transcended in a Christian marriage."[37] He further adds, "Submission in marriage was the type of moral conduct required at the time, certainly by Jews and also by many Gentiles. Christians were to live at least at that level."[38] What he means by "at least at that level" is what he means by "transcending": Christian wives who truly love their husbands in the way Jesus exhorted them to love and in the way Paul exhorts them to love will be more than submissive. They will be so loving that the term "submission" can hardly describe their relationship.

One time I was in a car with a well-known evangelical scholar, and we were discussing our wives. The conversation eventually flowed into the matter of submission, partly out of curiosity to what we each

---

35. I. H. Marshall, *1 Peter*, 99.

36. K. R. Snodgrass, "Galatians 3:28: Conundrum or Solution?" in *Women, Authority and the Bible*, ed. A. Mickelsen (Downers Grove, Ill.: InterVarsity, 1986), 181.

37. I. H. Marshall, *1 Peter*, 100. He draws an analogy to Old Testament laws that have been transcended by Christians who fulfill the Old Testament law in behavior that is consistent with the teachings of Jesus about the kingdom of God.

38. Ibid., 101.

believed. A statement he made illustrates the previous paragraph: "I believe in a wife submitting to her husband, but I don't believe the husband ever has the right to demand it. In fact, I know that when I am worthy of submission, my wife submits; and when I am unworthy of it, she does not." His final words send up all the fireworks: "My responsibility as a husband is to be worthy." That is the point! When a husband focuses on submission and the wife worries about it, the image of marriage is distorted. But when each focuses on the mutual responsibility to love and serve one another, the image of marriage is clear and beautiful.[39]

In our previous paragraphs the issue of feminism has been vying for discussion. This, then, is a good place to survey how modern feminists, and some of their opponents, interpret Scripture.[40] Feminist hermeneutics describes how the various branches of the modern-day feminist movement interpret the Bible and examines the various ways that movement seeks to apply (or deny) the relevance of the biblical text. *Radical feminist hermeneutics* is suspicious of the text, ultimately repudiating the revelatory value of the text in many (if not all) of its dimensions because of an ideological agenda that drives the interests of the interpreter. Such interpreters see a chauvinistic world inherent in a text that is ultimately used in manipulating and subjugating women. The appeal to Sarah in our text, it is argued, is because she legitimates male dominance. The text for these interpreters has no value except to point to error.

Liberal feminist hermeneutics tones down some of the starker proposals of the radical feminists. Here there is a desire to retrieve what is good, even if heavily suppressed, in the ancient text, while there is also a clear decision to reject what is unacceptable to modern feminist experience and ideology. While the text is clearly influenced by a hierar-

---

39. In saying this, however, I do not deny that some men are, for whatever reasons, perpetually unworthy of submission, but the wife's responsibility remains to live in a godly manner with that (unworthy) husband in an "orderly manner"; also, some wives are prone to resist the order God has ordained even when the husband is altogether worthy. Such problems make particular situations especially difficult for the marriage. I still maintain, however, that focusing on submission (by either partner) distorts a Christian concept of marriage.

40. I am dependent here on the masterful survey of feminist hermeneutics by A. C. Thiselton, *New Horizons in Hermeneutics* (Grand Rapids: Zondervan, 1992), 430–62. For the reader who wishes to follow up my summary, Thiselton's book provides a comprehensive bibliography.

chical and patriarchal world, there are features of that text that can be sustained across the centuries.

Within the orbit of evangelicalism, an *evangelical feminist hermeneutic* argues for a hermeneutic of understanding that is both socio-critical with respect to the text as well as mildly submissive to the text. This approach sees the text of 1 Peter 3:1—6 as a text for its time, accommodated to its cultural context. While it is not a chauvinistic act of manipulation, it is still heavily dominated by a male culture, and to that degree it must be reconstructed or altered. In other words, the text must be understood in its own terms, decoded, and then restructured to speak to modern women. While one might wonder if the text is allowed here to speak for itself, it should be pointed out that there is a living dialectic in this movement between the authority of the text and the modern world, creating what is clearly a living synthesis of how Christians ought to understand the Bible.

Finally, the *hermeneutic of many conservatives is one of tradition*. The text is timeless; a patriarchal world is what God intends, and women are to be submissive to the divinely ordained order, which has men as God's appointed heads of authority. To be sure, there are abuses, but in the main the cultural changes we find today are inconsistent with biblical notions and therefore ought to be criticized. The key for this approach to our text (and other texts of the same ilk) is to understand it and apply it, though a minimal amount of restructuring may be necessary.

It is impossible for me to evaluate each of these methods here, nor is it necessary. The alternatives for evangelical scholars nearly always fall into the latter two camps: evangelical feminism or traditionalism. To the degree that one believes the text must be updated, to that degree the interpreter is feminist in orientation. However, rather than be labeled in this camp, I urge that each interpreter look long and hard at his or her own principles and see if consistency is achieved in the process of interpretation. It will simply not do for someone to dismiss slavery as outmoded, or to contend for civil disobedience to governmental authorities, or to argue for some kind of "Mr. Mom" theory, and then not be consistent in permitting to women the same freedom and change of application. Nor is it fair to argue without substantial reasoning for some things being cultural (like wearing jewelry or fancy clothing) and other things being transcultural. Above all, we must be both biblically anchored and culturally reasonable if we are to let the gospel have its way of power today.

 TRAGICALLY, WHILE MODERN society has made great strides in the direction of equality of all peoples, men have remained behind the times in learning how to love their wives respectfully and treat women appropriately. Too frequently interpreters have become so preoccupied with the verses about women that they have neglected the impact Peter's exhortation to men ought to have on our world. But the words of Peter to husbands are highly relevant; therefore, I will devote my attention here to those words.[41]

There are, in the United States alone, around sixty thousand reported cases of rape a year, not to mention many more that are left unreported. That there are between three to six million women per year who are victims of some form of physical violence in their homes staggers the imagination. In addition, it is women (or the elderly) who are the favorite targets of robbery and assault. In each of these kinds of sinful, social deviance, the prominent issue is a violent act by a man who takes advantage of a woman because of his superior strength. In my judgment, the most blatant and pervasive form of men using violence against women is at the emotional and mental level—husbands intimidating, threatening, and manipulating their wives in countless ways. Anger is the foundation of it all; angry men at home may be the biggest problem in our society, however they appear in the public square. This problem of anger-induced violence, or violence against women in general, is not just found among non-Christians. The typical pastor sees over a dozen persons per year who are involved in family violence.[42]

---

41. This reflects a typical feature of application: Interpreters often focus on a section or idea in a passage that is especially relevant to that interpreter's culture and situation, where the Word of God needs to be heard. We can do no other. However, in doing this we must make sure that we are not avoiding difficult issues, and we must be careful to teach the entire text for what it says. It is also too typical for interpreters only to examine the ideas that are socially hot. This makes the text only a convenient stopping place for discussing our social agenda. Balance must be maintained.

42. This number, from a study of Marie Fortune, appeared in *Theology, News, and Notes* (June, 1982), 17 (from Fuller Theological Seminary); I found this in G. L. Martin, *Counseling for Family Violence and Abuse*, 15; see further in the discussion on pp. 19–27.

Against each of these acts of violence the words of Peter could be cited. Some (too many) men, for whatever reason,[43] try to strengthen their own egos by bully behavior and refuse to live within the limitations of their own inadequacies. Instead of living with the tension created by their inability to persuade or their inability to love or feel loved, they resort to violent activity targeted for a vulnerable woman. When the wife has small children, she becomes doubly addicted to staying with the abusive man: She both loves him (in spite of his violence) and loves her children. Furthermore, acts of violence against wives are often followed by some form of remorse, guilt, and apology, leading the wife to think things will get better. But the man will only change when he becomes convinced that the wife will no longer tolerate his abuse. Total separation is about the only hope for the wife and nearly the only form of communication that can get through to the husband. In some cases, the cycle of violence can be broken and restoration can take place.[44]

When violence takes place in a Christian home, it is sickening, both because of what happens to the wife (and children) but also because of the negative social implications it has for the impact of the gospel. Pastors, Sunday school teachers, parents, and Christian media need to devote large amounts of time and space to the instruction of boys and young men, not to mention adult men, in order to inform them of the hideousness of acts of violence against women and to guide them through and out of any feelings of violence or assaults of women. The church may pretend that acts of violence do not take place within its walls, but they do; and the church has this small word of Peter regarding any kind of violence against wives, daughters, and women.

---

43. Psychiatrists (and psychologists) have clearly worked out the kind of background typical of violent men; having such a background in violence, however, does not excuse the behavior. "Abusive men are likely to have come from violent homes, where they witnessed wife-beating or were abused themselves as children. The act itself is reinforcing; once a man has beaten his wife, he is likely to do so again. Abusive husbands tend to be immature, dependent, and nonassertive, and to suffer from strong feelings of inadequacy." So H. I. Kaplan and B. J. Sadock, *Synopsis of Psychiatry: Behavioral Sciences, Clinical Psychiatry,* 5th ed. (Baltimore: Williams and Wilkins, 1988), 378; see also the discussion of G. L. Martin, *Counseling for Family Violence and Abuse,* 31–38.

44. See G. L. Martin, *Counseling for Family Violence and Abuse,* 97–122, where the author details treatment of abusive men.

Peter's advice is rooted in the notion that Christian husbands need to understand their wives.[45] To be sure, wives need to understand their husbands as much as husbands need to understand their wives, but we are not talking here about what women need to understand. Husbands need not only a crash course[46] in understanding their wives, but they need to become lifelong learners of them because, just as husbands change over the years, so also do wives. Gary Smalley's conclusion is as humorous as it is helpful:

> I would venture to say that most marital difficulties center around one fact—men and women are TOTALLY different. The differences (emotional, mental, and physical) are so extreme that without a *concentrated effort* to understand them, it is nearly impossible to have a happy marriage. A famous psychiatrist once said, "After thirty years of studying women, I ask myself, 'What is it that they really want?'" If this was his conclusion, just imagine how little we know about our wives.[47]

It would be foolish for me to think I could sketch here a "view of women," but I do think that my experience of over twenty years of marriage to a wonderful (and challenging!) woman, my experience in studying the Bible, and my reading about marriage entitle me to a couple pieces of advice. Truly, no marriage is perfect because, as sinners, we all have personal problems that prevent us from being all that we could and should be to our mates. But that is no basis for excuse-making, nor is it any reason to avoid working hard at being a good husband.

First, I believe that wives want a husband who is loving, caring, sensitive, and understanding. Men may strut around thinking that what a woman wants is a strong man, a hulk, or a successful man who drives fancy cars and wears flashy suits; but when the doors are shut in the house, those things disappear into a mist. What remains is a desire by

---

45. Peter uses the expression "according to knowledge" (*kata gnosin*). This expression is buried in the NIV's use of "be considerate."

46. While I am not conversant with lots of literature in this regard, a book I can recommend is Gary Smalley, with Steve Scott, *If Only He Knew*, rev. ed. (Grand Rapids: Zondervan, 1982).

47. Gary Smalley and S. Scott, *If Only He Knew*, 17. Smalley and Scott go on to list what they perceive to be the major differences between men and women, describing mental/emotional differences, physical differences, sexual differences, and intuitive differences.

a woman to have a husband that understands her and loves her. A wife responds to a husband who showers all of his attention on her all the time, not just when he wants something. A wife wants a husband who calls her during the day to tell her an important piece of news because he can't wait to share it with her—because she is his best friend. A wife wants a husband who listens to her, really listens and learns in each conversation just what she is saying. In other words, a woman wants to be "number one" to her husband (just as a husband wants to be "number one" to his wife). A good test here might be that you imaginatively eliminate your wife's last birthday, the last Christmas, and your last anniversary, and ask yourself, "Are there any other special days during the year that I showered her with my love?" If not, you have much to learn about what it means to make your wife number one, to show her your love and affection, to show her that you care.[48]

Second, I believe that a wife wants a husband who is respectable and worthy of honor. Men are powerful at work and weak at home; men are famous in the public square but unauthoritative in the home. The reason for such a dramatic shift is that the wife knows what her husband is "really like," and there is no pretense inside the home. What a woman wants is a man who is consistent and therefore respectable, a man who lives his life with personal integrity in such a manner that he is justly "famous in his living room" as well as at work.

Perhaps it is because I have been married to a psychologist for so long, but I rarely trust the "public image" of professional athletes, those who are in the media, or those whom we see often in public (at work, at school, etc.). What I like to know is, "What are they really like at home?" When we hear of the breakdown of marriages of people in the public eye, we are usually confronted with the obvious problem of someone whose public persona is quite different from the private reality (call it "hypocrisy," if you want). Wives know these things, and what our wives want from us is integrity—and that means being who we are wherever we are. In other words, that means extending our private lives into the public, not creating two different personas.

I could go on about the implications of Peter's advice to husbands to be considerate in their relationship with their wives. The above

---

48. My wife, on reading this paragraph, reminds me that now that this is in print, she can hold me to its standards!

two pieces of advice only begin to illustrate what it means to "live with our wives knowledgeably." Other points could be made, involving such things as leadership, responsibility, planning, caring for children, and taking time for vacations. But they will only strengthen the observations about what wives want from their husbands. If I go much further, my wife will have me cornered for the rest of my life.

Socially, those who believe men need to treat women considerately and kindly and who also believe, with Peter, that violence against women is morally despicable, need to agitate for stiffer punishment for those who abuse women. It is a blot against our society that abusive men—men who have raped women, who have had incestuous relations, and who have beaten women—can be sentenced and then freed all too quickly, only to commit the same or worse crimes. As Christians, we ought to speak vocally against light punishments and to argue instead for "truth in sentencing." We ought to write to our public leaders and express our outrage about leniency for violent crimes. Furthermore, we ought to elect judges who take a stand against violence against women, just as we ought to protest against judges who are lenient with violent husbands and fathers.[49]

---

49. There are other pertinent points in our world to which this text speaks. For example, Peter's words about true beauty are important in a world where some women have been driven, by the desire to fulfill the American male's dream woman, to eating disorders that rack the body and soul. Some women have resorted to sexual promiscuity in their desire to fulfill the same dream. Identity has too easily slid into image, and that image is too often unavailable. See the insightful comments of I. H. Marshall, *1 Peter*, 101–2. Long ago, James Dobson wrote a book that speaks to this issue as much today as it did then (see his perceptive chapter "Beauty: The Gold Coin of Human Worth," in his *Hide or Seek*, rev. ed. [Old Tappan, N.J.: Revell, 1979]), 23–41.

1 Peter 3:8–12

FINALLY, ALL OF you, live in harmony with one another; be sympathetic, love as brothers, be compassionate and humble. 9Do not repay evil with evil or insult with insult, but with blessing, because to this you were called so that you may inherit a blessing. 10For,

"Whoever would love life
    and see good days
must keep his tongue from evil
    and his lips from deceitful speech.
He must turn from evil and do good;
    he must seek peace and pursue it.
For the eyes of the Lord are on the righteous
    and his ears are attentive to their prayer,
but the face of the Lord is against those who do evil."

Original
Meaning

THE FIFTH AND final[1] section of Peter's "Guidelines to Social Groups" (i.e., household codes) expresses his concern with everyone in the churches, and his regulations exhort Christians on how they are to behave in general. Accordingly, this section records the general ethical principles required of believers who want to live circumspectly in a world that opposes both their lifestyle and existence.

Peter begins with a brief listing of virtues concerning harmonious social relations (3:8); these are immediately followed by two clauses that deal with an appropriate Christian response to opposition (3:9). These exhortations are then buttressed in 3:10–11 by a quotation from Psalm 34:13–17, reexpressing the virtues of 3:8–9 and ground-

---

1. Peter begins with *to telos*, "Finally." One might translate this, "The sum of the matter is this: . . . ." Here he reexpresses what he said in 2:11–12, the various virtues listed in 3:8–11 being specific instances of "good conduct" and "abstaining from sin."

ing the motivation of living this way by an appeal to the omnipresence and omniscience of God (3:12). Peter calls his readers' attention to this passage from Psalms especially because of its last verse.

The interpreter must decide whether 3:8 is concerned with "insider" ethics (how individual members are to interact with one another) and 3:9 with "outsider" ethics, or whether both verses are concerned with how Christians are to relate to the world. To begin with, Peter's exhortations here are applicable to every encounter Christians have with others. To be sure, (1) his concern from the beginning has been with how various Christians relate to the outside world (Christians to government, slaves to unbelieving masters, wives to unbelieving husbands, and husbands to wives in general); (2) there is nothing in 3:8 that makes us think exclusively in terms of insiders; and (3) 3:9 is clearly concerned with outsiders. The flow of the text, then, makes us think almost exclusively in terms of how Christians are to relate to the outside world. In other words, we would be on sure footing if we read 3:8 as providing ethics for general relations in society rather than for relations within the Christian community, and particularly for how the church ought to relate to a hostile society (3:9). In this interpretation, Peter then grounds this ethics in the important observation that "God is watching us" (3:10–12).

However, to balance the evidence properly, we must note that the specific words Peter uses in verse 8 are used elsewhere in the New Testament (documented below) for the ideal relations of Christians to one another. I contend, then, that Peter begins by exhorting all Christians to relate to one another in a certain way, both because it is right for them to relate this way and because it provides them with a family of acceptance in the face of a hostile world.[2]

Ethics for General Relations in the Church (3:8). While the previous three sections were addressed to specific kinds of people (slaves, wives, husbands), this exhortation is for "all of you." All his addressees are to "live in harmony with one another;[3] be sympathetic, love as brothers, be compassionate and humble." If our conclusion above is accurate, the

---

2. See J. H. Elliott, *Home for the Homeless*, 165–266.

3. The NIV adds "with one another," giving the impression that the ethics are concerned exclusively for insiders. But the contextual flow does not suggest this. However, Peter may have in mind a harmony within that gives them a better status with the outsiders. See here J. N. D. Kelly, *Peter and Jude*, 135; J. R. Michaels, *1 Peter*, 176.

focus in these virtues is on how Christians demonstrate these virtues as they live with one another in a hostile world. They must begin with "harmony" (cf. Acts 4:32; Rom. 12:16; 15:5; 1 Cor. 1:10; Phil. 2:2; 4:2) in both mind and spirit. When this virtue is present, "what results from this is not uniformity but unanimity."[4] Harmony is, in part, a development of being "sympathetic" (cf. Rom. 12:15; 1 Cor. 12:26; Heb. 4:15; 10:34). It is both compassion and understanding.

In addition, believers are to "love as brothers" (1 Peter 1:22; 2:17; 1 Thess. 4:9). Such a virtue characterized much of early Christianity, though because of human nature, it was always under threat. Christians are to love one another and any whom they encounter as good neighbors. Those who love others are also "compassionate" (Eph. 4:32) and "humble" (Phil. 2:3).

Ethics for Relations to a Hostile Society (3:9). Since it is difficult to imagine Peter thinking of Christians throwing hostile barbs at one another, we are probably justified in thinking he has here moved from "inter-Christian" ethics to "outsider" ethics—to how believers should relate to the hostile world in which they live. "Do not repay evil with evil or insult with insult, but with blessing," just as Jesus lived (cf. 2:21, 23). Once again, Peter sees the Christian response to pressures from the outside world as one of passivity and grace, not aggressive retaliation. Why? "Because to this you were called so that[5] you may inherit a blessing." Peter anchors their relationships to outsiders in their calling and promises them a "blessing."

While some have seen this blessing as the final state of salvation,[6] others find here a promise for some kind of blessing in this life, perhaps a longer life or greater toleration for Christian faith.[7] In light of Peter's citation of Psalm 34, where the beginning emphasis is on "see[ing] good days" (3:10), he likely has in mind a prolonged life on this earth because of Christian goodness, in spite of persecution. In line with his emphasis at 2:11–12, he imagines it will be a much better life for the churches if they are quiet, humble, and gentle, and if they

---

4. L. Goppelt, *1 Peter*, 233.

5. Some see this expression (*eis touto*) to refer back to blessing those who curse you (J. R. Michaels, *1 Peter*, 178), while others see it pointing forward (NIV; L. Goppelt, *1 Peter*, 234).

6. See J. R. Michaels, *1 Peter*, 179; L. Goppelt, *1 Peter*, 234–35; E. Clowney, *1 Peter*, 141–42.

7. Cf. the extensive documentation in W. A. Grudem, *1 Peter*, 148–49.

refrain from retaliation and vindication. One might dub this orientation as "optimistic," but it is a conclusion drawn by a victim of persecution who knows, from tough times, how life works.

Foundation for Ethics: God Is Watching Us (3:10–12). In Peter's principle that believers are to absorb some injustices for the sake of the gospel by not returning evil with evil, the apostle expresses a theological anchor that goes deep into the network of New Testament theology. The Christian is supposed to be motivated by a desire to receive a "blessing from God" (3:9), a desire grounded in the fact that God is the final Judge. Christians have been called to inherit a blessing, which is God's reward for an obedient life. Peter supports his exhortation by quoting an Old Testament text that describes the close relationship between one's life and God's assessment of that person. Knowing that God knows everything and is control of everything gives Christians a serenity and acceptance of injustices while they await the truthfulness of God's final assessment.

Psalm 34 is particularly suitable for a situation of being harassed and persecuted. Its theme is that the one who wants to "get along in this world" must be peace-seeking, gentle-spoken, and good. Yet the fundamental point Peter makes is that God is omniscient and omnipresent—he sees all, knows all, and is always present. People must not think that they can get by with evil behavior, for God is watching and evaluating; his eyes are on the righteous. Moreover, he hears their prayers—that is, God is on their side, protecting and shielding them. At the same time, the Lord's face is turned against those who are wicked. Once again we are drawn back to 1 Peter 2:12: Those who live righteously before God will, in the end, be vindicated by God on the great day of glory, but those who live sinfully and oppressively will receive condemnation from God Almighty on that same day of his glory.

Bridging Contexts

IT REQUIRES NO special knack to understand abstract moral principles and see their *general* relevance to one's everyday Christian life. Texts that exhort Christians to "live in harmony with one another" are not hard to apply, since "living in harmony" is so flexible a principle and so clear an order that a special context is not required to discern its relevance. Texts that are specific and intricately linked with a cultural context (e.g., shaking the dust from your feet at Matt. 10:14) require the interpreter to generalize a specific practice into a transcultural principle that can then be applied to his or her target audience.[8] But if the principle is general, specific applications need to be discerned for that principle to be practiced in various cultures.[9] Our passage here provides an abstract principle ("live in harmony") for us apply to our cultures in various ways.

To be sure, to say "live in harmony" in Ireland may be different from saying it in the Netherlands, but the point remains the same: Abstract moral principles are not hard to understand. Their *specific* application in particular contexts, however, may be especially difficult to put into actual practice. This passage, then, is filled with abstract moral principles (be sympathetic; live in light of the judgment) that are not hard to understand (Christians of all ages need to live in light of the judgment), but specific applications can be difficult.

What does it mean, for instance, to "live in harmony" when one Christian group disagrees theologically with another Christian group? As an example, for a post-World War II Confessing Christian survivor of a German concentration camp to be understanding of a German Lutheran State Church pastor who supported (indirectly or even directly) the Third Reich was more than difficult for many of them.[10] In the broader context of biblical theology, a statement like "live in harmony" cannot be given more than its due because it is not intended to be the only factor in determining relationships. Truth is not sacrificed on the altar of harmony, but personal feelings belong on that altar. I can live in harmony with the person who has offended me by worshiping with him and by serving him; I cannot live in harmony with the person who blasphemes the name of Jesus Christ. I can pray for him and I can evangelize him, but those activities are not what Peter has in mind when he speaks of harmony.

---

8. This is not to say that there are not some practices that are no longer relevant (like the mixing of cloths in the Levitical codes). I am speaking here only of practices that can be generalized.

9. W. C. Kaiser, Jr., calls this "principlization"; see his helpful analysis in *Toward an Exegetical Theology: Biblical Exegesis for Preaching and Teaching* (Grand Rapids: Baker, 1981), 149–63.

10. See the exposition of this in F. A. Schaeffer, *The Mark of the Christian* (Downers Grove, Ill.: InterVarsity, 1971), 31–33.

Thus, in moving this text into our world, we must take into consideration Peter's setting as well as consider the meaning of his words and the function they were to have in his setting. He is exhorting communities under stress to live in harmony so that the gospel can have its desired effects. He is not speaking of the attempts of some Roman Catholics and Anglicans to unite their respective congregations into one large, catholic communion (though his point about harmony might apply in some senses). For true application to take place, the context of Peter must be considered carefully.

If Peter's words here are driven by the contextual situation of Christians under stress, then they need to be applied especially to any situation where Christians are experiencing persecution. Whenever Christians are under threat,[11] they need to be harmonious and love one another if they are going to be able to make an impact on the outside world; in fact, they may need to unify *simply in order to survive.* In the introduction to this commentary, I called attention to the work of J. H. Elliott.[12] One major element of his understanding of 1 Peter is his accurate emphasis on the church as the household of God. Elliott develops this emphasis in the direction of self-identity; that is, the church developed its own identity through its reliance on other members who could become an extended family and allow that very identity to nurture itself and grow. Two Christian fundamental ethical principles were brotherly love and not retaliating when injustices occurred. I believe Peter's exhortations here are not only Christian theology and ethics, but also important common sense at the social and pragmatic level: If his audience wants to survive and live God's will in this world, then they must be loving and kind people.

To bring this passage into our modern world, then, and to apply it the way Peter did, we should find analogous circumstances of Christian communities under threat. In fact, this context is more important for application than is sometimes recognized, for this text is only *indirectly* about social influence. It is about how to live together under stress in such a way that the community can survive. The impact this community may have on its surrounding environment is indirect; that is, if believers live together harmoniously, they will be able to survive;

---

11. In the "Bridging Contexts" section at 2:11–12, I examined the sociological theory of Bernard J. Siegel. One of the traits of a "community under threat" is its need to unify.
12. *Home for the Homeless.*

if they meet injustices with non-retaliatory attitudes, they may have an influence on their world. But this text is not a strategy for evangelizing the world. Life among the outsiders is here described as a life known for being nonvindictive (3:9, 10–11). One has to think that the peace that is enjoined in 3:11 is along the line of being harmonious, gentle, and "submissive" (2:13, 18; 3:1, 7).

If it is Christian high school students experiencing opposition at the public schools for meeting with one another "at the pole"[13] to pray for the school, or if it is the Christian businessman or businesswoman finding it tough going in an unsanctified environment, or if it is some local church in a difficult area of China, the words of Peter are especially important: Stay together, live peacefully, do not retaliate. Christians ought to be good citizens and be obedient to their superiors; wives ought to win their husbands by good behavior, and husbands ought to live with their wives sensitively. These short exhortations, then, are timeless words, but I doubt that they are a timeless or a "situationless" strategy for every Christian facing persecution.

My daughter and her friends, for instance, can write to the school newspaper and appeal to their civil rights for free speech; a Christian businesswoman can appeal to the same or to "fair trade" laws; a local church in Saudi Arabia, however, may have no other option. That last situation is analogous to Peter's situation. But what should Christians do when they face persecution and can do something about it? This is exactly the kind of question we need to ask and probe in order to find out how to apply this text to our world.

I contend, above all, that regardless of whether we can do something about our situation, the gentleness and "general pacifistic" nature of Peter's exhortations are fundamental to how Christians are to relate to the outside world. We ought not to be known for fighting and quarreling, nor ought we to become an unruly mob that is always agitating for one thing or another. Instead, we ought to be seen as peace-loving people who are good citizens. This is what I mean by "pacifistic" (the word comes from *pax*, the Latin word for "peace"). Christians are to be known not only for their love (John 13:34), but also for their peacefulness.

---

13. The expression "at the pole" has become a rallying cry for Christians to pray together at a visible place (at a flagpole) on a school campus.

Arguing that Christians ought to be peaceful does not mean they ought to opt out of culture and the public forum. There is a time when they ought to act, just as there is a time when they ought to wait. But, Peter urges us, when they do act, it should be in a gentle, law-abiding manner and in consort with one another; they live before the holy God who will judge them for their behavior.

Another point worthy of consideration is whether words like these apply when severe differences over the nature of the gospel are at stake. In other words, does the exhortation to live in harmony apply when the minister has gone off the deep end theologically or when someone in the church has ransacked his own family through hideous sins? I doubt it. Peter's words are not "situationless." They no more apply to the sinning husband in such a way that the wife must stay with him than they do when a leader argues that Christ is but one way of salvation. Harmony and unity are important, but that unity is not to be preserved by sacrificing what unites Christians: Christ and the gospel.

THE CHRISTIAN CHURCH should be seen as a *community*, a family. A local church ought to be the model *par excellence* in its own community of what it means to live harmoniously, lovingly, righteously, and peacefully. When disruptions are necessary, even these ought to be done in as peaceful a manner as possible.

John R. W. Stott has insightful words in regard to this issue:

> The problem we experience, whenever we think about the church, concerns the tension between the ideal and the reality. The ideal is beautiful. The church is the chosen and beloved people of God, his own special treasure, the covenant community to whom he has committed himself for ever, engaged in continuous worship of God and in compassionate outreach to the world, a haven of love and peace, and pilgrim people headed for the eternal city. But in reality we who claim to be the church are often a motley rabble of rather scruffy individuals, half-educated and half-saved, uninspired in our worship, constantly bickering with each other, concerned more for our maintenance

than our mission, struggling and stumbling along the road, needing constant rebuke and exhortation, which are readily available from both Old Testament prophets and New Testament apostles.[14]

Stott contends that there are at least three challenges from the secular world to the church today: the challenge for transcendence, the challenge for significance, and the challenge for community. The church, in other words, ought to be a living embodiment of what God wants for people in social relations. Simon and Garfunkel sang the song that reflected individualism at its highest when they sang, "I am a rock . . . I am an island . . . a rock never cries . . . and an island feels no pain." But what people continually return to is the *need for community that is driven by the divinely created need for love*. The church of Jesus Christ, in its deepest sense, is to be precisely that: the living incarnation of the love of Christ that is expressed for one another and the world.

The great Russian novelist Dostoevsky once said that "hell is the punishment of being *unable* to love."[15] This places love where it ought to be: the most important virtue of the virtues, the leading note of all our relationships. This is the love Peter calls his churches to have as they live in harmony and in community. "Love cures. It cures those who give it and it cures those who receive it."[16] But love must be worked at because those with whom we live in our communities are not, unfortunately, innately lovable. All we can offer to others is who we are: "The primary gift of love is the offering of one's most honest self through one's most honest self-disclosure."[17] When we truly open ourselves to one another, we pave the way for love, and love creates community. But until we open up, we will retain worldly values and blockade the creation of community. This, too, prevents growth, both personal and communitarian, for, as Harry Stack Sullivan said, "All personal growth,

---

14. J. R. W. Stott, *The Contemporary Christian: Applying God's Word to Today's World* (Downers Grove, Ill.: InterVarsity, 1992), 219–20. Another lucid exposition of this same problem can be seen in H. A. Snyder, *The Problem of Wineskins: Church Structure in a Technological Society* (Downers Grove, Ill.: InterVarsity, 1975), 89–99. See further his *The Community of the King* (Downers Grove, Ill.: InterVarsity, 1977); *Liberating the Church: The Ecology of Church and Kingdom* (Downers Grove, Ill.: InterVarsity, 1983), 112–31.

15. From N. Turner, *Christian Words*, 262.

16. Dr. Karl Menninger, in J. Powell, *Unconditional Love: Love Without Limits*, rev. ed. (Allen, Tex.: Tabor, 1989), 90.

17. J. Powell, *Unconditional Love*, 82.

all personal damage ... as well as all personal healing and growth, come through our relationship with others."[18]

Churches throughout the world need to examine their constitutions and confessions, and then thoroughly analyze their practices to see if the idea of the "church as community" defines their existence. I am not speaking here just of programs, like "coffee hour" or "prayer meetings"—both good ideas that may well encourage community. Nor am I speaking here only of "church growth" and its apparent development of a larger community.[19] Rather, what I have in mind is a perceptive discernment of our local churches to see if they truly function as a community where people are led to the holy love of God (the Father of the family), where that same love dominates the relationships and programs within that church (the nerve of the family), and where that love is known in the larger society as the characteristic of that church (the mark of the family).

Many kinds of suggestions have been made on how the church can "live as a community." One might think of the *individual home model*, where Christian families begin to become "open" to having others live with them;[20] or one might think of the *community church model*, where churches strive to be an alternative society.[21] Neither of these models is the superior, though the latter is our concern in this section. Unfortunately, many churches are not defined in light of the biblical category of "community." Instead, they are defined by how many people attend, on how tight their doctrinal statement is, or by some other measure. While we have to be balanced, arguing that community, evangelism, and doctrine each have their place in the definition and organization of the local church, we must also admit that far too few churches are defined by how they foster community—and, tragically, in a time when community is fundamentally needed.

A sure indicator of how "community oriented" a church is, in my experience, is how one is greeted and incorporated into a church as a

---

18. From J. Powell, *Who I Am*, 43.

19. See the critique of David Wells, *God in the Wilderness: The Reality of Truth in a World of Fading Dreams* (Grand Rapids: Eerdmans, 1994), 68–72.

20. An example of this can be found in David Watson, *I Believe in the Church* (Grand Rapids: Eerdmans, 1978), 84–95.

21. This older model that has inspired many churches is described in R. Stedman, *Body Life* (Glendale, Calif.: Regal, 1972).

first-time attendee. Both words are important: "greeted" *and* "incorporated." Some churches are gregarious at greeting new people but seem unable to incorporate; other churches may be a little bashful at "greeting" but work strenuously and sensitively at incorporating new people. A church that sees itself as a community welcomes new people and finds a place for them within its fellowship. While it may be normal for a three-year-old to resent the new infant mommy brings home from the hospital, such an attitude among Christians when new (and sometimes gifted!) people enter their community is repugnant. Churches ought to be welcoming, expanding, and developing as they grow with the gifts of new members.

In fact, it is precisely here that we see the fundamental nature of Christian community. When nothing changes and the church stays the same, no one gets upset. But when new people invade the community, as when a transfer student invades a student group or a neighborhood clique, we find out whether or not the church is a true community. When it can reach out and include *because the other person is a Christian*, then the church is operating as a community. But when it finds the poor person unacceptable, the African-American suspicious, or the Irishman intolerable, we are seeing the opposite of what Peter wants in the church. Differences create the need for sympathy and brotherly love. The churches of God are supposed to be communities, and that means expanding, welcoming, and incorporating *all kinds of believers*.

For Peter's day, as for ours, the church as community was vital for survival, for sustaining one's faith in the midst of threats and violence. We cannot compare our "Western trials with society" as identical to the Diaspora churches' experience of persecution, but such an analogy can be made as long as we recognize its distance. If the early church was a community in which Christians found strength to carry on in the midst of troubled times, then the church today ought to play the same role in our world, whatever the "trouble" might be. If our society is noted by an absence of moral values, then Christians need the family of believers to reinforce and strengthen their resolve to inculcate morals in their children and live a life of righteousness. If our society is noted by pluralism and skepticism about knowing "truth," then Christians need the family of believers to confirm their grasp of the truth as taught in the Bible and to hold that truth high. If our society is noted by psychological battery with its increase in technology and its absence of treating workers as genuine individuals in need of love, then Christians need the family of believers to be a society in which they are treated as those worthy of love and affection.

In a brilliant examination of the problem of self-identity in modern society,[22] Anthony Giddens, a noted British sociologist, contends for elements in a "pure relationship" that characterize meaningful relationships and are the desire of people in modern society. He finds seven characteristics of pure relationships: They (1) are not anchored in social or economic life but in the relationship itself; (2) are sought only for what the relationship itself can do for the parties involved; (3) continue to be based on self-examination of its value for the persons involved; (4) root themselves in commitment to one another rather than in some kinship relationship or economical relationship; (5) focus their attention on intimacy in a world that is characterized by a lack of privacy, thus leading to the idea that a pure relationship is in part a haven in an invasive world; (6) base themselves on mutual trust by the persons involved; and (7) create and sustain self-identity in our world.

Giddens has made some penetrating insights into our modern culture. While marriage and family are two areas where the "pure relationship" ought to be found today, the *pure relationship of which he speaks ought also to be a fundamental trait of the church*. In the church people ought to find trust, commitment, the development of self-identity, and growth in one's understanding of what it means to be a Christian in relationship with others. It can be easily said that what the world needs from the church is an alternative society, a society in which people are treated as genuine individuals worthy of love and instruction. Instead, the church has too often repeated those characteristics of society that are sources of despair and pain, instead of offering an alternative to a hurting people. Put differently, if Peter's churches were havens in which people could endure persecution, ours today ought to be havens in which people can endure the onslaught against personal morals and identity. The church is the house of God, and God is holy and loving. He calls people to be holy and loving *in community*.

---

22. A. Giddens, *Modernity and Self-Identity: Self and Society in the Late Modern Age* (Stanford, Calif.: Stanford Univ. Press, 1991). I borrow in what follows from his section on the pure relationship (pp. 88–98).

1 Peter 3:13–22

WHO IS GOING to harm you if you are eager to do good? [14]But even if you should suffer for what is right, you are blessed. "Do not fear what they fear; do not be frightened." [15]But in your hearts set apart Christ as Lord. Always be prepared to give an answer to everyone who asks you to give the reason for the hope that you have. But do this with gentleness and respect, [16]keeping a clear conscience, so that those who speak maliciously against your good behavior in Christ may be ashamed of their slander. [17]It is better, if it is God's will, to suffer for doing good than for doing evil. [18]For Christ died for sins once for all, the righteous for the unrighteous, to bring you to God. He was put to death in the body but made alive by the Spirit, [19]through whom also he went and preached to the spirits in prison [20]who disobeyed long ago when God waited patiently in the days of Noah while the ark was being built. In it only a few people, eight in all, were saved through water, [21]and this water symbolizes baptism that now saves you also—not the removal of dirt from the body but the pledge of a good conscience toward God. It saves you by the resurrection of Jesus Christ, [22]who has gone into heaven and is at God's right hand—with angels, authorities and powers in submission to him.

Original Meaning

PETER HAS NOW instructed various groups with specific guidelines on how to live in a world that is hostile to their presence. What has surrounded the discussion has been the problem of suffering; that is, his guidelines for these groups have been shaped under the fire of persecution. Peter now gives his principles for enduring suffering in a way that is thoroughly Christian.[1] His first guideline, that good behavior will ultimately lead to victory (3:13–22), is followed in chapter 4 with the present value of suffering (4:1–6).

Peter begins the first section with an exhortation to be good, based on the pragmatic concern that such behavior will be less likely to bring persecution (3:13). This, in turn, leads into a discussion on the possible problem: suffering in spite of doing good (3:14). Regardless of what is going on, Peter adds, Christians must be ready always to explain their hope in an unassuming manner (3:15–16). He then repeats (in different terms) the point made in 3:13: The perfect way for the Christian is to do good, for it is better to suffer for doing good than for doing bad (3:17).

Attached to that section on the importance of being good in order to alleviate suffering are some verses about Jesus that have stirred up considerable controversy in the history of the church, not to mention the idea that Jesus "descended into hell" (see the Apostles' Creed). As will be seen below, I believe these verses are attached here to emphasize the *victory* that Jesus achieved in order that the readers can perceive that, if they live the way Jesus did (doing good), they also will find ultimate victory in spite of the persecutions that loom on their horizon. When the next chapter begins, we find ourselves back at the themes discussed at 3:13–18: The suffering of Christ is a model of how to endure suffering. This confirms that 3:18–22 begins with the themes of 3:13–17 but extends them into a digression on more than what was brought up in Peter's concerns for his readers.

The Pragmatic Issue (3:13). While it may be naive for someone to think that good behavior will *always* save the Christian from persecution,[2] such naiveté does not characterize Peter here. To be sure, he asks this question somewhat rhetorically ("Who is going to harm you

---

1. The precise relationship of 3:13–17 to what precedes is not immediately clear. J. N. D. Kelly contends that "the transition seems abrupt" (*Peter and Jude*, 139). However, he goes on to show that the pragmatic concern of being treated more fairly by doing good actually derives from the Old Testament quotation in 3:8–12 itself: The one who wants to see good days ought to live honorably before God.

2. J. N. D. Kelly argues that "harm" here is ultimate harm (*Peter and Jude*, 140), while F. W. Beare sees too much naiveté on the part of the author (*1 Peter*, 162). I contend that all Peter has in mind is the normal deliverance from persecution that (often) comes to the Christian who lives peacefully and winsomely in the face of persecution. See the fine discussion in L. Goppelt, *1 Peter*, 240–41.

if you are eager to do good?"), but he is clearly aware that believers will nonetheless have to endure suffering (cf. 1:6–7; 2:11–12, 15, 18–25; 3:9). But this pragmatic argument fascinates Peter; he has raised the issue in different forms already and uses it particularly as a tool for evangelism (2:11–12, 14–15; 3:1–2, 9, 10–12). The followers of Jesus have been taught this (Matt. 5:16), and early Christian experience for the Petrine churches confirmed it (1 Peter 2:11–12; 3:1–2). What we have, then, is a stance of hope that is baptized into a context of realism (cf. 3:14, 16–17). But ultimately, Peter's assurances are grounded in his final hope: God will eventually (even if not now) establish complete justice.[3]

The Possible Problem (3:14). Showing that he is not naive about this issue of suffering, Peter continues by saying that "even if you should suffer[4] for what is right, you are blessed." While he believes generally in the rule that good behavior will alleviate suffering, he knows that not all opponents will be lenient. Even here he finds something positive: As Jesus taught, those who suffer because of doing what is right will be blessed by God (Matt. 5:10). Peter's exhortation to his readers, when they do have to endure suffering, is not to fear the oppressors. Once again, he draws this teaching from Jesus (Matt. 10:26–33).

The Need for Preparation (3:15–16). Instead of fear, believers are to honor the Lord Christ by being ready to speak boldly about their hope. That is, they are to acknowledge as holy the Lord himself and refuse to profane his name or breach his covenant with them by fearing someone else more than him. But such a disposition is not relegated to one's mental or spiritual attitudes. Rather, to set apart the Lord is a dimension of Peter's exhortation to holy living (1:2, 13, 22; 2:1–2, 5, 24; 4:1–6). This implies a constant willingness to speak up for him,[5] to confess one's allegiance to him, and to witness fearlessly to his saving grace.

---

3. So also J. R. Michaels, *1 Peter*, 184–85.

4. Its likelihood is lessened in this text by Peter's use of the optative mood. By 4:12 the likelihood of suffering seems greater. See the excellent discussion of J. R. Michaels, *1 Peter*, 186. In Greek the optative mood is used to describe an action that is only remotely possible.

5. Some have argued that this defense may have taken place in a courtroom (F. W. Beare, *1 Peter*, 164–65), but most think it better to see this as various kinds of informal defense (e.g., J. R. Michaels, *1 Peter*, 188).

The defense of the Christian concerns their[6] "hope." This term is not to be thought of specifically, in categories like "millennium" or "rewards." Rather, it is to be understood comprehensively, as all that drives the present history toward its destined future. Thus, this term includes terms like "salvation," "inheritance," "hope" (e.g., 1:21), and final vindication (3:18–22). Christians are, in other words, expected to be prepared to speak at any moment about God's salvation of his people through Jesus Christ and how that salvation will manifest itself at the end of history. This very hope sustains them through persecution and gives them strength to carry on when everything looks dismal (cf. 1:6–9).

Such a boldness, Peter warns, ought not to lead to a haughty, ugly defensiveness but to "gentleness and respect, keeping a clear conscience, so that those who speak maliciously against your good behavior in Christ may be ashamed of their slander." Instead of brash defensiveness (which is frequently nothing more than an expression of insecurity), Christians ought to defend the Lord in a humble and respectful manner. Such a manner can lead both to conversions (3:1–2) and to leniency when persecution strikes (3:13). Moreover, if they live a good life before their opponents, they can have a "clear conscience" (Rom. 2:15; 9:1; 2 Cor. 1:12).

The Perfect Way (3:17). Once again, Peter returns to the pragmatic situation: "It is better, if it is God's will, to suffer for doing good than for doing evil." That is, "it is better" both before God and in the practical results for living if people live a godly life. If God wills that they are to suffer,[7] it is better that such takes place when the Christians are doing good rather than evil.

A Digression on the Example of Jesus (3:18–22). These verses begin with the example of Jesus as worthy of understanding and imitating in order to cope with persecution (when God so wills). Jesus suffered as a righteous man (for the unrighteous), but he was also vindicated and now sits at the right hand of God. Between the statement of Jesus' suffering and his vindication Peter brings up some kind of preaching of Jesus

---

6. The text does not make it clear whether "in you" is to be understood corporately (a hope that pervades the Christian community) or individualistically (a hope that prompts the heart of every Christian).

7. Again, Peter uses the optative mood to show that the actual prospects of suffering are far from certain.

to spirits (3:19). These spirits are then subjected to further scrutiny as Peter identifies them with the spirits who were alive at the time of Noah, which in turn gives rise to a Petrine comparison of the delivery of God's people during the Flood (through the ark) with the delivery of contemporary Christians through baptism (3:20–21).[8] All of this is tied off with a conclusion about the vindication of Jesus. Even though Jesus suffered (3:18), he was ultimately vindicated by God (3:22).

Few passages have so many themes and different ideas intertwined. It is no wonder that commentators have shaken their heads in despair! But the main point is not complex. Just as Jesus suffered as a righteous man and was vindicated, so too if the churches of Peter live righteously (as he has exhorted them to do), they will be vindicated and sit with Jesus in the presence of God. Such an understanding of this passage is a typical way of putting this section into focus with the previous verses (3:13–17).

At this point, however, the discussion becomes highly complex and controversial.[9] It has led to three main views: (1) the descent-into-hell view, (2) the preexistent Christ view, and (3) the triumphal proclamation over the spirit-world view. Rather than seeking to defend or to refute any of these views at length, I will briefly explain each view and show how each position fits into the overall theme of this section in 1 Peter.[10]

---

8. This text has also generated considerable discussion in the history of the church. What Peter apparently does is connect the "water delivery" of the ark with the "water delivery" of baptism. What is fundamental to understanding the early church's attitude toward baptism is (1) that early Christians were much more ritualistic than most moderns, and (2) that all early Christians were baptized. Thus, there was no such thing as an "unbaptized believer" in Peter's day. This approach to the rite permits Peter to say things about baptism that many modern Christians would not want to say. The best book I know on baptism is G. R. Beasley-Murray, *Baptism in the New Testament* (Grand Rapids: Eerdmans, 1973); for a survey of the Jewish context, cf. Scot McKnight, *A Light Among the Gentiles: Jewish Missionary Activity in the Second Temple Period* (Minneapolis: Fortress, 1991), 82–85; see further at L. Hartman, "Baptism," *ABD*, 1:583–93.

9. Martin Luther: "A wonderful text is this, and a more obscure passage perhaps than any other in the New Testament, so that I do not know for a certainty just what Peter means." See *Peter and Jude*, 166.

10. It needs to be emphasized that scholars differ seriously with one another here; furthermore, even within the various parts of each general view there are often disagreements. For the first view, see L. Goppelt, *1 Peter*, 255–63; for the second view, see W. A. Grudem, *1 Peter*, 203–39; for the third view, see J. R. Michaels, *1 Peter*, 194–222 (see also R. T. France, "Exegesis in Practice: Two Examples," in *New Testament Interpretation: Essays on Principles and Methods*, ed. I. H. Marshall [Grand Rapids: Eerdmans, 1977], 264–81).

(1) For those who believe Peter is here describing the descent of Jesus into hell after his death, the prominent features are as follows: (a) "through whom" refers to Christ in his disembodied spirit and prior to his resurrection, (b) the "spirits" refer either to the fallen angels of Genesis 6:1–4 or to the spirits of those who died prior to the Flood, (c) the "prison" refers to the underworld, (d) the expression "he went" describes a descent into the underworld, and (e) "preached" refers to a genuine offer of salvation to those who had never had an opportunity to hear the gospel. In general, then, while the text does bring in some extraneous factors, it deals with the vindication of Jesus and his continued ministry in spite of death. As the text goes on, the theme of vindication becomes more prominent.

(2) The view that Peter is describing the preexistent Christ understands the same elements as follows: (a) "through whom" describes the preexistent Christ in the person of Noah, (b) the "spirits" are the contemporaries of Noah who needed to hear the word of God, (c) the "prison" is a metaphor for sin and ignorance or a literal description of their location now, (d) "he went" refers neither to a descent nor an ascent but rather describes simply that Jesus spoke to that generation, and (e) the verb "preached" describes a genuine presentation of the gospel of salvation to the contemporaries of Noah. Once again, the overall compatibility of this view with the theme of 3:13–17 is not hard to understand: Just as Jesus endured suffering in different ways and experienced opposition to his preaching, though he remained faithful, so also the Christians Peter is addressing must remain faithful in spite of suffering.

(3) The view that Peter is here describing a triumphal proclamation of Jesus Christ after his resurrection and prior to his exaltation assumes a Jewish context[11] and takes the following views: (a) "through whom" refers to some kind of spiritual existence of Christ after his resurrection (as the chronology of the text suggests), (b) the "spirits" refer to the fallen angels of Genesis 6:1–4, (c) the "prison" describes the upper regions of binding or, in the words of 2 Peter 2:4, the "pits of darkness," (d) "he went" refers to an *ascent* of Jesus, and (e) "he preached" describes

---

11. So much is the Jewish context important here that R. T. France ("Exegesis in Practice," 265) said: "To try to understand 1 Peter 3:19–20 without a copy of the Book of Enoch at your elbow is to condemn yourself to failure."

the proclamation of victory that Jesus announced over the spirit world as he ascended to the right hand of God. Once again, the compatibility of this view with the theme of 3:13–17 is obvious: Just as Jesus was vindicated before his opponents, so also will the Christians be, if they, like Jesus, remain faithful and righteous to the tasks God has called them to do.

I prefer the third view, but regardless of the view one takes, I would emphasize at this point the need to see this passage in light of its context:[12] the overall theme of vindication. Jesus was righteous and suffered for the unrighteous; God vindicated him by exalting him to his right hand. The churches of Peter need to know that if they remain faithful, like Jesus they too will be vindicated. That is the hope that ought to sustain them as they endure suffering, the hope of which they are to be ready to speak, and the hope that Peter urges them to embrace.

 IN INTERPRETING THIS passage, one needs to recognize how easy it is to drift into the problem verses (3:19, 21) and lose sight of the way in which these particularly disputable passages fit into the general theme of persecution and suffering. That is, focusing on these verses tips the balance against the weight of the passage—how the example of Jesus becomes a source of encouragement for those who are facing suffering. While I would not want to minimize the significance of this passage for formulating special ideas (though I doubt debate about the location of Jesus after his death and before his exaltation advances theology much), it is fundamentally important to interpret these problem verses in light of their overall context.

Furthermore, interpreting problem passages in light of their overall context permits us to see the more basic point of the author here: *vindication*. Vindication, not the precise nuances of baptism (for infants or adults? by immersion or by sprinkling?), is a significant point with many ramifications for Christian living today. That is, while the context is one of suffering—and suffering is comparably rarer today than

---

12. See J. S. Feinberg, "1 Peter 3:18–20, Ancient Mythology, and the Intermediate State," *WTJ* 48 (1986): 303–36, who presents a view much like Grudem but focuses on how the unit fits into the larger context.

in Peter's day—the theme of vindication applies more readily to our world. In general, then, we learn how to move a text into our world today more effectively if we learn to interpret specific elements of a text in light of the larger picture.

On the other hand, I do not want to minimize the importance of examining difficult passages and learning how to make applications of such passages in our world. But such passages need to be dealt with fairly; we need to canvass the interpretations to find the options. As seen above, there are three broad views of the difficult expressions in 3:19. Then we need to examine the evidence for each viewpoint, a procedure that is beyond the scope of this commentary, though I have pointed the reader to a significant piece of bibliography for each view. Finally, we need to come to a conclusion for ourselves. After analyzing the evidence myself, mostly in preparation for class lectures at Trinity Evangelical Divinity School, where students are quick to challenge a professor's points of view, I came to agree with those who thought that Peter was utilizing a view about spirits that was current in the Judaism of his time. Inheriting this tradition, probably from *1 Enoch* (a Jewish pseudepigraph), Peter adds color to it by having Jesus announce his victory over the nether world in his exaltation to the Father.

Finally, we need to be humble about conclusions to passages that are "clearly unclear." Accordingly, while I prefer the view stated above, I am by no means certain (and neither was Martin Luther—a man who did not lack confidence in his interpretations!) that this view is vastly superior to the others. Knowing this, we must respect other views and live with the diversity such interpretations create. We do not often find a passage where its central ideas are so much in dispute; when we do, we need to admit that there is great debate over the meaning of the passage.

Another idea worthy of our attention for application is that of the "pragmatic value of doing good." Several times in this letter, and a couple of times in our passage in particular, Peter urges his fellow Christians to live godly lives *because it will make their difficult situation better.* It would be foolhardy to think Peter was prescribing some surefire method for escaping opposition to the gospel or for a style of living that would make everyone like the churches. His optimistic hope about the value of doing good is tempered by a genuine realism, for in several places he suggests the likelihood of being persecuted. Thus, it is important that his pragmatic argument not be given too much weight in his overall strategy for living Christianly in the world. But the argument is nonetheless valid: If we assume (1) the similarity of human nature and (2) the general limitation of such an argument, then it becomes important to urge Christians who are being persecuted to live godly and good lives *so that those who are against them might be more tolerant of them.* That is, human beings in general do appreciate being respected, and when they are respected, they will be kinder.

Along this same line it makes sense that people who are being opposed will get defensive, even churlish and petulant. For this reason Peter has to urge his readers to be humble and respectful (3:16). In our day, we must remind those who are being opposed for their faithfulness to Christ to avoid using any bitter language and retaliatory speech, however great a temptation it may be. Instead, they must learn to be respectful and humble in their responses to suffering.

Once again, we need to remind ourselves what Peter means by "harm" and "suffering" in our passage. He is not talking about human pains, about children being sassy, or about things not "going our way" in social events. Rather, he is talking about the fundamental opposition to the gospel in society when it is confronted with the truth of the gospel. The way to move this text into our society, then, is to find examples and scenarios where Christians are being persecuted for their faith and where they need to hear both about the pragmatic effects of good behavior and the hope of vindication. That is, we must find those who need to be sustained by the prospect of following the vindication path of Jesus.

FOR THE THEME of vindication to have meaning in our day, we must emphasize both the need to *believe in final justice* and to *live in light of that justice.* Perhaps we have been worn down by the seeming lack of justice in our world, worn down into living in apathy about justice—and especially final justice. Justice in our world seems to be haphazard, even chaotic, and it seems extremely slow in its realization. All of us have followed news stories of murderers or criminals who got "off the hook," received some minor punishment, or were released from jail far too early, only to find that they were arrested shortly thereafter for the same violent crime. When events like this take place before our eyes, it is not surprising that a sense of justice is eroded. Before long we can slide into a state of not believing in ultimate justice.

It is true that sometimes justice does seem to take place in our world; right is rewarded and wrongdoing punished. Our government and its judicial system seem particularly just when it comes to drug busts and abuse of children, and we applaud the government and its officials when they seek to bring a swift and enduring judgment on criminal activity. But we are perplexed when white-collar crime goes unpunished or people who have ruined countless lives can somehow be set free on some "legal technicality." Such haphazard realization of justice erodes our confidence and belief in justice. It is not my task here to criticize or evaluate the legal system, for my readers may come from different countries or different parts of the same country and may have different perceptions of legal systems and justice. My point is merely that we live in a day when many people *have surrendered their belief in justice to the winds of modernity and relativism.* I suspect that many people in our world have simply given up on any sense of justice.

We must attempt to regain a belief in justice, but we must transfer our hope away from governmental officials to God, to his actions both in this world and especially in the next. It is in that future that we need to focus our hope for final vindication and justice. I can weep about children who are abused by their parents, and I can work until my bones grow weary so that less abuse takes place. But I can also be dismayed when I read in the morning newspaper that some judge has released an accused abuser because of a lack of evidence when nearly all followers of the case were certain of the parent's guilt. To be sure, the legal system demands that evidence be clear and incontrovertible to convict someone of abuse. Nonetheless, I still stand aghast when I see abusers released to commit the same crime. What I argue here is that I can cope more readily with this kind of limitation and chaos in society *because I know that someday all will be rectified, the guilty will be fairly punished, and the innocent victims will be vindicated to enjoy the life that God wants for them.*

But dealing with the theme of justice and vindication has a special angle in Peter's letter. We would be unfair to Peter if we left this theme of vindication at the broadest level. We need to apply *his own angle on vindication* in order to be true to the text. And Peter's angle is that vindication will come to the faithful Christians who are being persecuted because of their faith, obedience, and refusal to participate in the sins of their society. Once again, this leads us into the need for finding analogies in our Christian world, analogies of persecution for being a Christian. In such context the message of vindication needs to be heard.

The critical issue here is to think clearly: Where do Christians suffer injustice *because they are Christians?* Such people need to hear the message of Peter, the message of Christ's vindication and ours, and then to learn to live in light of that message so they can live beyond and through the persecution itself.[13] I have known people who were fired because they were honest, people whose children suffered severe forms of ostracism because they sought to live Christian lives, people whose careers were jeopardized because of their faith and denominational affiliations, and people who simply felt "out of it" because they refused to "run with the crowd." Such people readily discover the message of Peter applicable to their own lives and can find solace in the midst of their trouble by reflecting thoughtfully on the ultimate vindication of God. They can learn to say, "Someday—" and so can learn to live in joy today.

Imagine you are teenager where the majority of high schoolers drink alcohol to the point of drunkenness on a semiregular basis, where many of them smoke pot or use addictive drugs, where they go to bed with other teenagers in a casual manner, and where that same teenage society knows who does these things and who does not. Then imagine that you would not be accepted (to some degree) if you refused to go along with these activities. Peter's message says something to you about your situation. He knows how difficult it is to fight off pressures for acceptance and conformity; he knows that Christians seek to live holy and good lives and so refrain from sinful behaviors; and he knows that you will need to have special faith and courage to endure. My contention is that Peter wants you to focus on the final day when God will bring about ultimate justice. He wants you to say: (1) I will

---

13. See D. A. Carson, *How Long, O Lord? Reflections on Suffering and Evil* (Grand Rapids: Baker, 1990), esp. 81–91.

not conform to the sinful habits of my peers and friends; (2) I will remain faithful to the teachings of Jesus by living faithfully and obediently; (3) I will endure lonely nights and few friends; (4) I will find my friends in those who seek, with me, to be obedient; and (5) I will look forward to the day when God shows that faithfulness rather than acceptance is the truer virtue.

Maybe I am sensitive to these issues because I have two teenagers and because I coach basketball at a high school. But these issues are the very ones our youth are constantly facing. Furthermore, whether we are aware of them or not, similar kinds of peer pressure to conform also face adults. These pressures are "a form of persecution" in the sense that they are socially driven institutions that seek to prevent us from obeying the words of the apostles and the teachings of Jesus. We need to learn, with Jesus, to be just; we need to listen to Peter and seek to be obedient. And we especially need to get our eyes off the problems of acceptance and get them focused squarely on God's final day of vindication, when all will be made right and all true virtues will appear for what they are: the will of God, now done on earth as it is heaven.

1 Peter 4:1–6

THEREFORE, SINCE CHRIST suffered in his body, arm yourselves also with the same attitude, because he who has suffered in his body is done with sin. ²As a result, he does not live the rest of his earthly life for evil human desires, but rather for the will of God. ³For you have spent enough time in the past doing what pagans choose to do—living in debauchery, lust, drunkenness, orgies, carousing and detestable idolatry. ⁴They think it strange that you do not plunge with them into the same flood of dissipation, and they heap abuse on you. ⁵But they will have to give account to him who is ready to judge the living and the dead. ⁶For this is the reason the gospel was preached even to those who are now dead, so that they might be judged according to men in regard to the body, but live according to God in regard to the spirit.

Original Meaning

IN THE CENTRAL section of 1 Peter, extending from 2:11–4:11, Peter covers several topics, including his general principles (2:11–12), the specific application of these principles for special groups (2:13–3:12), guidelines for those who are enduring suffering (3:13–4:6), and advice for the family of God (4:7–11). Our present section (4:1–6) is the second piece of advice Peter gives to those who face suffering for their Christian faith. In the first piece (3:13–22), Peter encouraged the Christians to remain faithful to their tasks in light of the coming vindication of God. Now he focuses on the effects of suffering on the Christian life.

After giving his exhortation to be like Christ (4:1a), Peter gives a reason for suffering like Christ: "because he who has suffered in his body is done with sin" (4:1b). This point is carried on in 4:2 as Peter shows the meaning of "done with sin." He then gives another reason for learning to suffer like Christ: "For you have spent enough time in the past doing what pagans choose to do" (4:3). Not only have they "spent enough time," but those with whom they had lived are themselves surprised at their conversions, to the point that they are abusing them (4:4). Peter warns that such people will have to answer to God for their abuse (4:5; cf. 2:12). In verse 6, Peter appends a comment on an issue raised in 4:5, that the opponents of the gospel will have to answer for their behavior to the God will "judge the living and the dead." He observes that this is "the reason the gospel was preached even to those who are now dead." In other words, the odd expression about preaching to the dead must be understood as a comment on verse 5.

The Exhortation (4:1a). In 3:18, Peter started to talk about the suffering of Jesus but went hurriedly to the end of his life, a vindication (3:22). He now begins again at the same point (suffering),[1] but this time contends with his readers that suffering is good for the Christian life. His strategy is for the mental dimension of life. To survive persecution in an obedient manner, Christians must have proper mental preparation (cf. 1:13): "Arm yourselves also with the same attitude" that Christ had. In the context of Peter's letter, the proper attitude includes a steadfast hope for vindication (1:13; 3:18–22), a fear of God (3:15), and a commitment to live (including suffering) in such a way that outsiders see the grace of God (cf. 2:18–25; 3:1–2, 15–16). But the fundamental attitude is that Christ surrendered himself to the God whom he knew would judge justly and save (2:23).

Reason Number One: It Helps Your Obedience (4:1b–2). Christians ought to have the same mental approach as Jesus had "because he who has suffered in his body is done with sin." This verse has generated several explanations, and it is worth our while, because of the importance of this verse in the overall point of the paragraph, to consider the views and the evidence called in for each, and then to consider which option is the strongest.[2]

---

1. Many commentators maintain that Peter is focusing on the death of Jesus in this verse, but such a view makes his point much more difficult to understand. How, we might ask, does "death" help one to cease from sin in any meaningful way? Is it not obvious to say that death stops sin in one's life? But, if we ask instead how suffering in this life helps, we find clues in 4:2–5: Suffering helps to purge one's life of sin. Thus, I suggest that, while Christ's suffering did include his death, this passage is not concerned with his "suffering unto death" but with his "suffering" as such. For discussion, see L. Goppelt, *1 Peter*, 279.

2. See the lengthy discussions in J. R. Michaels, *1 Peter*, 225–29; L. Goppelt, *1 Peter*, 278–82; see also W. A. Grudem, *1 Peter*, 166–67; P. Davids, *1 Peter*, 148–50.

Some argue that Peter has in mind only the inevitable transfer (seen here as a suffering death) from a sinful to a saved state that takes place at conversion (or baptism), as can be seen in Paul (cf. Rom. 6:1–12) and John (1 John 5:18–19).[3] Others contend that Peter is dealing more generically: The one who suffers physically learns from such experiences not to sin but to value the obedient life.[4] A variation of this second view is that the one who suffers has chosen to break definitively from sin.[5] A final view particularizes the phrase "he who has suffered" so that it refers only to the suffering Christ. That is, "he who has suffered" is Christ, and he is the example to whom Peter is appealing. In this context, "is done with sin" means that Christ did away with sin.[6]

It is hard to decide what evidence counts the most in deciding among these options. I would eliminate the third option (the variation of the second view) because it seems to be little more than a nuancing of the first and second views. Since the first two views are similar except on the precise meaning of "suffer," it is best to decide between them by examining what "suffer" means in 1 Peter. Clearly, the term refers too consistently to "physical suffering" to expect readers to read this as a conversion term.[7] Thus, the options reduce themselves down to who is suffering. Is it Christ? Or is it the Christians?

In my judgment, since Peter has moved in this verse from Christ ("since Christ suffered in his body") to Christians ("arm yourselves also with the same attitude"), it makes more sense to think he is still speaking of Christians in the next clause ("because he who has suffered in his body is done with sin"). Furthermore, the use of "is done with sin" for describing the work of Christ is unusual and inconsistent with Peter's other expressions for the achievements of the cross (cf. 1:18; 2:21, 24; 3:18). Finally, 4:2 goes on to explain the Christian's subsequent life; this suggests Peter has the Christian (not Christ) in mind at 4:1b. Thus, the most likely interpretation of this difficult expression

---

3. See, e.g., J. N. D. Kelly, *Peter and Jude*, 166–69; F. W. Beare, *1 Peter*, 179. The particular expression in Paul is "because anyone who has died has been freed from sin" (Rom. 6:17). See also E. Clowney, *1 Peter*, 169–71.

4. So E. G. Selwyn, *1 Peter*, 209–10 (cf. 1 Cor. 5:5).

5. W. A. Grudem, *1 Peter*, 167.

6. For this fourth view, see L. Goppelt, *1 Peter*, 280–82; J. R. Michaels, *1 Peter*, 225–29.

7. See 1 Peter 2:19, 20, 21, 23; 3:14, 17, 18; 4:1a, 15, 19; 5:10.

is that it refers to Christians who are suffering and that they learn not to sin by undergoing persecution.

However, to be fair to all sides, we do recognize another possibility: that Peter is summing the Christian's entire life on earth as a life of suffering. In this case, "is done with sin" describes not some state on earth (post-conversion/suffering holiness) but their eternal reward. Just as Christ got to sit down at his Father's right hand and enjoy his victory, so also will the Christians.[8] While there is some contextual analogy (3:18—22) for this view, 4:2—5 leads the reader to think not in terms of the eternal reward for obedience, but rather in terms of a kind of life on earth—a life not so much of sinlessness, but of obedience.[9] Thus, the theme of 4:2 follows naturally from our interpretation of 4:1b: "As a result, he does not live the rest of his earthly life for evil human desires, but rather for the will of God."

Reason Number Two: You Have Done Enough Sin (4:3). That suffering can work obedience into a Christian's life is an early Christian theme (James 1:2—4), but Peter's next idea is not so common: "After all," he says in essence, "you have sinned enough"[10] (4:3). While it is difficult to know what to infer from such a comment (e.g., did Peter think everyone was appointed to a certain amount of sin?), it is clear that his pragmatism takes over again: Just as good behavior will help get Christians out of tough situations, and just as suffering purges the Christian from sin, so also these same Christians have sinned more than enough for a lifetime,[11] and it is time for them to get on with a life of obedience.

Explanation of the Former Crowd (4:4—5). The very sins that once characterized the Christians' patterns of behavior have now been abandoned, partly because of the healing effects of suffering. But those behaviors continued among their old friends, who, Peter tells us, "think it strange that you do not plunge with them into the same flood of dissipation, and they heap abuse on you" (cf. 1:18). These surprised former friends, who now abuse them verbally, are ultimately blasphemers

---

8. On this see P. Davids, *1 Peter*, 149—50.

9. So W. A. Grudem, *1 Peter*, 167.

10. J. N. D. Kelly suggests that "enough" means "more than enough." See *Peter and Jude*, 169. J. R. Michaels adds "too much in fact"; *1 Peter*, 230.

11. On the list of sins, which focus on drinking and sexual sins, see esp. J. R. Michaels, *1 Peter*, 230—32.

(cf. 2:12; 3:16).[12] Accordingly, Peter informs the Christians of Asia Minor that "they will have to give account to him[13] who is ready to judge the living and the dead" (4:5). As at 2:12, so here the idea is less one of hopeful expectation of final reward than a threat of judgment on those who sin.

An Added Note (4:6). Almost as an afterthought Peter adds, "For this is the reason the gospel was preached[14] even to those who are now[15] dead, so that they might be judged according to men in regard to the body, but live according to God in regard to the spirit." This afterthought has spirited a great discussion. Are the "dead" those to whom Christ preached after his crucifixion (3:19), the spiritually dead who are now alive, or the Christians of Peter's churches who have already died?[16] The vast majority of commentators today argue that Peter is referring to Christians in Asia Minor who heard the gospel while alive but are now physically dead.

Because this life is only a prelude to life after death, the gospel was preached to those who are (now) dead. And because those people will have to give an account to God for their life, everyone must hear the gospel. Finally, Peter expresses the ultimate purpose of preaching, that people, regardless of what happens to them in this life, might be able to live eternally (i.e., in "spirit") with God.[17] The gospel is preached to all, including the (now) dead, because ultimately this life is only a pre-

---

12. Some have understood the "heap abuse on you" (Gk. *blasphemountes*) as a vocative ("those blasphemers") and even attached it to 4:5. So J. R. Michaels, *1 Peter*, 233—34.

13. This could be either the Father (Rom. 2:6; 3:6) or the Son (cf. Matt. 25:31—46; Luke 21:34—36; Acts 10:42; Rom. 14:9; 2 Tim. 4:1). The evidence of 1 Peter tips the balance in favor of the Father (cf. 1:17; 2:23), but evidence from Acts 10:42, in a speech of Peter, makes one cautious. See the discussion in J. R. Michaels, *1 Peter*, 235.

14. Who the evangelist is in this verse depends on how one interprets "dead." It could refer to Christ or, more likely, to the evangelists in Peter's churches, including Peter himself. See J. N. D. Kelly, *Peter and Jude*, 172—75.

15. The word "now" has been added by the NIV. Such a translation, while possibly correct, leads the reader to exclude other interpretations. The NRSV has just "dead."

16. For the discussion, cf. J. R. Michaels, *1 Peter*, 235—38.

17. The NRSV reads, "though they had been judged in the flesh as everyone is judged, they might live in the spirit as God does." This suggests a judgment for our present life but the option of eternal life in the spirit for those who survive God's judgment. I prefer the positions taken in the NIV; Peter's idea here is similar to that in 2:4. Thus, he has in mind the distinction between what happens to the righteous in this life (suffering and martyred) and what happens before God (vindication). See the excellent discussion of J. R. Michaels, *1 Peter*, 238—41.

lude to a greater and endless world beyond. Those who hear the gospel and respond, *even if they are killed for their faith*, will be vindicated ultimately before God.

INTERPRETING ANCIENT TEXTS that touch on expressions and ideas that are more than a little problematic makes it doubly difficult to move the same texts into our modern world. In my nearly three decades of sitting in Sunday school and listening to sermons, both in a house of worship and in a seminary chapel, I have never heard a sermon on this passage, nor I have ever preached on this passage myself. However, I have often heard messages about the positive effects of suffering, and I have heard many sermons rooted in the idea of needing to preach to all people because someday we will have to answer to God.

One of the reasons expository preaching[18] is healthy for the church is because it does what has not been done in my experience: expose the church *to every passage in the Bible*, whether they are simple and transparent (like Matt. 5–7) or exceedingly difficult (like Heb. 6:4–6). In moving this text into our world, I begin with the observation that we must do this *simply because it is there and is the Word of God*. I am not denying that there are some difficult things to interpret and apply in this text; I am saying that we need to struggle to bring all of the text into our world.

To be sure, some things are readily transparent and valuable—for instance, that *suffering improves the moral life of the believer*. Most Christians have experienced some kind of opposition because of their faith, whether it is a blank stare at a suggestion they make or outright physical persecution. And those who have endured that can readily testify that such an experience has strengthened their faith (even if they failed in some way). I remember as a high schooler being laughed at for being a Christian; I remember that it hurt, but I also remember that such opposition aided in confirming my faith and strengthening my trust in God. But what we ought to admit even here is that our kind

---

18. See esp. J. R. W. Stott, *Between Two Worlds: The Art of Preaching in the Twentieth Century* (Grand Rapids: Eerdmans, 1982), 125–33.

of suffering is still strikingly unlike the persecution the Christians in Asia Minor endured, for their suffering could end up quickly in death. So even here, when we have struggled to find something relevant, we may still be considerably different in our orientation than the ancient world.

Sometimes passages raise issues that are distant from our modern world, even though there are invariably other ideas in that passage that are relevant to our lives. It is my belief that the most important applications of Scripture can only be made when the *central thrust of the passage* is the *central thrust of the application*. But what if the central thrust of the text is completely at variance with one's life and one's culture? It is important, then, that the interpreter and reader find applications that are meaningful, even if not central to the passage. In other words, sometimes a secondary meaning or a secondary application has to be made. While I find this kind of application taking place regularly in sermons and Bible studies (and sometimes I am disappointed that more struggle did not take place to find a more central application), such a procedure is necessary at times and becomes a regular part of applying the Bible. Applications like this express the fundamental belief that the whole Bible is valuable for Christian living (2 Tim. 3:16–17). Even here, however, the meaning and application must be taken from the text and not from ideas not in the text.

In the present passage, the main thrust is the moral value of suffering, a thrust that is largely outside the normal experience of the vast majority of Western Christians today. I have, in several instances, attempted to show how Peter's teaching addressed to sufferers can be made relevant in our world, applying such teachings to those in the business world and those in school (especially secular university) settings. I do not want to minimize either of these contexts, nor am I suggesting that there are not other areas where applications could be made. However, we do want to have applications for as broad a reach of our audience as is possible, and thus we may at times need to move to less central ideas in a passage.[19]

What are some examples of this kind of procedure? One thing Peter does here is to contrast Christian morality and non-Christian lifestyles. Thus, some interpreters may choose to focus on this contrast

---

19. Once again, however, this should not be done frequently. If we find that we do this frequently we need to look to other passages or we need to ask ourselves if we are truly submissive to God's Word.

even though it is less central to the passage than the value of suffering. Thus, we can explore the nature of Christian morality in various environments (business, neighborhood relations, social practices, or parties). Or we can explore this theme in more than one culture, insofar as each culture has its own set of mores that dominate the ethical values of that society. Contrasts can made because Christian morality constructs a different lifestyle. Still another example, one that we will look at briefly in our next section, is the example of Jesus. Peter begins our section on the note of Jesus' suffering as a paradigm for Christian suffering, even though he does not develop this theme here. Interpreters could choose to look at this theme more closely by placing 4:1a into the larger context of 1 Peter, taking special note of 2:18–25 and 3:18.

Another final path for bringing this word into our world is to focus on the judgment of God because this is a transcultural feature of Peter's message. We may face different cultures (e.g., a massively pluralistic one or a massively unified, Buddhist one), but we must all be prepared to give an account of our lives to God at the end of history. While I may not stare suffering in the face every day and you may, each of us will be judged by God. This permits an application that is as easy as it is universal. Focusing on the common, broader elements of a passage can often lead to penetrating applications. To this we can now turn.

Contemporary Significance

IT IS NOT difficult to extend the principle of 4:5–6 into our world by observing that we need to live in light of the Judgment Day. The threat of judgment is healthy to the Christian life, however unpopular it might be in our world. Recently at a gathering I attended, a young lady began to speak up about her church. She informed us that "when she grew up," the entire emphasis was on "hell, the devil, and the judgment;" but now, she continued, "all we are permitted to talk about is love. Love is all that matters now." She said this with considerable approval, and it is this kind of mental outlook that deserves careful analysis.

It may be the case that this woman's upbringing was in some kind of Christian church that did (over)emphasize judgment and hell (she called it, rather humorously, "fire and brinestone"). We find ourselves at the opposite extreme today: no threat of judgment—anywhere. We do find no threat of judgment in theology or morals, in our legal system (where a good lawyer seems able to get anyone off the hook), or in our social world. But what makes a moral life healthy is the *threat of judgment that derives from an appreciation of the holiness of God.* To be sure, it can be overdone, just as love or anything else can be overdone. But the solution to an overemphasis is not its neglect; rather, it is to bring the emphasized idea back into its biblical and realistic perspective. I do not want to go to bed at night worrying about whether I will be damned by God, but neither do I want a God who is so soft that I do not have to fear him or stand in awe of his judgment if I live in sin. In the word of John Stott: "To live, work and witness in conscious antic-ipation of Christ's parousia and judgment is a wholesome stimulus to faithfulness."[20]

Consequences for our behavior, then, is an important theme for our world. The threat of judgment here is part of Peter's encouragement to live faithfully in the context of persecution. But that threat can be removed, for the moment, from its context and treated separately because it is a fundamental principle that transcends its context. Judg-ment is, after all, the foundation for all kinds of ethical exhortations. So even if we separate this theme from that of suffering, we are still in conformity to the text's concern for us to live in light of God's judg-ment.

At the same time, it is best to treat the theme of judgment in its fuller context (preserving its connection to suffering) because (1) it forces us to treat the text *as it is* rather than as we would like it to be, and (2) it gives the "threat of judgment theme" its special context. That is, peo-ple who are being persecuted find special comfort in knowing that God is Judge because they are experiencing an unjust judgment from other humans. When the context of the interpreter is analogous to the context of the original text, then special resonances can be found.

A suggestive direction in applying this passage begins with the importance of *the example of Christ* for Christian living. Verse 1 begins with the example of Christ and roots its exhortation in that example: Just as Christ suffered, so we should be prepared to *follow his example,*

---

20. J. R. W. Stott, *The Contemporary Christian: Applying God's Word to Today's World* (Down-ers Grove, Ill.: InterVarsity, 1992), 373.

regardless of our situation and our context. If we are following him, learning to live the way he lived, and seeking to shape our lives after his life, then it is *natural* for us to encounter any kind of persecution with a proper mindset. Maybe Peter mentions the example of Christ because of what he thinks *will happen* more than what he knows *is already happening*, though I tend to think he knows that suffering is already happening. He exhorts his churches to assume the stance of Jesus as they live in an unbelieving world.

I know of no better way to put this into practice than to learn to ask ourselves, "What would Jesus do here?"[21] Clearly there are many things about the life of Jesus that cannot be imitated. We cannot die a substitutionary death or be raised for others, nor can we do stupendous things like walking on water. But in the general patterns of life we can live in such a way that we can constantly ask ourselves how Jesus would act in a given situation. Peter's concern is with responding the way Jesus did when he was persecuted (2:21–25; 3:18–19; 4:1), and the exemplary nature of Jesus' life is still in force.

We see here the *Christocentric* nature of early Christian theology, which I contrast with the *moralistic* nature of much of modern Christian theology. It is not uncommon to hear today that Gandhi was Christian in much of what he did, especially in his pacifistic and gentle wisdom; but if we say this, we lose the Christocentric anchor of our faith. To be sure, Gandhi was a wonderful, pious man, but behavior is only Christian when it is consciously obedient to Jesus Christ. There are clear parallels, particularly at the moral level, among various religions in our world; but if Jesus Christ is eliminated from the picture, a moral practice is not Christian. Peter anchors his moral practice (suffering unjustly) in the example of Jesus, thus giving it a different basis and motivation. Christians are to suffer, not because suffering makes them better people (which it can do), nor because it makes them conscious of a higher world (which it can also do), but because Jesus himself suffered—and they are his followers.

In his excellent book *The Contemporary Christian*, John Stott gets to the heart of this issue when he surveys the Christian idea of mission.[22]

---

21. The classic treatment of following Jesus is Thomas à Kempis, *The Imitation of Christ* (Grand Rapids: Zondervan, 1983 [reprint ed. 1418]).

22. See J. R. W. Stott, *The Contemporary Christian*, 356–74.

Each aspect of this theme is anchored in Christology, permitting him to expound mission in a truly Christocentric form. The *model* for mission is the incarnation of Christ, the *cost* of mission finds its parallel in the cross of Christ, the *mandate* for mission is founded on the authority granted to Jesus as a result of his resurrection, the *incentive* for mission is the exaltation of Christ, the *power* for mission comes from the "Spirit-gift" of Christ, and the *urgency* for mission is the parousia of Christ. Each aspect of the church's mission is anchored in the ministry of Jesus Christ, permitting Stott to title his chapter the "Christology of Mission." When Christians learn to think Christocentrically, they begin to think and act in a fully Christian manner. Peter was like this: He anchored his exhortation to suffer in the life of Jesus and gave to his exhortation an indelible Christian stamp.

A final consideration is the *change of life* that Christians in Asia Minor had experienced. Peter's words in 4:3 reveal a group of converts whose former lives were anything but virtuous; they did more than their share of sexual sins and alcoholic excesses. Now, however, their former "comrades in sin" are shocked at their newly formed holy lifestyles (4:4). Such changes are normal in the stories of Christians of all ages. The fundamental feature is the radical change of life that occurs in those who become Christians and begin to follow Jesus. Mental habits, sexual behaviors, social interactions—each of these areas reveal serious changes on the part of many Christians. And it is not at all unusual to find that believers speak of "former friends," not because they no longer like their former "comrades in sin," but because they have found their new lifestyle of following Jesus makes them uncomfortable with those people,[23] and, more importantly, because those former friends no longer find any "common bond" with Christians.

One of my friends has told me how he had to leave his "B. C. Group" (Before Christ Group) when he became a Christian because all they did together was drink to the point of drunkenness or take drugs until they were high. He missed them and longed for their conversion (and he shared the gospel with them frequently), but he knew he had to restrict his times with them because he was, due to his carnal nature, tempted to drink and do drugs. By the time he was "cured" of his desire

---

23. Many times the former group becomes a source of serious temptation for the convert; as a result, the convert feels compelled to restrict social communication with it.

for mind-altering substances, he had graduated from college and moved on to better things. His story is but one example of countless Christians who have experienced, as a result of their conversion, a complete change of social groups. Peter's churches had gone through that kind of change. They therefore provide an early example of what happens when people establish a lifestyle that follows Jesus.

1 Peter 4:7–11

T HE END OF all things is near. Therefore be clear
minded and self-controlled so that you can pray.
⁸Above all, love each other deeply, because love
covers over a multitude of sins. ⁹Offer hospitality to one
another without grumbling. ¹⁰Each one should use whatever gift he has received to serve others, faithfully
administering God's grace in its various forms. ¹¹If anyone speaks, he should do it as one speaking the very
words of God. If anyone serves, he should do it with the
strength God provides, so that in all things God may be
praised through Jesus Christ. To him be the glory and
the power for ever and ever. Amen.

Original Meaning

T HESE VERSES FORM the fourth and final section of Peter's exhortations to various social
groups (2:11–4:11). Here he provides general instructions for the entire family of God.
In essence, these exhortations can be summarized as *eschatological ethics*.
That is, Peter exhorts believers to pray (v. 7b), to love one another
(v. 8), to be hospitable (v. 9) and to exercise their spiritual gifts (vv. 10–
11a) *in light of the End*. The foundation is stated in verse 7a: "The end of
all things is near." Put differently, believers ought to govern their lives
by the perception that since the end of the world is near, they should
live in light of God's judgment.[1]

This paragraph is not to be seen as some tag-on at the end of a
section.[2] Rather, it pulls together some important themes in the letter, highlighting the dominance of eschatology for Christian ethics
(cf. 1:3–5, 7, 9, 13; 2:12; 3:15; 4:5–6, 13, 17–19; 5:1, 4, 6). It also

---

1. Peter ends the unit, revealing some kind of climax to a major section, with a doxology (4:11b).

2. In fact, the section reads almost the like the conclusion to a letter. With the doxology at 4:11, one could easily think the letter is over. Many have concluded that 4:12–5:14
(or perhaps 4:12–5:11) were added on after the completion of this letter. But see J. N. D.
Kelly, *Peter and Jude*, 182.

recapitulates the centrality of the church in Peter's understanding of Christian ethics (1:1–2, 10–12, 22; 2:1–10; 3:8–12; 5:1–4). The people of God is the church and the church is the people of God, which should live with integrity, love, and holiness as it awaits the Lord's return. The church is the eschatological people of God, and it is dominated by the hope of the Last Day as much as it lives in the awe of God's final discerning judgment (4:17–19).

The Coming Day: The Foundation of Ethics (4:7a). To say that "the end of all things is near" is to say that Peter believed, in some sense, that the end[3] of history was imminent.[4] That End involved the Final Judgment (4:6), and it was "near."[5] It is important for us to realize that Peter roots his ethical exhortations in 4:7b–11 in this perception of history and the judgment.

However, the history of scholarship has been dotted with scholars who have argued that because Peter (and others) believed that the end of history was imminent but did not take place as they thought it would, they were therefore wrong and the Christian conception of history is wrong. The weaknesses of this position cannot be addressed here in depth, but several considerations are important here. (1) A belief that the next event would usher in the end events was typical of Jewish prophecy. Jewish prophets always envisioned the next big event on their "prophetic calendar" as the event that would usher in the last days—*and it never did*. (2) When the next event did not usher in the last days, no one thought the Jewish prophets were wrong. (3) The reason they thought this way was not some kind of psychological denial but because the people of God recognized that a Jewish prophets'

---

3. Some have argued that "end" here might mean little more than that all of the decisive events in God's redemptive plan have now been revealed; all that remains is the final act to bring history to a close. The idea of imminency, therefore, is simply the unknown state in which the church must live. But, if we understand Jewish prophecy properly, then imminency can mean what it seems to mean (they believed the end of the world would come soon), and the issue of there being some kind of enthusiastic foolishness in all this can be swept away.

4. The term "imminent" includes, but is not to be restricted to, the idea that the End may occur suddenly and within a few moments. Such a concept includes the perception that history may come to an end "within a generation" or "in conjunction with the next event on God's calendar."

5. The Greek word behind our "near" is *engiken*, meaning "has drawn near" (see Matt. 3:2; 4:17; 10:7; 21:1, 34; Luke 7:12; 15:1; Rom. 13:12; James 5:8); BAGD, 213.

vision was shortsighted in that they could not see the entire chronology of God's plan.[6] Thus, while I do think Peter presented his ethical exhortations in light of a view that the end of history was imminent, I do not think such a view was mistaken. Rather, it was how Jewish prophecy worked.[7]

Exhortation Number 1: Pray (4:7b). Like 1:13, Peter's first bit of advice is that Christians keep themselves mentally and spiritually alert: "Therefore be clear minded and self-controlled so that you can pray." The expressions here are to be understood as a twofold injunction to mental alertness, with the goal of having an effective prayer life. As was the case with the alert husband (3:7) and the obedient community (3:12), so here with the entire church: If they stay alert, they will be effective in prayer (cf. Eph. 6:18; Col. 4:2). Thinking that the end of history is at the door and the Judge is about to enter through it can energize one's prayers and lead to a specially effective focus in those prayers.

Exhortation Number 2: Love (4:8). Earlier in the letter Peter's ethics found one of their core values in "love" (cf. 1:22–25; 2:17; 3:8); now this communal ethic rises powerfully to the top.[8] When the church is being threatened by persecution and takes comfort in the coming end of history because God will judge justly, that same church strengthens its faith by relating to one another in love. Peter's exhortation is that they are to love one another "deeply" (cf. 1:22); that is, they are to work at loving one another because doing so in the midst of stress is difficult. Since familial, business, and social relationships tend to become frayed and tested when difficulties arise, Peter urges them to love one

---

6. For a more complete discussion of the nature of prophetic language, see G. B. Caird, *The Language and Imagery of the Bible* (Philadelphia: Westminster, 1980), 243–71; see also his *New Testament Theology*, ed. L. D. Hurst (New York: Oxford, 1994), 250–67. While there may be little consensus here, I contend that Peter's vision of the future was most conditioned by his perception of A.D. 70 as the critical event on the horizon. Peter is among the vast majority of early Christians who inferred from the presence of persecution that the end must be near. See also I. H. Marshall, *1 Peter*, 140–41.

7. See also B. Witherington III, *Jesus, Paul, and the End of the World: A Comparative Study in New Testament Eschatology* (Downers Grove, Ill.: InterVarsity, 1992), though he does not discuss 1 Peter. See also R. H. Stein, *Playing by the Rules: A Basic Guide to Interpreting the Bible* (Grand Rapids: Baker, 1994), 89–100 (who uses "impressionism" as an analogy to the nature of prophetic language); W. W. Klein, C. L. Blomberg, and R. L. Hubbard, Jr., *Introduction to Biblical Interpretation* (Dallas: Word, 1993), 292–312.

8. See L. L. Morris, *The Testaments of Love: A Study of Love in the Bible* (Grand Rapids: Eerdmans, 1981), esp. 193–227.

another with great effort because he knows how much work it takes with the dark cloud of persecution and stress hovering above.

Loving one another when things are tough is important "because love covers over a multitude of sins."[9] We have all probably heard this statement bandied about to justify many kinds of behaviors, but what does this saying mean for Peter? That loving others now will procure forgiveness from God at the end[10] (cf. Matt. 25:31–46)? That loving others leads a community to holier and more forgiving behaviors[11] (cf. 1 Cor. 13:7)? Or, developing this second view, that loving others is the sure sign that they have put away sinful behaviors[12] (2:24; 4:1–2)? The essential ambiguity of the proverb, as well as the lack of substantial parallel ideas in 1 Peter, means that we are not able to know for sure. But in light of how the saying came to be connected in the early church with the second view, I contend that we are probably better off understanding the saying to be a social one by Peter: The community that loves one another is able to forgive one another more rapidly when minor issues arise.

Exhortation Number 3: Be Hospitable (4:9). Hospitality is a specific example of loving one another—this time by receiving others into our homes, making them feel welcome, meeting their needs, and providing for them a place of fellowship and acceptance. But Peter knows that people are better at conforming externally than at doing something from the heart. Accordingly, he adds "without grumbling." Hospitality formed the foundation of the Christian movement.[13] When Jesus sent out the Twelve, they were to find places to stay that offered hospitality (Matt. 10:11–13). When he needed a place for the Last Supper, he assumed a place of hospitality would be found (26:17–19). And the early church's practice of celebrating the Lord's Supper together (1 Cor. 11:17–34) is rooted in Jesus' practice of eating with

---

9. Proverbs 10:12 reads, "Love covers over all wrongs"; many think Peter is either quoting (though not literally) or at least alluding to that verse. Others have argued, perhaps more accurately, that Peter is simply quoting a long line of others who have appealed to the same set of words to express a variety of ideas (cf. J. R. Michaels, *1 Peter*, 246–47). Accordingly, a saying like this is found at James 5:20; 1 Clement 49:5; 2 Clement 16:4.

10. See the sensitive remarks of J. N. D. Kelly, *Peter and Jude*, 178.

11. So, for example, F. W. Beare, *1 Peter*, 184–85; L. Goppelt, *1 Peter*, 298–99; W. A. Grudem, *1 Peter*, 173–74.

12. J. R. Michaels, *1 Peter*, 247.

13. See J. N. D. Kelly, *Peter and Jude*, 178–79; esp. J. Koenig, "Hospitality," *ABD*, 3:299–301.

his disciples (Matt. 9:9–13). Thus, the early church regularly expressed its love for one another within the context of hospitality.

Exhortation Number 4: Exercise Your Gifts (4:10–11a). That the End is near prompts Peter to exhort believers to love one another beyond the idea of hospitality; they are to use their gifts "to serve others, faithfully administering God's grace[14] in its various forms" (4:10). Loving one another enables one to put up with others (4:8), instigates hospitality (4:9), and means using one's gifts to help other people (4:10–11). Spiritual gifts is a special topic in Paul's letters (cf. Rom. 12:6–8; 1 Cor. 12:8–10, 28–30; Eph. 4:11), and some maintain that Peter is echoing Paul's ideas here. Whatever the origin of Peter's ideas—and a Pauline or an early Christian tradition is likely—the purpose of Peter's use of the theme of spiritual gifts is to illustrate the importance of loving one another in the Christian community. Thus, as in 1 Corinthians 12–14, love is the context for the exercise of spiritual gifts in the church.

Whatever Christians are gifted to do, those gifts are to be exercised in such a way that they reflect their divine origin and purposes: "If anyone speaks, he should do it as one speaking the very words of God. If anyone serves, he should do it with the strength God provides, so that in all things God may be praised through Jesus Christ." That is, if someone is called on to speak in the presence of believers or if God's Spirit prompts a person to speak to the congregation, that person ought to take the opportunity so seriously that the words spoken be considered with reverence.[15]

To God Be the Glory! (4:11b). Peter concludes his exhortation to use all gifts from God in a way that brings him glory with a doxology. This is a short prayer of praise to God—or is praise ascribed to Jesus Christ? Because it would be unnecessarily redundant to ascribe praise once again to God (4:11a does that), it seems more probable that this doxology has Jesus Christ as its object.[16] God glorifies himself through his Son, and the Son is at work in the prayer and loving ministries of the church.

---

14. The words "grace" and "gifts" are derived from the same root; that is, a gift is an individual expression of God's grace.

15. So W. A. Grudem, *The Gift of Prophecy in the New Testament and Today* (Westchester, Ill.: Crossway, 1988), 105.

16. So J. R. Michaels, *1 Peter*, 252–53. In Greek the natural antecedent of "to him" is Jesus Christ, not God (the Father).

Bridging Contexts

THESE VERSES CONTAIN both difficult and specific directives for Peter's churches. In what follows I have chosen to focus on the larger pattern of his thought—the eschatological context for ethics. In so doing, however, I do not want to minimize the importance of other considerations. If Peter's primary thrust here is to drive home the urgency of the hour and the consequent need for prayer (4:7b) and love (4:8–11), then there is much that needs to be done to bring this text into our world *because our world has almost no belief in a "divine end" to history*. In fact, even Christians today seem to have lost much of their moral nerve about the end of history climaxing in a judgment that will decide the fate of all people. Such ideas are clearly found in the Bible, but they have sometimes become an outright embarrassment to Christians.

In the place of the final judgment, the modern Westerner has substituted what sociologist Christopher Lasch has called the "Myth of Progress."[17] What once drove Christians to look forward to final justice and impelled them to holy living has dissipated today into a feeble idea that somehow, through better methods, better techniques, better therapy, better self-development, better science, and better computer know-how, the world is actually getting better. Whether it is the myth that the rural is better than the urban, or that the frontier will get us to the promised land, or that childlike innocence needs to be recaptured, our Western world is somehow caught in a web of believing that if we can only take a different road, we will somehow arrive at the Celestial City of Optimistic Dreams.

Indeed, in science things get better. We can now heat things quicker, more effectively, and with less fuss because the old wood stove has given way to the microwave. As I sit typing away (now called "word processing") at a portable computer, I am conscious of the typewriter I grew up with (a Royal manual typewriter, which my dad told me was a superb machine!), of the electric typewriter I once owned, of its newer form in an IBM Selectric (which had a "ball" that could be changed so I could type in Greek and Hebrew!), of a Macintosh 512K that jump-started me into the computer world, of the external drives

---

17. See C. Lasch, *The True and Only Heaven: Progress and Its Critics* (New York: W. W. Norton and Co., 1991).

that doubled my capacities, and now of a portable computer—with 12 megabytes of RAM and 160 megabytes of memory, a battery that makes the machine portable, and all kinds of new gadgets on screen that make the work easier.

I am also aware that I can instantly send my current screen to my secretary, with a message attached, so she can make copies for my classes. I can send letters to my professor in northern England, I can gain access to the major newspapers of the United States and the holdings of major libraries, and I can carry on conversations with millions of unknown users of various on-line services. As I stare at this technological marvel, I can ask, along with the rest of the users of computers, "What next? Can it really get that much better?" The answer of scientists and technicians the world over is that everything will get better, faster, and easier until the whole world is at our fingertips.

This *fact* about the world of technology constantly improving has been transferred by the majority of Westerners to moral and social realms. That is, from the infinite progresses of science moderns have inferred that, given time, techniques, and the right people, we can make the world a better place. Thus, our modern musicians sing utopian songs about making the world better, and the modern listeners believe them. It is a fact, of course, that my computer is better (in every way—except when the electricity goes out!) than my old manual typewriter. Yet however nice technological advances are, it is not a fact that our society is getting better.

In fact, in my judgment, society remains about the same. We still have massive discrimination against other races, the poor, the powerless, and the uneducated. The myth of progress may form a solid core to the way most middle-class people perceive the world around them, but that theory is but a myth; our world is hardly getting "better" in every way. This optimistic outlook, I am contending, conditions the way Westerners as a whole read the Bible. Moreover, it has virtually stripped us from a capacity to understand and apply the significance of the biblical outlook on the End as a violent event of judgment and salvation. In other words, the "Myth of Progress" has replaced the "Fact of Final Judgment" in our modern perception of what is coming down the road. Because of this replacement, there is little urgency in our exhortations and even less backbone in our moral warnings.

What shall we do? Above I mentioned that many Bible readers today are embarrassed by the popular presentations of eschatology. I am thinking here of the countless preachers and teachers who have gone on public record, especially since World War I, asserting that the end of history will be soon, only to be disappointed to discover that history kept moving on.[18] I can think of one preacher who, when I was a teenager, proclaimed to our church that the Rapture would occur before 1973. What ran through my mind was not whether he was right (he seemed so compelling and confident), but whether I should even bother to apply for admission to college. My pastor, a wiser man than the prophet, suggested I ought to prepare, "just in case the prophet is wrong." Twenty-three years of preparation and study have made me wiser and more temperate about prophets and their predictions.[19]

Examples of this type of prophecy preaching and belief could be offered at length. To aid us in seeing what has caused many to become either despondent or cynical, we should mention a few items. Prophecy preachers and those who follow such ideas have fastened onto many events or people in the current world scene as direct fulfillments of biblical prophecies, only to be proven false over time. Included in such would be Hitler and Mussolini, Kissinger, Gorbachev—each presented as fulfilling the requirements for the Antichrist. Others have pointed to the reestablishment of Israel as a nation (1948) and argued that within a generation,[20] usually calculated to be 30—40 years, the End will come. Still others have become convinced that the development of nuclear weapons, or the world oil crisis, or the recent war in the gulf states, or the cryptic signs read into the bar codes of stores are all signs of the End.

---

18. Jack Kuhatschek, *Taking the Guesswork Out of Applying the Bible* (Downers Grove, Ill.: InterVarsity, 1990), 145–46. For a more scholarly study, see R. A. Doan, *The Miller Heresy, Millennialism, and American Culture* (Philadelphia: Temple Univ. Press, 1987).

19. A brilliant analysis of modern popular prophets and their beliefs can be found in Paul Boyer, *When Time Shall Be No More: Prophecy Belief in Modern American Culture* (Cambridge, Mass.: Harvard Univ. Press [Belknap], 1992). Former President Ronald Reagan was known for his occasional comment about some fulfillment of a prophetic scripture; but less is known of how much an impact Christian belief in prophecy has made on current American policies. Boyer explores such a topic.

20. Some argue that Matthew 24:34 indicates that within a generation of the establishment of Israel (argued parabolically, and mistakenly, from Matt. 24:32–33), the Lord will return.

Christians might be forgiven if they become despondent or even cynical about our actual knowledge of the future; the endless suggestions and flexibility of these prophets have become more a measure of their ingenuity than their faithfulness to interpreting the Bible correctly. As Christians, we want to sustain the grand vision of Bible: the establishment of God's will on earth, while we counsel the prophets to keep themselves to what can actually be known. Sadly, our tendency has been to abandon belief in prophecy or belief in the ultimate establishment of God's will. In the place of such a conviction, many Christians have instead embraced, unreflectively, the myth of progress, or they have simply despaired of knowing anything substantial about the future by reading the Bible.

These are the two contexts in which our modern readers encounter a statement like that of 4:7 that "The end of all things is near": either a context in which the optimism of our age[21] drowns out the tunes of a final judgment that is absolutely just, or a context in which we are cynical about knowing God's scheme of history because we have been burned by (false) prophets who spoke well beyond a sense of moderation and temperance.

I STILL BELIEVE, no matter how disappointed I may be with modern-day prophets, in a climactic display of God's justice and love that will bring our world to its knees and God's people to their final reward of endless praise to God. And I still believe, no matter how optimistic our world might be, that this world is not getting better and that it will only "get better" as a result of God's infusion of grace and justice. And I look forward to the Day when Christ will be praised by all, when God will be acknowledged by all to be God, when the lion will lie down with the lamb, when swords will be reforged to become instruments of peace, and when peoples of all races, tribes, and sexes will be eternally united and put millennia of hostilities and prejudices aside permanently.

But I believe all this will happen *only as a result of God's grace and*

---

21. See also W. A. Dyrness, *How Does America Hear the Gospel?* (Grand Rapids: Eerdmans, 1989), 61–81 (on the American Dream).

intervention into history. I do not believe we have either the capacity (because we are sinners and limited) or the technology (because science cannot change human nature) to bring this about by ourselves. However hard we work for justice and peace, ultimately only God can bring the desired changes. And so we work and pray for God's sovereign intervention: "May your kingdom come."[22]

Looking forward to that Day, we need to hear the exhortations to pray, love, be hospitable, and exercise our spiritual gifts. And we need to do these things *because someday we will be judged for how we did these things*. I often wonder how frequently we examine our lives in the light of eternity or of God's just and fair judgment. Once again, we find ourselves (most probably) in a situation where we have overreacted. The Christians of one and two generations ago, and beyond, were surely subject to far too many threats and sermons on hell-fire. Our response has been one of embarrassment, so that we have neglected the theme of judgment altogether. Yet that very theme is foundational to a Christian view of ethics—the foundation that God is the Judge and that we are accountable to him for our behavior.

If we keep moving in this direction, no doubt, we will eventually forget about the holiness of God in our perceptions of him and in our teaching-preaching ministries. But in reality, God's holiness ought to lead us to confess our sins, repent, and live lives of fear before him (1:17). God's judgment is rooted in his holiness: *Because God is holy, he is Judge*. That is, because God is holy and simply cannot tolerate sin in his presence, he must act as Judge in purging sin from his world and presence.

If we can raise Christian consciousness about sexual equality or racial unity, then surely we as Christians can unite to raise once again a Christian consciousness of God's holy judgment. Recently, my son (Lukas) and I had a profitable conversation about what I will call "Christian conversation"—what we as Christians permit ourselves to say, what we permit ourselves to write, and what we permit ourselves to be involved in with others who are communicating. My point was this: Others may say certain things, tell certain kinds of jokes, and use certain kinds of communication devices, but we as Christians must

---

22. See also D. A. Carson, *How Long, O Lord? Reflection on Suffering and Evil* (Grand Rapids: Baker, 1990), 133–52.

learn to communicate *in light of the fact that we will someday have to answer before God for how we communicate.* We as Christian parents must begin to teach our kids how to live in light of the Judgment Day. We need to have Sunday school teachers who teach their charges that God is the Judge. We need to have pastors who preach the awful implications of falling into the hands of holy and angry God. And we need to stop being embarrassed by this message. This will raise Christian consciousness, and eventually social consciousness, about living now in light of the End.

As I read 1 Peter, I see a Christian community seeking to survive as a Christian community in the face of persecution. I see the importance of a loving Christian community for coping with unbelief and opposition to the gospel. Prayer for one another, love of one another, hospitality shown to one another, and exercising gifts so as to strengthen one another are clear methods for sustaining faith and for coping with opposition to the gospel. The effect of such ministries is, according to our text, the praise of God through Jesus Christ (4:11).

Particular attention needs to be given here to the *prominence of love.* Peter says, "Above all, love each other deeply, because love covers over a multitude of sins." The expression "above all" speaks to the priority and preeminence of love as a Christian virtue as we wait for the Day of the Lord and learn to live in light of that Day. It is the MVP of Christian virtues and deserves all the media's attention. Furthermore, it needs to be worked at, for that is what "deeply" means. A love for others that transforms a society into a true church is more than a response to people we like; it is a virtue that dominates our thinking so that we ask, "How can I act lovingly to that person?" There are people in our church with whom we have disagreements; how do we respond lovingly to these people? Do we ignore them so as to avoid conflict? Do we gossip about them so as to strengthen our ego and damage their reputation? Do we pray against them and their ambitions? Or do we seek them out so as to create reconciliation? Do we pray for them and their ambitions? Do we speak kindly to them and of them? When love is preeminent among Christian virtues, then we behave differently.

And when we are dominated by love, we "cover over a multitude of sins." As stated above, such a proverb implies that a loving community is able to tolerate more differences, forgive more wrongs, and grow into more effective prayers. It will inevitably be a community noted by its hospitality and warmth. Love is a perennial solution to problems in the Christian community. We do not call on it sporadically or occasionally to enter into the fray, nor do we pray for its presence only when things have gotten totally out of hand. Instead, love is what we ought to pray for *all the time* because it is the "above all" virtue.

1 Peter 4:12–19

۱۶

DEAR FRIENDS, DO not be surprised at the painful trial you are suffering, as though something strange were happening to you. ¹³But rejoice that you participate in the sufferings of Christ, so that you may be overjoyed when his glory is revealed. ¹⁴If you are insulted because of the name of Christ, you are blessed, for the Spirit of glory and of God rests on you. ¹⁵If you suffer, it should not be as a murderer or thief or any other kind of criminal, or even as a meddler. ¹⁶However, if you suffer as a Christian, do not be ashamed, but praise God that you bear that name. ¹⁷For it is time for judgment to begin with the family of God; and if it begins with us, what will the outcome be for those who do not obey the gospel of God? ¹⁸And,

> "If it is hard for the righteous to be saved,
> what will become of the ungodly and the sinner?"

¹⁹So then, those who suffer according to God's will should commit themselves to their faithful Creator and continue to do good.

Original Meaning

PETER HAS SKETCHED the glories and implications of salvation (1:3–2:10) and spelled out how Christians are to live honorably within the context of a hostile society (2:11–4:11); he now turns to his final concerns. The major theme of 4:12–5:11 revolves around exhortations based on the life *within* the church. Peter speaks here again about how to cope with suffering, but this time adds a note of urgency.¹ He then addresses the leaders of the churches (5:1–9) and concludes with a doxology (5:10–11).

---

1. It has been argued that 4:12–19 demonstrates a new (and later) situation in that the experiences of persecution seem more present. Thus, writes C. E. B. Cranfield: "In the earlier passage [he is referring to 3:14–4:6] persecution would seem to be still a comparatively

Peter begins by *exhorting* his churches not to be surprised at the sufferings they are experiencing (4:12); instead, he contends in a *counterproposal*, they are to rejoice in their sufferings because it is participation in both the sufferings and glory of Christ (4:13). He reminds them of the one *condition* (emphasized in 2:18—20; 3:13—17) that is to obtain: If they are to suffer, it must be because of doing good, not because of rebellious behavior (4:14—16). Finally, he reminds them of the *foundation* of their perspective on suffering: They are to live in light of God's judgment instead of in light of earthly pleasures (4:17—19).

Exhortation (4:12). As at 2:11, Peter marks the beginning of a major section with "Dear friends" and exhorts his readers to avoid being surprised[2] by the "painful trial you are suffering." Presumably, the early Christians were not generally surprised by opposition to the gospel (cf. 1 John 3:13), but the actual turn of events among Peter's audience may have caught them off guard or shocked them. They were encountering a "painful trial" (lit., "the fiery ordeal that is taking place among you to test you," NRSV).[3] "Trial" denotes an experience that is either positive (God is testing you; cf. 1:6—7) or negative (it is a painful experience or an occasion for temptation). While the latter may be true, the primary sense is surely to be found in the former.[4]

Counterproposal (4:13). Instead of being shocked by these events and turning inward to wonder and doubt, Peter's readers are to "rejoice."[5] Their lives will be tied into the patterns of Jesus' life (2:18—25; 3:15, 16; 4:1; cf. Mark 8:34—38), which should shape their *fundamental* attitude as they encounter persecution. Though they may now be somewhat surprised at the intensity of the heat they have stirred up by

---

remote possibility, while in the present section the fiery trial is apparently already beginning" (*First Peter*, 100). However, L. Goppelt (*1 Peter*, 310—12) argues that what has changed is only the author's point of view: He now sees it as an enduring situation, and his presentation is more concrete.

2. Peter said previously that their pagan friends were "surprised" when the Christians changed their moral behavior (4:4).

3. The NIV has translated "fiery" with the word "pain" and placed "to test you" in a more prominent position by translating it "trial"—thus, a "painful trial."

4. So also J. N. D. Kelly, *Peter and Jude*, 184—85; L. Goppelt, *1 Peter*, 313—14. The clearest use of the two senses of *peirasmos* (as either "test" or "temptation") can be seen in James 1:12—14.

5. See the enlightening discussion on joy in the midst of suffering by L. Goppelt, *1 Peter*, 316—21.

following Jesus, that very heat is an opportunity to "participate[6] in the sufferings of Christ." As Paul taught his own sufferings completed the sufferings of Jesus (Col. 1:24), so Peter sees the sufferings of ordinary believers as a special bond with their Lord.

But this attitude is only a preparation: Being able to rejoice now in the midst of suffering prepares one for being "overjoyed[7] when his glory is revealed." What seems presently unjust and difficult to face can be turned into a celebration of joy when one understands that Jesus endured the same; but even that celebration of joy is nothing compared with the abundant joy that will be experienced when the glory of Christ (cf. 1 Peter 1:5, 7, 13; 3:18–22) is revealed to vindicate God's people and usher them into his pure joy, peace, and love (cf. Rom. 8:18–21).

Condition (4:14–16). Having lifted his readers spirits, Peter now reminds them of one important condition for enjoying that final, inexhaustible glory: They must remain faithful in doing good and not incur suffering because they deserve it. The first comment (4:14) is reiterated by the third comment (4:16): that is, being blessed if you suffer in the name of Christ is essentially the same as not being ashamed for suffering as a Christian. These two comments surround another one, about not suffering because they are evildoers (4:15).

The first comment speaks of being "insulted."[8] Because the first-century Mediterranean society was an honor-shame culture,[9] an "insult" was much more than a form of criticism. Criticisms can be deflected; being shamed, however, irreparably damages one's social

---

6. The Greek term is *koinoneite* and is usually translated "fellowship with" (see also 5:1).

7. The Greek reads *"rejoice* as you participate in the sufferings of Christ, so that you may *rejoice* exceedingly at the revelation of his glory." The verbal identity is obscured when the translators use "rejoice" and "overjoyed."

8. The early Christians were frequently insulted (cf. Matt. 5:11–12; 27:44; Rom. 15:3; Heb. 11:26; 13:13). See the excellent summary of C. Spicq, *Theological Lexicon of the New Testament,* 2:585–87.

9. See J. Plevnick, "Honor/Shame," in J. J. Pilch and B. J. Malina, *Biblical Social Values and Their Meaning: A Handbook* (Peabody, Mass.: Hendrickson, 1993), 95–104. Honor is a group value that expresses one's worth in a public manner; to be shamed (cf. our text, v. 16) is to have that honor either unexpressed or to have one's honor attacked by public criticism. For further information, see B. J. Malina, *The New Testament World: Insight from Cultural Anthropology* (rev. ed.; Louisville: Westminster/John Knox Press, 1993), 28–62 (with extensive bibliography). Our culture, in contrast, is driven much more by a sense of guilt than of honor and shame.

standing. This is why in 4:16, Peter writes: "Do not be *ashamed*." What these Christians must learn to cope with is the loss of social standing involved with conversion and consistent Christian living (though this does not imply they were previously in the upper class).

Rather than taking these insults personally, Peter's readers must take these insults as an occasion to see that they are blessed (4:14), for Jesus taught that way (Matt. 5:10, 11–12; cf. 10:24–25). Peter therefore exhorts them to glorify God for their being identified with the name of Jesus (4:16); they are to wear his name proudly.[10] The reason they are to assume this stance against persecution is because "the Spirit of glory[11] and of God rests on you" (4:14). That is, they are blessed by God and are to glorify him because of the presence of his Spirit on them. This resting of the Spirit may refer to an occasional presence of the Spirit (as in Matt. 10:20), but it more likely means the constant indwelling of the Spirit in the community of saints, for the same Spirit rested on Jesus (Isa. 11:2; Matt. 3:13–17). This Spirit, especially when the saints are in stress, reveals the power, patience, and goodness of God to those who witness such events (cf. 1 Peter 2:12; 3:1, 16; cf. e.g., Acts 7:55).

No matter what happens, however, Peter offers a warning: "If you suffer, it should not be as a murderer or thief or any other kind of criminal, or even as a meddler." Suffering for the name of Christ or for being a Christian is acceptable; suffering for doing bad things is unacceptable and deserving. Once again, the social context highlights the importance of Peter's exhortations: The Christian household is under a severe threat of extinction, and any kind of behavior[12] that jeopardizes an already difficult situation must be eliminated. Instead, as Peter says in 2:11–12, Christians should live good lives (which includes suffering for doing Christian kinds of things), so that there may be no just cause of suffering.

Foundation (4:17–19). The Christians of Asia Minor are to rejoice because they are participating in the sufferings of Jesus; they are also

---

10. Instead of "name," some mss. read "matter" (see J. R. Michaels, *1 Peter*, 257, 269–70).

11. A special connection is made between the Spirit and glory in 2 Cor. 3:8, 17–18. See G. D. Fee, *God's Empowering Presence: The Holy Spirit in the Letters of Paul* (Peabody, Mass.: Hendrickson, 1994), 307–20.

12. On Peter's list of evildoers here, see the extensive comments of J. R. Michaels, *1 Peter*, 266–68.

to make sure that, if they do suffer, it is because they are doing good. Peter now gives the foundation for both exhortations: *They will some-day have to answer to God for their behavior.* He begins with the statement: "For it is time for judgment to begin with the family[13] of God" (4:17a). Judgment is an important motif in 1 Peter and, as observed at 4:7, serves as the foundation for motivating early Christians to live faith-fully before God (cf. 1:17; 2:23; 4:5).

That God's judgment begins with the people of God is familiar to any reader, whether ancient Jewish or modern Westerner, of the Old Testament.[14] For instance, Amos 3:2 says, "You only have I chosen of all the families of the earth; therefore I will punish you for all your sins."[15] While the threat of judgment was for everyone, the actual judg-ment would begin with God's people, resulting in the salvation of the faithful and the condemnation of the unfaithful. Such a condemnation would then extend to all the nations of the earth. A similar threat of a judgment of all is found throughout the New Testament (cf. Matt. 25:31–46; 1 Cor. 11:28; 2 Cor. 5:10), and it is clear that the early church saw persecution as the first stage of the coming judgment (cf. Phil. 2:28–30; 1 Thess. 3:3–4; 2 Thess. 1:4; Revelation). This threat of judgment formed the basis for exhorting Christians to live faithfully.

It is not enough for us to say simply that the final judgment will begin with the family of God; rather, we must understand that such *per-secution is the beginning* of that judgment.[16] In other words, the persecution these Christians are experiencing is the act of God whereby he purges his people to prepare them for his final display of salvation, insofar as he makes them fit for that judgment through suffering. So, for example, Paul says in 1 Corinthians 11:32, "When we are judged by the Lord, we are being disciplined so that we will not be condemned with the world."[17] This may be the context for understanding 1 Peter 4:1: Suf-fering purges sin from one's Christian living. What Peter is saying here,

---

13. The term "family" translates the Greek word *oikos*, normally translated "house." It is possible that Peter has in mind the temple of Jerusalem and that the imminent judgment of God will begin there. See the comments of J. R. Michaels, *1 Peter*, 271, but see also L. Gop-pelt, *1 Peter*, 329.

14. See the lucid exposition of this theme in E. G. Selwyn, *1 Peter*, 299–303.

15. See also Jer. 7–9; 25:17–26 (begins with Jerusalem); Zeph. 1:4–2:15 (begins with Jerusalem).

16. See L. Goppelt, *1 Peter*, 330–32.

17. See further at *2 Baruch* 32:5.

therefore, is as much related to persecution and suffering as it is to the final judgment, though the two are closely related. Those who are purged through suffering are the ones who inherit final salvation.

In light of this statement, Peter then asks rhetorically: "If it begins with us, what will the outcome be for those who do not obey the gospel of God?" (4:17b). That is, if the judgment is so severe that it deals a harsh blow for those associated with the family of God, then surely the pagans, who have no connection whatsoever with God's people or salvation, will be cut off entirely (cf. 2:7–8). The apostle then reiterates this rhetorical question in 4:18 with another question, this time a question from Proverbs 11:31: "If it is hard for the righteous to be saved, what will become of the ungodly and the sinner?"[18]

Because of the severity of God's penetrating judgment, Peter exhorts these Christians to submit themselves to God by living a good life (4:19). If it is God's will for some to suffer, then those same people must, like Jesus (2:23), surrender themselves to the faithful Creator. Peter's construction makes it clear that the trust of these suffering Christians is to be exhibited by means of, or in the context of, doing good works. That is, they are to live honorably within their cultural context (2:11–12; 2:13–3:12) in such a way that there is no room for accusing them of sinfulness and rebellion. As Goppelt has written: "This 'handing over' of one's own 'I' to the Creator, which liberates a person from fear, takes place, amid the danger of losing one's life, through prayer and through action arising from hopeful faith."[19]

Bridging Contexts

ONCE AGAIN, WE are confronted with a text whose main direction is considerably remote from the normative experience of most Westerners. While we do occasionally hear reports of suffering in the name of Christ in the Western world, such reports are noteworthy only because they are unusual. For Peter's churches, however, such experiences were the norm. Once again, therefore, we must protect the integrity of the text and give adequate

---

18. The NIV reads at Proverbs 11:31: "If the righteous receive their due on earth, how much more the ungodly and the sinner!" Peter quotes the LXX of this verse (omitting the needless particle *men*).

19. L. Goppelt, *1 Peter*, 336.

respect to our brothers and sisters throughout the world and history of the church who have truly suffered in the name of Jesus. This means we must not cheapen the message of this text in our haste to make it relevant. After all, what really does an American Christian businessman have to do with suffering when he drives a $20,000 car, has media access to all his connections wherever he finds himself (in a car, on a golf course, at home, or a work), takes lush vacations several times a year to exotic places, and buys whatever his heart desires? To make our text relevant to such a man by suggesting that his tithing dedication is something that prevents him from advancing in today's markets is, in my opinion, to make a mockery of the millions of Christians who have suffered extensively simply because they are Christians and want to meet to worship.

However, within this text is a concept that might help us make a transition into our modern context—the concept is *honor and shame*. While it would be foolish for us to think that our culture is as much honor-bound or shame-bound as an ancient Mediterranean culture, such a mechanism is not entirely absent from our modern world. When a new employee assumes the tasks of a former employee, that former employee can feel a sense of a "lack of status" or "shame" if the new employee is more competent, whereas a sense of honor is preserved when the new employee cannot handle the tasks with the same competence. When a parent discovers that one of her children knows more than she does or can perform a task with greater efficiency and skill, that parent can sense of lowering of status and hence feel some shame. When your pastor comes to you to ask you what you think about a certain program or plan in the church, you might feel honored, even elevated in your status, to be asked such a question by a pastor. These are all instances that show the presence of honor and shame in our culture.

Where we might be able to make this text more relevant to ours are those times when we lose some status (are shamed) or gain more status (are honored) because of our allegiance to Jesus Christ. Recently I heard a professional baseball player speak of his embarrassment over the continuing threat of a strike by the Player's Association and how he had lost respect from other ballplayers because he was opposed to that decision. He was concerned about the impression of greed and wrong priorities that the players were giving to our society and its youth, and his judgment about these issues was entirely formed on the basis of his Christian faith. Such a "loss of status," and therefore the presence of shame, was the direct result of his faith. We can only imagine how he will be treated during the season. In such a case, I believe we are bringing Peter's text directly into our world, regardless of how different the situation might be.

Christians in the first century undoubtedly frequently experienced loss of respect and shame to a degree that we probably never will. But we are not amiss if we try to find analogies to this in our society—to the occasional presence of shame in our world for being Christians. This can happen whenever a supervisor speaks for honesty instead of greed or for fairness to workers instead of profits, whenever a Christian worker opts for respect of an employer over adopting an adversarial relationship, whenever a family member loses power or influence within a family structure because of conversion to Christ, or whenever the Christian student refuses to participate in the party spirit at the college campus. In each of these the Christian alternative may very well lead to social shame, to the loss of status and influence; such shame is to be endured with joy.

In 1 Peter 4:15, the author records prohibitions for which Christians are not to suffer. His concern is with the reason for suffering; he says, in effect, "Do not let it come about because you deserve it." This does not mean people can do these things as long as they do not get caught, as long as it does not cause problems for the Christian community, or even as long as they do not find themselves suffering for such behavior. In other words, applications can be made indirectly: If these prohibitions are given to keep the churches from suffering for doing bad things, it follows that the churches are not to do those things even when the prospect of suffering is less likely. Furthermore, such prohibitions are founded on the law of Moses and biblical principles. This makes them even more readily applicable.

IF INDEED THIS text speaks of learning how to cope with the shame that can be caused by following Christ, we need to begin here with discovering the contemporary significance of the text. Put differently, we can draw up some guidelines of what happens when we feel the lowering of our status because we confess our allegiance to Jesus Christ and compose a list of considerations we need to pursue for how to cope with the ensuing shame. A list of principles, some of which may be more pertinent than others (depending on the person and the situation), includes the following nine items.

(1) Christians ought not to be surprised if they suffer shame and loss of status because of their faith (4:12). Instead, they ought to know that in the history of Israel and of the church, God's people have always been opposed by the Prince of Darkness, by the flesh, and by people who refuse to submit to God's will. Whether we think of Joseph, Moses, Elijah, Jeremiah, Jesus, or the apostles, or whether we think of ordinary Christians in mainland China or in some Muslim countries, persecution is a theme woven tightly and boldly into the fabric of the Christian story. When it does occur, we ought not to be surprised.

(2) Suffering shame for Jesus should be understood as a test to prepare us for God's final judgment (4:12). Although Peter may have drawn this theme from Jewish eschatology, wherein persecution was connected with the final age as a preparatory device, it speaks to the human condition whenever Christians endure unjust suffering. Our lives now prepare us for our final exam with God; even our suffering is one way God prepares us to be fit for his presence.

(3) Christians ought to welcome the opportunity to share in the sufferings of Christ (4:13). When we realize that losing status puts us right into the company of Jesus, we should be able to cope much more easily with suffering. Jesus has gone before us, he has suffered like us, he has endured and gives us encouragement to go on, and, in the categories of Hebrews 4:14–16, he is a sympathetic high priest who intercedes for us.

(4) Christians ought to be able to transcend their present pain by reflecting on the transcendent glory that awaits God's people (4:13; cf. 1:3–9). It is of no small consolation to the sufferer to know there is something infinitely greater in his or her hope. In spite of injustices, there is a glory for the Christian because God is just. "That means that [Christians] do not always have ready answers; they have, instead, a reasonable confidence in One who does have the answers and the

power to impose them. God will have the last word; we dare to wait for that."[20]

(5) Even if anxieties and cares jump up to terrify Christians at every turn when facing suffering, they should be able to thank God for the Spirit, who will enable them to continue in doing good and in bringing glory to God (4:14). Jesus taught this (Matt. 10:20) and clearly endured it (chaps. 26–27); other Christians have witnessed to the same confidence and thankfulness that Stephen had (Acts 7:54–8:1).

(6) When facing suffering, the Christian needs to remind himself or herself to guard good behavior with a firm shield (4:15). Whatever happens to us, Peter reminds us, we are not to ruin the cause of the gospel with filthy works of evil. Once again, Christian wisdom has taught us the same thing: nothing is more damaging to the glory of God and the growth of the gospel than the sins of his people, especially those of well-known Christian leaders.

(7) Christians are to take their eyes off themselves, endure shame, and turn their eyes on the glory of God as they face injustice because they are following Jesus (4:16). Shame is the heart of peer pressure, and peer pressure may never conquer our resolve to be obedient, loving, and peaceful. We must learn to put aside what others think and care only about what God thinks.

(8) Because Christians realize that the final day of reckoning is yet to come and is a firm, fixed date in God's diary, they must strengthen their resolve to obey God in the face of suffering and injustice (4:17–18). Here they need to develop a stubborn streak, that no matter what happens to them, they must live their lives in light of God's judgment. Whether the IRS knows or not is not the issue; God knows. Whether the boss knows or not is not the issue; God knows. Whether your family knows or not is not the issue; God knows. And because God knows everything, we must learn to submit everything in our lives to his final assessment.

(9) Finally, when facing suffering in the name of Christ, Christians must continue to do good works as an expression of their trust (4:19). Obedience in the Bible is not an appendix to faith. These two

---

20. D. A. Carson, *How Long, O Lord? Reflections on Suffering and Evil* (Grand Rapids: Baker, 1990), 151.

(obedience and faith) are so connected in the Bible that they are insep-
arable. Believers are obedient, and the obedient ones believe. Consequently, Peter exhorts his readers to hand over their lives to the faithful
Creator by living a life of good deeds no matter what happens to them.

1 Peter 5:1–5

〰️

TO THE ELDERS among you, I appeal as a fellow elder, a witness of Christ's sufferings and one who also will share in the glory to be revealed: ²Be shepherds of God's flock that is under your care, serving as overseers—not because you must, but because you are willing, as God wants you to be; not greedy for money, but eager to serve; ³not lording it over those entrusted to you, but being examples to the flock. ⁴And when the Chief Shepherd appears, you will receive the crown of glory that will never fade away.

⁵Young men, in the same way be submissive to those who are older. All of you, clothe yourselves with humility toward one another, because,

"God opposes the proud
but gives grace to the humble."

THE PERIL OF suffering has preoccupied Peter's attention. From the beginning of the letter (1:3–12) to the end of chapter 4, he has exhorted his churches to live faithful lives before God, constantly placing these exhortations against the backdrop of persecution. Having given his final exhortation to the churches to suffer as Christians (4:12–19), he now turns to specific groups within the churches for special instructions (5:1–5), after which he will offer some final remarks (5:6–14). The present section contains three units: an address to the "elders" (5:1–4), an address to the "young men" (5:5a), and an address to "all of them" (5:5b). Since the three sections are joined by a common form,[1] we will treat them together.

---

1. That is, each section addresses a specific group with specific instructions for that unique group. The verses that follow (5:6–14) are not directed toward a specific group. Thus, our unit here is concerned with instructions for two groups of men and then the entire body. Its concern with specific groups makes it similar to 2:13–3:12, but its focus on specific groups within the church, as opposed to within society, gives it a different orientation.

The address to the elders begins with the *basis of an exhortation* (5:1), provides *an exhortation* (5:2—3), and then offers a *promise* to those who carry out the exhortation (5:4). The address to the "young men"[2] contains *an exhortation to submit* (5:5a). The third unit, addressed to "all of you," is an *exhortation to humility* and closes with a *reason for this exhortation* (5:5b).

The Address to Elders (5:1—4). Peter begins by defining his personal relationship to the elders (5:1), which serves as the *basis* for his exhortations: He is "a fellow elder, a witness of Christ's sufferings and one who also will share in the glory to be revealed."[3] He cites three traits they have in common: (1) They are all elders,[4] (2) they are all[5] witnesses of Christ's sufferings, and (3) they will all partake of the future glory.

That Peter calls himself a "fellow elder" is both a statement of modesty (he is also an apostle; cf. 1:1) and sympathy. As an elder, he knows both the temptations these elders encounter and the joys. More importantly, he knows the essence of the calling he needs to spell out in 5:2—3. While it may be argued that Peter condescends to their level, it is more likely that he is elevating their ministries and incorporating their work into his. As a "witness" to the sufferings of Christ,[6] Peter can

---

2. On whether "young men" refers only to males, see the discussion below.

3. The NIV does not translate the inferential particle that begins this verse; the Greek has *oun* ("therefore"). The NRSV appears to have "now" as the translation. It is possible that Peter intended to see the logical connection as follows: "In light of the coming judgment that will begin with house of God, and since the elders are responsible for the house of God, I exhort you elders to be faithful in the task God has given you." However, some mss. omit the Greek word altogether, which may explain why the NIV does not have it.

4. Peter uses a rare Greek word, *sumpresbuteros*; see J. R. Michaels, *1 Peter*, 279—80. On elders in the early church, see R. Alastair Campbell, *The Elders: Seniority Within Earliest Christianity* (Studies of the New Testament and Its World; Edinburgh: T. & T. Clark, 1994). Campbell argues that the term "elder," however imprecise, refers mostly to the status of household heads and to the senior status these people had in the early house churches.

5. The *sym-* is not carried over to the term "witness" but is implicit because there is only one article connecting the two nouns: he is a "fellow-elder and -witness." It follows, then, that the same relationship pertains to the "partaker" as well. Also, it makes little sense for Peter to appeal to the churches on the basis of his relationship if that relationship is completely unlike the elders in those churches.

6. Some argue Peter means "eyewitness" here; however, as others have argued, he has in mind one who testifies about the sufferings of Christ in its saving and exemplary benefits and who participates in that suffering through experiences (so J. N. D. Kelly, *Peter and Jude*, 198—99; L. Goppelt, *1 Peter*, 341—42; J. R. Michaels, *1 Peter*, 280—81).

appeal to them to endure hardship, suffering, and persecution because of the example of Jesus (2:18–25; 3:18; 4:1, 13). That is, Peter and the other elders both preach the significance of the sufferings of Jesus (as Peter has admirably done) and endure such sufferings. Since Jesus was vindicated by God, he knows that he, like all the faithful elders, is someone "who also will share[7] in the glory to be revealed." The apostle appears to be drawing again from the important connection he has made between suffering and being glorified (cf. 4:13), and he waits for the prize of the elder (5:4).

Having established the common traits of all elders, Peter turns to the *exhortation* itself (5:2). It is comprised of a *general exhortation* ("Be shepherds of God's flock that is under your care") and several *specific instances* of that general exhortation ("serving as overseers—not because you must, but because you are willing, as God wants you to be; not greedy for money, but eager to serve; not lording it over those entrusted to you, but being examples to the flock"). These specific instances begin with a general term ("serving as overseers") and move to three illustrations that contain both a negative and a positive point.

Elders are responsible to shepherd God's flock (5:2). Throughout the Bible, and mostly because Israel was composed of agrarian communities, the relationship of leaders to their charges was described metaphorically as a shepherd-like relationship. As shepherds cared for their flocks, so ought the leaders of Israel to care for Israelites. This is all rooted in the description of God as a Shepherd to his people. Besides the well-known Psalm 23 (which concerns the Lord's relationship to David), there are the important uses of this image in Isaiah 40:11 (God-Israel), Jeremiah 23:1–4 (Israel's corrupt shepherds will be replaced by good shepherds), Ezekiel 34:1–10 (God will rescue his people from selfish shepherds), Zechariah 11:4–18 (a caring shepherd is replaced by a worthless, uncaring shepherd), Matthew 9:35–38 (Jesus appoints new shepherds for his people), John 10:1–18 (Jesus is the good shepherd), and John 21:15–17 (Peter is to be a shepherd).

Peter exhorts his fellow shepherds to tend to the flock that God has appointed to them. What he has in mind is almost certainly the role

---

7. Some argue that Peter is alluding to his experience of the Transfiguration (cf. Matt. 17:6; 2 Peter 1:16–21). However, the glory he describes here is something future.

that individual leaders played in a given house church—to tend to that house church as a group assigned to them by God.[8] Without question, Peter ends any sense of possession by stating that it is *"God's flock,"* not theirs.

Peter goes on to list, in contrasting pairs, the *specific instances* of what shepherding ought to involve and not involve. It begins with an expression that both resumes what 5:2a has said and carries the notion of shepherding further: "serving as overseers."[9] Their ministry of leading these churches was:

Not to be	To be
not because you must,	but because you are willing, as God wants you to be;
not greedy for money,	but eager to serve;
not lording it over those entrusted to you,	but being examples to the flock.

Here Peter lists some of the tasks involved and the personal characteristics of early church leaders (as Paul does in his listing of elders in the Pastoral Letters). Service in the church ought to be done with the proper motive, that is, with personal willingness[10] and a sense of divine calling, not because of a sense of internal or external compulsion. As E. G. Selwyn says, "There is all the difference, especially in spiritual matters, between the man who does his work for no other reason than that he has to do it, and the man who does it willingly, as being in God's service."[11] If, as many think, age played a critical role in the assignment of the pastoral ministry, then personal willingness and eagerness become even more important.

Besides compulsion, greed is also an unworthy motivation for leading in God's house. Jesus had no fixed income and consequently had to trust in God for his daily provisions (Matt. 6:11, 25–34; 8:20); he

---

8. In Greek, the expression is "the among-you flock of God": that is, that part of God's flock assigned to you.

9. "Overseers" translates the Greek term *episkopos*, another popular term for church leaders in the earliest churches (see, e.g., Acts 20:28; Phil. 1:1; 1 Tim. 3:2; Titus 1:7). For further study, see L. Coenen, "Bishop, Presbyter, Elder," in *NIDNTT*, 1:188–92 (bishop), 192–200 (elder), and the extensive bibliography on pp. 200–201.

10. See the discussion in J. R. Michaels, *1 Peter*, 284.

11. E. G. Selwyn, *1 Peter*, 230.

taught his disciples that they, too, were to live by faith (10:8–13). This early church squeamishness about reputation and ministry not done for profit leads Peter to reflect on the importance of the same principle: The elders are not to serve in the churches in order to gain a profit.[12] Instead, they are to do their ministry eagerly. Peter's concerns possibly reflect a period when the elder of a local church was paid a fixed income, though he may be thinking of gifts in return for their ministries. More important, his instructions are concerned with the social impact of how Christian ministers acquired their living (cf. 2:11–12).

Finally, Peter urges the elders to lead by example, not by authoritative domination of their local churches.[13] Again he seems to be reflecting a saying of Jesus (Mark 10:42). Power, no more today than in the first century, is addictive. It leads to unworthy motives and pollutes decisions that are to be made under the guidance of the Spirit. Instead of seeking God's agenda, power-hungry church leaders pursue their own, doing what they can to increase their own reputation. Instead of leading by dominating power, Peter urges elders to lead by example, as Jesus has been their example (1 Peter 2:18–25). Note how Paul had been an "example" to his churches (1 Cor. 11:1; Phil. 3:17; 4:9; 1 Thess. 1:7; 2 Thess. 3:9; 1 Tim. 3:9; Titus 2:7).

Peter's exhortation to elders to carry on their ministries with the proper motivations was founded on his relationship to the elders (5:1); he now incites them to the appropriate behavior by appealing to the *promise* they will receive for faithful discharge of their calling (5:4): "When the Chief Shepherd appears, you will receive the crown of glory that will never fade away." If Peter is a "fellow elder" (5:1), he is nonetheless an "undershepherd," under Jesus himself (cf. 2:25). Once again, understanding all elders as equals reflects an important saying of Jesus: We are all brothers, and there is but one Teacher (Matt. 23:8–12). When Jesus returns as Savior and Judge (cf. 1 Peter 1:3–5, 9, 13,

---

12. That support of itinerants was a hot issue can be seen in R. F. Hock, *The Social Context of Paul's Ministry: Tentmaking and Apostleship* (Philadelphia: Fortress, 1980), 52–59. Paul, too, worried about what others would think about his receiving of money. See S. McKnight, "Collection for the Saints," *DPL*, 143–47; P. W. Barnett, "Tentmaking," *DPL*, 925–27; J. M. Everts, "Financial Support," *DPL*, 295–300.

13. Peter uses the term *kleroi* to describe the sphere of their ministry; this most likely refers to a specific church. See, e.g., F. W. Beare, *1 Peter*, 200; J. R. Michaels, *1 Peter*, 285–86.

20; 2:12; 3:9–12; 4:5–6, 7, 13, 17–19), he will give (cf. 1:9) them a "crown of glory" for their faithfulness to him. It is unwise to think here of a physical crown; rather, the crown is the glory of being accepted by God[14]—a reward for those elders who conduct themselves as elders should, by serving under God those whom God has given them to serve. Until then they are to serve because of God's call and the joy that comes from doing his work.

The Address to the Young (5:5a). Peter now addresses a different group, the "young men," instructing them "in the same way[15] [to] be submissive to those who are older." Some have argued that the "young men" are not just men younger in age but refer to a more specific group within the churches: the "elders-to-be."[16] But we have no evidence that any such group existed in the early churches.

Is Peter addressing just men here? Perhaps, though the majority of scholars argue[17] that he is speaking generically of all those who are under the authority of the elders, both men and women. Since Peter probably does not have in mind a specific group of younger men who are waiting until they can assume elderships, it seems best to me to translate "young men" (NIV) as "younger ones," referring generically to *all members of the house churches.* Furthermore, if the elder was in effect the sole leader of a local house church, then what remains were not just young men but both men and women. In fact, if we continue this line, it is likely that more women than men were left. At any rate, the younger ones are to defer to the elders. Dividing churches by age might seem odd to us, but in "the ancient world the division of society into older people and younger ... was just as much taken for granted as the division into men and women, free men and slaves, etc."[18]

---

14. The "of" in "of glory" is called an epexegetical or appositional genitive: the crown that is glory. A similar expression can be found in English when we say that the disobedient will drink a cup of sorrow; the cup is the experience of sorrow. For an excellent discussion of rewards, see C. L. Blomberg, "Degrees of Reward in the Kingdom of Heaven," *JETS* 35 (1992): 159–72. Blomberg dismisses the idea that Christians will be eternally distinguished from one another by some kind of reward system.

15. "In the same way" connects 5:5 to 5:1–4; the connection seems to be that just as the elders have a God-ordained task to perform, so also do the young men. As the elders lead their churches, so the young men should live in line with the elders' directions.

16. Some have appealed to Acts 5:6 or Luke 22:26. See the discussion of L. Goppelt, *1 Peter*, 350.

17. So E. G. Selwyn, *1 Peter*, 233; L. Goppelt, *1 Peter*, 350–51; J. R. Michaels, *1 Peter*, 289.

18. J. N. D. Kelly, *Peter and Jude*, 205.

The advice to this group is to listen to the wisdom of the elders and live in accordance with their instruction; that is, they are "to submit." As stated in 2:13, the term *submission* should be understood as "living according to some constituted order"—here, the order established by the directives of the elders. And since they have already been instructed to lead, not by domination but by example, we can assume that submission here was not some onerous task. Rather, it was joyfully acceptable to those who wanted to live in accordance with God's will. If it was possible for the churches to stand against the governmental authorities (see at 2:13–17), so it was possible that the younger members of the churches might want to resist the authority of the elders.[19]

The Address to All (5:5b). Finally, Peter addresses both the elders and the younger members of the churches with the following words: "All of you, clothe yourselves with humility toward one another, because, 'God opposes the proud but gives grace to the humble.'" Whether leader or laity, whether old or young, Christians are to develop a deferential and humble attitude toward one another. Peter hinted at this in 3:8–12 and 4:7–11; he now makes it more explicit. The elder is not to arrogate himself to the position of dominant partner, nor are the younger members to rebel against the authority of the elders; rather, they are to respect one another mutually. The elder's service is by way of leadership while the younger members' service is by way of conformity to the norm of the elders.

Once again, Peter grounds his exhortations in the threatening judgment of God (see at 4:7, 17–19). The Christians of his day do not want to assign themselves to the same fate of the persecuting pagans by living a life of pride and avarice; instead, they should live in accordance with God's will.

THE BULK OF this passage contains exhortations for pastors, teachers, elders, and church leaders; they are not designed primarily to speak to the typical person in a Christian church today (what we call the "laity"). That is not to say that there are not some lessons to learn for all, for there are. For instance, parents

---

19. Scholars have appealed to *1 Clement* 3:3; 44:3–6; 47:6 for evidence of such a problem.

can learn from this on how to deal more Christianly with the spiritual nurture of their children, and Bible study teachers, whether trained or not, can find in these exhortations lessons on how to lead. But those are derivative lessons from the main one, directed to the pastors and leaders of the house churches.

Thus, the first step in moving 5:1—4 into our world is to recognize that it is directed at leadership, at any who have been given the task of looking after the spirituality of people in the church. That is, it applies as much to what we call the "Senior Pastor" as to the "Youth Pastor," the "Visitation Pastor," the "Small Group Pastor," the "Christian Education Director," and the "Music Pastor." The reason we draw this conclusion is because Peter's churches knew of no such divisions of labor; his words are addressed to those who lead the churches in any way. In coming to this position, I am not arguing that pastors and ministers are somehow superior; rather, Peter recognized a "pastoral calling" and gave instructions to those who had that calling.

This means that the typical person in our churches today will feel no particular relevance to this text. However, it would be wise for the laity to understand the details of a text like this, not so they might usurp the callings of others, but so they might pray for their leaders, understand and sympathize with that calling, and institute policies in the churches that protect such callings. Just as a pastor needs to understand the callings of his "parishioners" in order to be more effective in serving them, so the parishioner needs to understand the calling of the pastor to be able to support such a calling.

Returning again to the general or derived application of this text to the laity,[20] I contend that this text can be used *indirectly* to apply to *any situation in which a Christian is called to serve another for spiritual growth*. It is important to recognize that such a move is indirect (e.g., the text does not directly concern a mother's teaching her children how to pray) and that there will undoubtedly be things that are not applicable (e.g., mothers always teach their children without pay!). Nonetheless, whoever is exercising a spiritual service to others can learn things here about leadership. For instance, when a Bible study teacher goes out of his way to work with one of his "students," he is exercising a

---

20. I am "low church" in my perceptions of the relationship of the pastor to the laity; thus, I do not make radical distinctions between what pastors can do and what laypersons can do.

ministry analogous to the service of elders. When a concerned church member visits a struggling brother or sister in the church, that church member is extending the pastoral ministry. In these and similar situations, the words of Peter are important: Do not do this work out of compulsion, or for financial gain, or for power. Instead, such acts need to be done willingly, eagerly, and in an exemplary manner.

Moving the text about the "younger ones" into our world has one important knotty issue: If the text is only about young *men*, then either the text is only for younger men in our churches, or it must be adjusted to a world that has changed with respect to patriarchalism. We argued above, however, that the text is about both men and women—all those who are being led by an elder. The application of such an injunction to our world is not difficult since, though changes have surely come, there are plenty of church members who are being led by elders. But is the term *submission* appropriate? The answer is not simple. If we understand *submission* to be *subservience*, with the result that the congregations *always* must go along with the plans and schemes of the elders, then the term is not appropriate to our world. But if we understand *submission* to be "living orderly under the leadership of the elder," then the term is appropriate: Elders are to exercise leadership, and congregations are to follow their lead.

This puts a finger on a touchy issue: leadership and authority. Ours is not a culture that easily adjusts itself to such an idea. Ours, in fact, is a society of mavericks and do-it-yourselfers. Consequently, not only does the term *submission* sound foreign, but even the idea of actually being led by a spiritual advisor/pastor is hard for many to comprehend. I am not convinced that our social makeup is an improvement. While I surely enjoy the freedom of independence that our culture affords, I am not sure that the pendulum swing away from authority and leadership is any healthier than total control.

What we need is able leadership; when able leadership is present, following the lead of the elders is healthy and effective.[21] Just as it is morally healthy for children to follow the good guidance of their parents, so it is spiritually satisfying and edifying for the churches to follow the guidance of the elders. It is important to remember God's call

---

21. See the excellent discussion of W. L. Liefeld, "Leadership and Authority in the Church," in *In God's Community: Essays on the Church and Its Ministry*, ed. D. J. Ellis and W. W Gasque (Wheaton, Ill.: Harold Shaw, 1979), 29–39.

on an elder's life and ministry as well as the high calling he or she has to preach the gospel and teach the truth of the Bible. Until we come to terms with that calling and with God's call on our lives to be recipients of that person's calling, we will fail to be what God has called us to be: church members.

Even while affirming the importance of leadership and authority on the part of the elders, we must not forget that there will be differences of opinion on matters, some small and some significant. After all, we live in a fallen world, and we simply do not come to concord on all issues. Thus, at times an individual member will disagree with the pastor and will want to pursue an alternative course of direction. Such a decision by a member ought to be done with humility, in conversation with the elders, and in such a way that is not disruptive (unless necessary).[22] When done in a spirit of humility and concern, disagreements can be minimized and the harmful effects of divisions reduced.

Accordingly, Peter's words to the churches to "submit" are not to be taken as a blanket endorsement of every elder in the world. Rather, he assumes spiritual healthiness at the top; when that leadership is corrupt, following it would be contrary to God's will (as Peter himself resisted leadership in Acts 4:1–22; Gal. 2:11–21). Indeed, I suspect that Peter was aware of differences between elders and the "younger ones" and urged them to submit as a principle consistent with true spiritual leadership.[23]

Peter's final words in this section are crucial for understanding the perspective of his instructions both to elders and the younger ones: Whatever is happening, everyone is to clothe himself or herself with the robes of humility. When everyone is so clothed, church dress is not shabby. That is, when everyone is concerned with serving others, the problems of leadership and authority are virtually eliminated. When both elders and laity are out to serve, the elders are no more authoritarian than the laity is rebellious.

---

22. If submission to elders and leaders were the only guiding principle, there would never have been a Protestant Reformation!

23. Though only directed to the preaching component of elders, the chapter of John Stott on contemporary problems with preaching discusses the subject of this paragraph admirably; see his *Between Two Worlds: The Art of Preaching in the Twentieth Century* (Grand Rapid Eerdmans, 1982), 50–91.

PETER PROVIDES A virtual checklist of proper and improper pastoral motives. The problems pastors in his day faced are essentially no different from the ones faced today by contemporary pastors. Admittedly, their society offered fewer temptations than what we face, and our pastors face challenges Peter's elders probably never thought of. Nonetheless, the essential temptations to greed and power have hardly changed, only their manifestations. What our text offers, then, is a list of three problems of motivation, and contemporary pastors and church leaders need to look over this list, examine their hearts, and ask themselves, "Why do I serve God in the church?"

First, are you as a church leader motivated to serve in the church *because you have to or because you want to?* I was once traveling with a pastor in England who frankly told me that he did not like the ministry. I could understand the pain that sometimes comes with people-oriented ministries because people are not always easy to work with. But I was not prepared for his next comment. I asked him, "Why then did you get into the ministry?" His answer was cold: "Because my parents demanded it, and now I have no other option." Here was a man in his late fifties who had no personal motivation to serve others in the ministry of the church of Christ.

Many pastors, Christian educators, and evangelists, if we can trust studies on job satisfaction, are carrying the same burden. They neither enjoy nor want to be pastors. Apart from an act of God's grace, through his mighty Spirit, such people cannot change. What these people need is time alone—time to spend with God in prayer so that he might either direct them out of the ministry of the church or renew the fires of ministry in their hearts.

There are at least two problems here, emotional-spiritual burnout and the normal trend for many to "cool down" after some years of service. Burnout, in our context, is a term that describes leaders who simply can no longer function at the appropriate energy level for their calling and job description. Christian leaders are called to a ministry of serving others; unfortunately, many of these same leaders have no ability to say "No" to the many demands on their time. Cloud and Townsend have expressed it perfectly:

Made in the image of God, we were created to take responsibility for certain tasks. Part of taking responsibility, or ownership, is knowing what *is* our job, and what *isn't*. Workers who continually take on duties that aren't theirs will eventually burn out. It takes wisdom to know what we should be doing and what we shouldn't. We can't do everything.[24]

To be sure, pastors suffer an enormous burden, and the Christian message of service suggests (to some) an unlimited availability to others for whatever they need—even mowing grass for others. And it sounds arrogantly selfish for the Christian leader to say that he or she needs to spend some time for leisure or for self-healing. But the wise leader sets boundaries that, while at times may be shifted, allow for healthy self-development.

Louis McBurney, a psychiatrist who specializes in working with Christian workers, both understands the pressures of ministry-oriented callings and has some important insights for ministering to those suffering in those callings.[25] Dropout is as pervasive a problem for Christian ministers as any vocation in our society. The clergy no longer command the same respect that they once had, divorce rates are up among them, they leave for "secular" jobs more than ever before, and they are fired more than ever before. These pressures create what McBurney calls a series of five crises: a crisis of authority, of identity, of priority, of integrity, and of dependency. In addition, pastors have a list of impossible tasks, a mandate to succeed, job insecurity, unexpressed anger, and financial pressure. To make matters worse, Christian workers tend to resist counseling because they are perceived (and therefore perceive themselves) as infallible, they are afraid of being exposed as failures or of being rejected, they seem to distrust psychology, they seem to lack funds for paying a therapist, and they do not deal with their feelings well.

This thorough analysis of the problem by McBurney, while it is more than we can deal with in detail here, demonstrates why Christian workers burn out and why the words of Peter are especially rel-

---

24. H. Cloud and J. Townsend, *Boundaries: When to Say Yes; When to Say No To Take Control of Your Life* (Grand Rapids: Zondervan, 1992), 25.

25. See L. McBurney, *Counseling Christian Workers* (Resources for Christian Counseling 2; Waco, Tex.: Word, 1986).

evant.[26] Are they doing their tasks because they want to or because they have to? Marble Retreat, McBurney's counseling center near Aspen, Colorado, is devoted to helping Christian workers emerge from the sea of burnout and broken marriages in a healthier way. Sometimes the Christian worker is performing tasks, not out of the great sense of calling from God, but because he or she simply feels the burden of having nothing else to do. Such a person needs to admit the symptoms of burnout, seek help, and pray to God that his Spirit will regenerate the spiritual passions for ministry. God is more than able.

But what about the problems that befall nearly all of us in the natural cooling down of our eagerness? This is common, and at times we need to go through the typical technique of "cold turkey obedience." That is, we get up and go about our ministries *even when we do not want to just because God has called us to do a certain task*. It is not unusual for a minister to awake some morning, perhaps not irregularly, and face the day with the wish that something else were to be done. Instead, that pastor can take time with God and ask him for the courage of obedience to do the tasks of ministry in spite of a lack of passion about it.

Further, what pastors need most is the constant stimulation that causes growth and development in their own lives. You cannot give to others if you are dried up yourself. Stimulation comes from spiritual disciplines, personal relationships, and physical rest. Psychologists tend to "burn out" because they have a pattern of overworking themselves. Pastors have the same tendencies, and churches, unfortunately, are good at exploiting those tendencies. Pastors need to feed themselves by reading new and interesting materials, by finding other pastors with whom they can share their lives (both joys and frustrations), by praying and meditating so they can deepen their knowledge and experience of God, by attending retreats and conferences that will challenge them to new and deeper ministries, and by investing their time in the love and joy that comes from their families. Pastors also need to take time off—weekly, quarterly, and annually. When they work too hard, they lose their joy for ministry and their willingness to serve. Before

---

26. Another insightful study, written over a century ago, is C. H. Spurgeon, *Lectures to My Students* (Grand Rapids: Zondervan, 1972), 154–65 ("The Minister's Fainting Fits"). See also D. M. Lloyd-Jones, *Spiritual Depression: Its Causes and Cure* (Grand Rapids: Eerdmans, 1965).

long their entire ministry is one of "cold turkey obedience," if not downright bitter compulsion.

In the last few months I have gotten phone calls from former students. One student shared with me the utter joy of serving God in the church. David was as joyous about his ministry now as he was when he was first called, nearly eight years ago. I asked him what he had been doing in the last year, and he shared a litany of things: reading a couple of new books by his favorite author, enjoying the growth of his two daughters, loving his supportive wife, following the Philadelphia Phillies, playing some golf, attending a Willow Creek Conference, spending a lot of time reading his Bible and praying, and so on. I contend that part of the reason for the joy in his life was the variety of stimulations he was enjoying. I did not hear one negative word about anyone in his congregation, even though the primary reason he called was ask my advice about dealing with a troubled person in his church who was disrupting things because of some strange views on how to interpret the Bible.

Contrast David with another student (whose name will go unmentioned), who, though trying to be positive, had obviously lost some fire. When I asked him what he was doing, there was only one comment: "Building program!" Enough said. In other words, he was spending so much time on the development of a new wing for his church that he had no time to feed his soul. He confessed that he hardly had time for prayer and Bible reading, found his time-squeeze affecting his relationship with his wife and his kids, did not take time to enjoy fishing or boating, and simply could not stoke the flames of godly desires. While there are certainly more things going on here than can be discussed (like his age and his diet), I noticed he lacked the eagerness to serve that he once had. Part of that, perhaps most of it, was caused by a lack of stimulation in his life. His priorities were messed up, and all that mattered to him was the building of some new wing in the church—and I told him that.

We can blame the pastors for a lot of this, and we always have, but the church too is to blame. Individual members of churches, beginning with the leadership committees, need to be sensitive to a pastor's schedule and do what they can to provide nourishment and edification. Elders need to grow, and the churches need to see to it that their elders are developing. When elder boards begin to see the care of the pastors as part of their ministry, pastors will repay them with more vital leadership.

Second, are you, as a church leader, motivated to serve in the church *because of the money you can acquire or because of your enthusiasm for ministry?* Love of money, Paul said, is "a root of all kinds of evil" (1 Tim. 6:10). The love of money is nowhere uglier than when it is found in Christian ministries. It is true, I believe, that the average pastor, the average Christian educator, the average youth pastor, and the average music leader of an average church are not motivated by money. This can be said for the average because for most, pay is by way of salary. But there are other places where motivation by money shows up: for example, when a minister says, "I won't do that because I'm not paid to do that!", when a pastor's work intensity heats up around church budget time, when calls come in for some extra ministries that have an honorarium attached to them, when certain people are given special priorities because they have money and helping them will increase one's opportunities, or when special ministries are developed so as to enable one to increase pay by serving in those ministries.

I believe the pastor today, as at no other time, needs to be above board and ruthlessly circumspect about the monetary side of the ministry. I also believe that the churches themselves need to be concerned about impressions given off by expenditures and salaries. When pastors are being paid salaries that permit them to live in $400,000 homes and when those same pastors drive exotic cars and take vacations to extravagant places, then churches need to ask if this is helpful for the gospel of Christ. So, too, pastors need to sit down with the board and ask not, "How much can you pay me?" but, "Will this salary figure and the lifestyle it permits be helpful for the cause of Christ in our community?" In saying these things, we need to recognize that a Christian worker deserves to be paid, but there is a difference between *making* money and *serving* money.

Elders and pastors need to examine themselves here and be penetratingly honest with themselves. They need to ask, "Lord, show me anywhere that I am being motivated by the money I can earn." In our world, Christian leaders need to be examples of financial responsibility (there is nothing wrong with a wise investment) and of simplicity in lifestyle so that outsiders have no reason to point fingers at local churches with respect to the financial component of ministry. Pastors are people, and people can spend their money where they want; but unlike most people, pastors are public figures, and where they spend money is known to all. Therefore, they need to be circumspect, wise, and simple in their spending so as to further the gospel.

Third, are you as a church leader motivated to serve in the church *because of your desire for power or because of the impact your life makes on others?* If loving money is a root of all kinds of evil, loving power is the earth in which it grows and the moisture that feeds it. Some church leaders serve because of the sense of power; others serve because they are called by God to serve; and still others do so because of the impact their lives make on others. The second and third motivations are godly; the first is despicable. Power, of course, is difficult to discern. How do we know when power and authoritarianism is part of the pastor's motivation?

One sure sign of being motivated by power surfaces when a church leader does not "get his way" in a particular matter. When that pastor stews, complains, threatens to leave, and appeals to authority and position, then he or she is not motivated by what is best but by what strengthens his or her fortress.

Another sign is when the pastor feels threatened by the divinely granted gifts of someone else or maneuvers to reestablish her position because of the positive comments made about another's giftedness. If a Christian mother expresses her appreciation for a certain radio teacher and says so to her pastor, and when that pastor wonders what she is lacking or wonders if she thinks that teacher is "better" than she is at teaching, then that pastor's motivations are stained with the guilt of wanting power. The true Christian leader rejoices with the lady and does not compare ministries to find out who is best.

Again, if a pastor makes sure he dresses himself in a way that conveys authority and power, then he may well be motivated by such things.

A fourth sign of domineering rather than leading by example occurs when a church leader refuses to delegate responsibilities and leadership. Hoarding all decisions and responsibilities is a clear sign of not trusting in God to guide and in the Spirit to work. The responsible Christian minister trains and delegates in such a way that all are led into their gifts and the entire church does the work (Eph. 4:11—16).

Pastors must desire to serve God, no matter what that means. They need to recognize that they are "undershepherds," like Peter (5:1, 4), and that they serve only to increase the Lordship of Christ. They have no power, only a temporary service in Christ, because only Jesus is Lord. Peter's alternative to domineering leadership is an exemplary lifestyle. When a Christian leader can stand up in all humility and ask others to follow as he or she follows Christ (cf. 1 Cor. 11:1), that leader is doing exactly what God has called. Life is more important than office, just as it is true that our children learn more from what is caught than what is taught.

1 Peter 5:6–14

❦

HUMBLE YOURSELVES, THEREFORE, under God's mighty hand, that he may lift you up in due time. ⁷Cast all your anxiety on him because he cares for you.

⁸Be self-controlled and alert. Your enemy the devil prowls around like a roaring lion looking for someone to devour. ⁹Resist him, standing firm in the faith, because you know that your brothers throughout the world are undergoing the same kind of sufferings.

¹⁰And the God of all grace, who called you to his eternal glory in Christ, after you have suffered a little while, will himself restore you and make you strong, firm and steadfast. ¹¹To him be the power for ever and ever. Amen.

¹²With the help of Silas, whom I regard as a faithful brother, I have written to you briefly, encouraging you and testifying that this is the true grace of God. Stand fast in it.

¹³She who is in Babylon, chosen together with you, sends you her greetings, and so does my son Mark. ¹⁴Greet one another with a kiss of love.

Peace to all of you who are in Christ.

AT THE LOGICAL level, 1 Peter 5:6–9 is an exposition of 5:5b, where Peter urged Christians to be humble and quoted Proverbs 3:34 in defense of his point. Here he develops the concept of humility and adds an exhortation to beware of Satan's schemes. Near the end of this unit (5:10–11) is a doxology in which he praises the God who protects his children. I have included 5:12–14 with this section for convenience sake; it parallels the many ancient letters that end with a formal greeting.[1]

---

1. See at 1:1–2, n. 2.

I could have included 5:6–7 with the previous section, but that would leave two short units, a rather minor exhortation (5:8–9) and a doxology, all by themselves. Admittedly, the exhortations of 5:6–9 are addressed to the "all of you" of 5:5b. But as they move along, the theme of suffering becomes apparent (5:9–10); this has led most commentators to see 5:6–11 as a separate section.[2] Peter introduces this theme by capitalizing on the word "humility" in 5:5b, creating a word connection with 5:6. There are four parts to this section: (1) the exhortation to *humility* (5:6–7); (2) the exhortation to *vigilance* (5:8–9); (3) the *doxology* (5:10–11); and (4) *final remarks* (5:12–14).

The Exhortation to Humility (5:6–7). Theses two verses bear a striking resemblance to James 4:6–7, 10.

1 Peter 5:5b–9	James 4:6–7, 10
"God opposes the proud but gives grace to the humble." Humble yourselves, therefore, under God's mighty hand, that he may lift you up in due time....	"God opposes the proud, but gives grace to the humble." Submit yourselves, then, to God.
Your enemy the devil prowls around like a roaring lion looking for someone to devour. Resist him, standing firm in the faith, because you know that your brothers throughout the world are undergoing the same kind of sufferings.	Resist the devil, and he will flee from you.
	Humble yourselves before the Lord, and he will lift you up.

Most scholars see here the reflection of an early Christian tradition that exhorted Christians to humility because of the presence of Satan.[3] Christians need God's grace to gain victory over the devil's assaults. Whereas James brings out the importance of humility for dealing with inner-church strife, Peter draws out the significance of humility and grace for the suffering believer. The humble wait for God's exaltation of believers at the end of time (cf. 2:12). "Humbling oneself 'under the mighty hand of God' is not an ethical admonition making a virtue

---

2. So, e.g., L. Goppelt, *1 Peter*, 355; J. R. Michaels, *1 Peter*, 293–95.

3. See L. Goppelt, *1 Peter*, 355–56; J. R. Michaels, *1 Peter*, 293–95 (who draws out the finer differences and similarities).

of necessity, but springs from the religious insight, that God alone can change the ultimate darkness of this world era, that only he can 'exalt you in the time of visitation' (5:6)."[4]

Believers are to "humble" themselves under "God's mighty hand." Peter seems to have in mind an eschatological persecution motif: As God's mighty hand was seen in the plagues of the Exodus (see Ex. 3:19; 6:1; 13:3, 9, 14, 16), so his mighty hand is now being seen in the persecution the believers in Asia Minor are experiencing. By submitting to and waiting out God's deliverance, they can expect that same mighty hand to deliver them (5:6b), just as the Lord delivered the children of Israel. While the word behind "due time" may be general (in God's own timing), that same term is used frequently in 1 Peter and early Christian literature for the final day of salvation (cf. 1:5, 7, 13; 2:12; 4:7).[5] It is more likely that Peter thinks of an eschatological vindication of God's suffering people than some kind of reward or vindication in this life.

Peter grounds their submission to God in his loving care and protection: "Cast all your anxiety on him because he cares for you" (5:7). If Peter has in mind the picturesque words of Jesus (Matt. 6:25–34), he has now taken them into the realm of persecution. Drawing on Psalm 55:22 (LXX 54:23), where the psalmist expresses confidence that God will never permit the righteous to be moved and will eventually bring evildoers to justice, Peter exhorts his churches to express a similar confidence in God's justice. By turning over their fears and worries to God, they express their trust in him and rely on him to bring about vindication and justice. The reason for turning over fears to God is because "he cares for you." In summary, these two verses are concerned with persecution and suffering and the appropriate Christian response. Believers are to humble themselves before God by submitting to his will, which now includes suffering; they are to turn over their worries to him and let him bring about the justice that he has promised in his own time. In submitting to God's will and enduring suffering for the sake of Christ, Christians are undergirded with the knowledge that God cares about and loves them.

---

4. R. Schnackenburg, *The Moral Teaching of the New Testament*, trans. J. Holland-Smith and W. J. O'Hara (New York: Seabury, 1965), 370.

5. So J. N. D. Kelly, *Peter and Jude*, 208; L. Goppelt, *1 Peter*, 357; J. R. Michaels, *1 Peter*, 296.

The Exhortation to Vigilance (5:8–9). The activity of Christians' submitting themselves to God in a confident trust of his ultimate triumph is suddenly interrupted with two sharp commands: "Be self-controlled and alert!" Or, as J. R. Michaels translates: "Pay attention! Wake up!"[6] Why? Because "your enemy the devil prowls around like a roaring lion looking for someone to devour" (5:8). Satan, it was believed, would be particularly active in the last days (2 Thess. 2:3–12; 2 Tim. 3:1–9; Revelation), and since the persecution Peter's readers are suffering is a harbinger of those last days, it is not surprising that he exhorts them to be alert to Satan's activity. The devil's roaring and devouring is possibly to be connected with insults (cf. 2:11–12; Ps. 21:14) or, more probably, with assaults aimed at physical death (2 Tim. 4:17).[7]

Peter exhorts the Christians facing the devil to "resist him, standing firm in the faith" (5:9). Christians resist Satan by refusing to succumb to his temptations to deny the Lord and to be faithless and fearful in the midst of suffering. They can do this "because you know that your brothers throughout the world are undergoing the same kind of sufferings." This expression makes it clear that Peter sees Satan's assaults (his roaring and swallowing) as connected with physical persecution; he exhorts them, therefore, to remain faithful and obedient. Their encouragement comes from the worldwide family of God, for everywhere Christians are suffering.

The Doxology (5:10–11). Peter's letter ends on a note of prayer, which he begins with a *theological reflection:* The God they worship and serve is a God of grace. That is, he is merciful and forgiving. He has brought them into covenantal relationship through no merit of their own; he has chosen (1:1–2) to make them his people (2:9–10) and promises his protection (1:3–8).

This theological reflection is then directed toward the *specific calling* God has given them: He has appointed them to "his eternal glory in Christ." From the outset of this letter, Peter has focused on the eschatological hope of believers, a hope that sustains them during their suffering. But this hope is not just something that permits them to cope with suffering; it is in fact the destined calling God has given them. He made them his people so they could be with him eternally and praise him forever.

---

6. J. R. Michaels, *1 Peter*, 292.
7. See the extended discussion in ibid., 298–99.

This calling has in it a *present condition*, one that is not pleasant: suffering for awhile. Once again, the reality of his readers' social condition shapes Peter's teaching and prayers.

Finally, Peter's *prayer* is for their strength—strength to endure, to remain faithful, and to resist the temptations to the flesh (2:11; 4:4). Peter's prayer reinforces his promise in 5:6 that God will lift them up by sustaining their lives on a daily basis.

Final Remarks (5:12–14). Peter concludes his letter in a manner similar to the endings of other letters: mentioning the amanuensis or deliverer of the letter (Silas), summarizing his intention (to exhort and testify), greeting them, and wishing them God's peace.[8] For years scholars have argued that the expression "with the help of Silas" described Silas's help in *writing* the letter. Such aid, it was argued, helps explain how "unschooled, ordinary men" (Acts 4:13), among whom was Peter, could write a letter as refined at 1 Peter.[9] Such a view is permissible.[10] On the other hand, some today argue that Silas was the one who delivered the letter.[11] The preponderance of literary evidence supports the second position, for ancient expressions similar to Peter's wording here speak almost uniformly of the carrier of the letter, not its amanuensis.[12]

Peter' intention in writing this letter has been to exhort, and the frequency of imperatives in 1 Peter proves he has been successful (e.g., 1:13–25; 2:11–3:12; 5:1). In addition, he contends that what he has written witnesses (cf. 5:1) "that this[13] is the true grace of God." The

---

8. Second Peter ends more on a note of exhortation and less in line with customary letters. On the various formal elements and their parallels, cf. J. R. Michaels, *1 Peter*, 305–6.

9. So, e.g., E. G. Selwyn, *1 Peter*, 9–17, 241; J. N. D. Kelly, *Peter and Jude*, 214–16; P. Davids, *1 Peter*, 198; C. P. Thiede, *Simon Peter: From Galilee to Rome* (Exeter: Paternoster, 1986), 175–76.

10. Literally, the Greek has, "Through Silas, to you, the faithful brother . . . I write." The issue is what "through" (Gk. *dia*) means here. Cf. 2 Thess. 2:2, where *dia* is used with the clear implication that it was written, not sent, "through us."

11. So, e.g., J. R. Michaels, *1 Peter*, 306–7; W. A. Grudem, *1 Peter*, 23–24, 199–200; N. Brox, *Der erste Petrusbrief*, 241–43.

12. The evidence includes Acts 15:23; Ignatius, *Romans* 10:1; *Philadelphians* 11:2; *Smyrnaeans* 12:1. Eusebius (*Ecclesiastical History*, 4.23.11) suggests the first view mentioned above. Romans 16:22 is ambiguous for, though it supports the existence of a secretary, it does not use the "through" expression.

13. The word "this" (Gk. *tauten*) refers back either to the whole letter or to those parts of the letter that speak of God's grace and truth.

apostle alludes here to the truthfulness of the gospel he has preached (1:10–12) and assumes that this is what his readers firmly believe. He only urges them to "stand fast in it." That is, they are to stand fast for the gospel and resist the temptation to cave in under the pressure of suffering.

Our letters begin with greetings; Peter's ends with greetings. "She who is in Babylon, chosen together with you, sends you her greetings, and so does my son Mark." Because Babylon was a notorious place of sin, it became a figurative expression for any place known for its sinfulness (cf. Rev. 14:8; 17:18; 18:2, 10, 21). However, it may be used here simply to describe where Christians have been deported from the homeland of Judea. In this case, it is the counterpart to "scattered" (Gk. *diaspora*) in 1:1.[14] The description of Babylon as "chosen" favors the second view; interestingly, election is also found in 1:1. In either case, it surely describes Rome,[15] and early Christian tradition confirms that Peter wrote from Rome.[16]

Both Peter and Mark share their greetings. Peter then urges his readers to "greet one another with a kiss of love," the standard form of greeting in the ancient world (cf. Rom. 16:16; 1 Cor. 16:20; 2 Cor. 13:12; 1 Thess. 5:26)[17] and in many parts of the world today. Americans tend to shake hands while other cultures hug one another or give one another a kiss. Peter's blessing then follows: "Peace to all of you who are in Christ."

WHILE THE PARTICULAR nuances Peter brings out are not the nuances we would bring out (since most of us are not in a context of suffering), the larger themes he deals with are as relevant now as they were then: Christians are to submit to God, wait for God's good time, and fight off the devil's schemes. Furthermore, Christians need both God's strengthening and his peace.

---

14. So J. R. Michaels, *1 Peter*, 311.

15. Ibid.

16. See Eusebius, *Ecclesiastical History*, 2.15.2: "He [Papias] also says that Peter mentions Mark in his first Epistle, and that he composed this in Rome itself, which they say that he himself indicates, referring to the city metaphorically as Babylon. . . ."

17. See the discussion of L. Goppelt, *1 Peter*, 377–78.

When texts are immediately relevant, it is not hard to bridge a New Testament text with our world. However, even here we must be careful to define our terms so that we can properly guard against interpreting a text in such a way that it simply confirms our culture. Thus, our text contains several critical terms that the modern interpreter may seize upon, but he or she needs to make sure that the application is in harmony with the ancient text.

For instance, when Peter promises that God will "lift you up" (5:6), it will not do to apply this to our world by suggesting it includes some kind of job promotion that a Christian sees as a reward for faithfulness. What Peter has in mind is final vindication at the end of history, not a present reward.[18] The expression "in due time" is similar to those at 1:5 and 4:17, where the end of time is clearly in view. Furthermore, the entire message of this letter is set over against a deep and abiding hope for the End to come to make all things right.[19] Eusebius is perhaps the best example of how this term is intended here. In speaking of the martyrs, he says, "They humbled themselves under the mighty hand and by it they have now been greatly exalted."[20]

Again, expressions like the devil's prowling, roaring, and seeking to devour (5:8) need to be understood as Satan's assault on the physical life of a Christian, not just any set of temptations. Even the term "peace" in 5:14 should be defined as God's salvation and the consequences it brings. No matter how much we might like terms like this to mean something vitally relevant to our political, business, or social situation, it is important for modern interpreters *to let the text say what it said and not ask it to say more than it did.*

The pursuit of the varied nuances of the text by seeking out carefully the meaning of our author does not, however, prohibit us from taking specific ideas and applying them more generally. For instance, I argued above that Peter's intention in 5:6 was along the line of submitting to God by waiting on his final display of salvation, when he will vindicate his people. The specific context to which Peter is speaking is surely that of suffering for Christ's sake, and it clearly applies to any context where the church is suffering. But in our context, suffering for

---

18. See J. R. Michaels, *1 Peter*, 296.
19. See the introduction, pp. xx.
20. Eusebius, *Ecclesiastical History*, 5.2.5. The term behind "greatly exalted" is *hupsomenoi*, the same term that is used for "lift you up."

Christ's sake is not as frequent. Are we then to drop this text and move on to another? Not always, though sometimes we frankly have to admit that a text "no longer speaks" to us. But we can sometimes generalize from a specific idea to a broader one. Thus, while 5:6 speaks of enduring persecution, we may also apply it to our world along the following lines: Inasmuch as God is faithful to his people and cares for them (5:7), we can expect our current obedience to be vindicated by God at the Final Day.[21]

Similarly, while Satan's assaults here are understood as his attempts to get Christians to crumble in the face of persecution, we can surely infer that this is but one method of getting Christians sidetracked from doing God's will. Therefore, we find it permissible, through inferential logic, to apply this text to any assaults by Satan to thwart God's plans. But inasmuch as Peter's concerns were serious, we will be most faithful to Peter's text if we apply these to large situations where God's will is being attacked. For instance, a crusade to evangelize one's city might be attacked by Satan through the political machinery of the city to prevent the gospel from being heard by those who are hard to reach any other way. It would be good to restrict our applications to those situations where we find a broader opposition to the church (5:9), though I do not deny that the personal oppositions each Christian encounters are included in Satan's overall scheme to stymie God's plan.

On another issue, I doubt that it is important for us to change our cultural form of greeting, from handshaking and hugging to the "double kiss on the cheek" simply because Peter instructs his readers to greet one another with a holy kiss. However culturally conditioned we may be about being kissed by total strangers, culturally conditioned we are. We must simply apply this text to our culture's institution of greeting; Christians ought to greet one another warmly everywhere, no matter how they express that greeting.

Finally, it is always wise to move the message of a passage of the New Testament into our world by seeking to relate the "big message." That is, while it may be fruitful to take a single verse (such as the "roaring lion") and make it relevant, it is even more fruitful to summarize

---

21. We cannot, however, transform the notion of "Final Day" into "Any Day," for Peter does not, nor do the other writers of the New Testament, believe there is any guarantee that current conditions will necessarily improve because one is a Christian. Sometimes they do, sometimes they don't. Waiting on God's timing is crucial.

the essential message of a passage and move it into our cultural setting. I have frequently heard sermons and Bible study lessons that focus on one minor point, however relevant it might be, to the neglect of the larger picture in which that minor point is found. And all too frequently, that minor point is a hobby horse of the preacher. We must be relevant, to be sure, but never at the expense of the essential theme of the text.

Therefore, we may ask, what essentially is Peter driving at in 5:6– 14? The answer is simple: He is both summing up his entire orientation (exhortation) and being specific at the same time. His central message is clear: You must remain faithful to Jesus Christ, in spite of your social condition and its potential dangers, by living obediently and in community with one another. This is the message we want to relate to our world, even though at times it may be difficult to do so.

PETER'S MAIN EXHORTATION of the importance of standing firm is expressed in several ways:

- by humbly submitting to God in faithful waiting
- by remaining vigilant and aware of Satan's schemes
- by praying for God's enablement to give us strength and solidity
- by affirming once again the truthfulness of God's grace.

Peter's whole letter is an exhortation designed to get the believers of Asia Minor to remain faithful, obedient, and good citizens, who will in no way damage the cause of Christ through bad behavior. That is what we need to apply to our world today: faithfulness to the gospel so that our society can see the glory of God.

I begin by reflecting on the reality that our enemy, the devil, is against us. As David Watson said, "Even amongst Christians who do believe in the devil's existence, there is often a marked blindness about the reality of spiritual warfare and the nature of the enemy's tactics."[22] Though Peter only addresses the significance of Satan in the persecution schemes of the pagans of Asia Minor once (5:8–9), his oppo-

---

22. David Watson, *Discipleship* (London: Hodder and Stoughton, 1981), 167.

sition is nonetheless real.[23] Satan still wants to ruin us and the impact of the gospel in our world. This places the theme of Peter's letter, the Christian's life in an unbelieving society, on a higher plane. Our lives are to be seen as part of a cosmic struggle (cf. Rev. 12:1–9). Though some Christians are a bit neurotic about the real presence of Satan and demonic forces in the normal struggles of life (like flat tires, long red lights, and bad prices at the supermarket), an overreaction that totally eliminates him from our lives is just as bad.

Satan's devices[24] include tempting us to sin (Gen. 3:1–6; Luke 22:31, 32), accusing us before God and making us fear our standing before God (Job 1:6–12; 2:1–7; Zech. 3:1–2; Rev. 12:10), opposing God's will in a multitude of ways (Matt. 13:19; Acts 13:8–10), confusing our minds regarding truth (2 Cor. 4:4; Eph. 2:2), inciting acts of idolatry and magic (Acts 8:9–11; 19:13–16; Col. 2:8–23), and overtly dominating people to the point of demonization (Mark 5:1–20). I also believe Satan can work his way into the political and structural machinery of society to the point of society itself becoming a tool of sin and oppression (cf. Dan. 10; John 8:44; 1 Thess. 2:18).[25]

But God is stronger than Satan, and he can reclaim those who have been demonized (Matt. 8:32; 17:18; Mark 5:1–20) and permit his people to escape the devil's tempting lures (Luke 4:1–13; 1 Cor. 10:13; Eph. 6:10–18; James 4:7). Those who seek to bring God's will to every venture will also work against the political machinery that opposes God. The everyday trust that Christians exercise protects them from Satan's assaults against God and his people. The temptation to deny association with Jesus can be overcome when we realize that God is Judge, remember that others have endured suffering on our behalf, and recognize that someday God will bring about total justice, everywhere and for everyone.

A second point in this connection is that *God's grace can sustain us* in our most difficult hour. Peter assures his readers that the God who

---

23. See S. McKnight, "Knowing Our Enemy: The Devil in Perspective," and "Knowing Our Enemy: Satan's Many Manifestations," *Moody Monthly* 89/10 (1989): 36–43; 89/11 (1989): 32–39.

24. A spiritual classic here is Thomas Brooks, *Precious Remedies Against Satan's Devices* (London: Banner of Truth Trust, 1968; originally published in 1652).

25. A creative presentation of this problem can be found in Os Guinness, *The Gravedigger File: Papers on the Subversion of the Modern Church* (Downers Grove, Ill.: InterVarsity, 1983).

called you by his grace "will himself restore you and make you strong, firm and steadfast" (5:10). Since Peter understands that the struggle his readers are facing is not just a social battle or a religious difference, but a cosmic battle in which God's glory is at stake, he prays that God will enable his churches to live faithfully, honorably, and obediently in the face of a hostile environment.

If we are tempted, God is on our side (1 Cor. 10:13); if we are fearful, God calls us to fearless obedience with the promise that confession will bring its reward (Matt. 10:32–33). In all of this, God's grace starts and sustains the spiritual energies required (Eph. 2:8–10). Peter began his letter by informing his readers that they were kept by God's power, so that what God began in his mercy will be completed (1 Peter 1:3–5). Even the faith that Christians have is a gift of God (Phil. 1:29). "It has been said that in the New Testament doctrine is grace, and ethics is gratitude; and something is wrong with any form of Christianity in which, experimentally and practically, this saying is not being verified."[26] Thus, what Peter is saying, and what we need to hear as well, is that the God of grace who called us will preserve us as we trust and obey him.

One of the most ennobling features of this text is that the God who called us to his eternal glory is indeed a God of grace. No matter what God has called us to do—whether that means living victoriously in some modern Christianized culture or living in the heat of suffering—as the God of grace, he will bring us to the end he desires. We do not have to earn that final state because as the God of grace, he has willed that it be ours. We do not have to worry about things, because as the God of grace, he has promised us eternal glory. When we are tempted to give up on the tasks God has given us, we need to remind ourselves that our gracious God has appointed us to those tasks and that he will give us strength and power until the End.

Third, Peter knows that the Christians of Asia Minor are fully responsible for their actions, so he exhorts them to humble themselves in trust before God (5:6), to hand over to God their fearful hearts (5:7), to be on the lookout for Satan's wily schemes, and, when seeing them, to resist his temptations (5:8–9, 12). These are their, and our, responsibilities before God—when facing temptation, to resist it;

---

26. J. I. Packer, *Knowing God* (Downers Grove, Ill.: InterVarsity, 1993), 137.

when seeing the reality of persecution, to commit the heart to God and wait for his vindication; when encountering the fear that comes from difficult stresses, to rid the anxiety by living in light of God's care.

Therefore, as we come to the end of a marvelous letter, we too are confronted with the same call to responsible living in our world. We are called to live honorably in our society so that there are no grounds of accusations against us and we can make the biggest possible impact on our world. We are called to live a holy life, abstaining from sin. We are called to live a loving life, serving our brothers and sisters in the Christian family. We are called to live in light of God's judgment, making sure that everything we do will be approved by God in that final hour. Our identity is not to be wrapped up in our social location, whether that be low (like Peter's churches) or high (like many churches today), but in the fact that we are God's family and are related to him. As such, we are to serve one another with the gifts God has granted and live orderly and lovingly with one another. No matter how many adjustments we have to make as we read Peter's letter in our world, we are anchored to his world by the fact of the common salvation that transforms our behavior (1:3–2:10), we are challenged to live circumspectly in our society (2:11–3:12), and we are expected to live as the family of God ought to live (3:13–5:11). When we live like this, people will glorify him on the day he visits us (2:12).

Scripture Index